Praise for *Sled Dogs to S*

An essential Minnesota story in the grand tradition of Minnesota storytelling . . . A must-read and a call to action for anyone concerned about the future of our environment and the place we call home.

Ali Selim, Writer and Director of the
Award-Winning Film *Sweet Land*

A really engaging and recommended Minnesota read.

Paul Thissen, Speaker of the
Minnesota House of Representatives

[T]he wilderness friendlies who worry that mining in the northeast inevitably will taint the Boundary Waters—literally and figuratively— have a formidable leader.

Dennis Anderson, Outdoor Columnist,
Minneapolis Star Tribune

Sled Dogs to Saint Paul is the story of a man's relationship to his dogs and his involvement with politics and environmental advocacy. He writes about mushing and sled dogs with honesty, and takes the reader with him in his sled during the Beargrease and other races. Finally, he recounts the decision to run a team of sled dogs to the Saint Paul capitol with a pile of petitions against sulfide mining in northeastern Minnesota. His team carries Moe through the streets of the city and as readers, we are witness to their bravery and get insight into the extraordinary ability of Alaskan Huskies.

Erin Altimus, Managing Editor,
Northern Wilds Magazine, Grand Marais, MN

Sled Dogs

to Saint Paul

Culicidae
PRESS, LLC
culicidaepress.com

Ames | Berlin | Gainesville | Rome

Frank Moe

Culicidae Press, LLC
918 5th Street
Ames, IA 50010
USA
www.culicidaepress.com

editor@culicidaepress.com

Culicidae
PRESS, LLC
culicidaepress.com

Ames | Berlin | Gainesville | Rome

SLED DOGS TO SAINT PAUL
Second Edition

For more information please visit www.culicidaepress.com

ISBN-13:   978-1-941892-01-5

ISBN-10:   1941892019

Cover photo by Bill Cady
Cover design and interior layout © 2014 by polytekton.com

For Mom and Sherri

❀

Thank you for never saying I should get rid of the dogs.

Acknowledgements

One March morning in 2009 I was sitting at my desk, staring at the computer, trying to focus on writing my PhD dissertation. I had been fortunate to receive a Bush Fellowship to finish my Doctorate at the University of Minnesota. My course work was done, and all I had to do was write that damn paper. My head continually drifted out to the dogyard and the past sled dog race season. That morning I did eventually begin to write but it wasn't my dissertation. Instead I started chronicling my experiences with our sled dogs. I never finished the dissertation, but some of those stories found their way into this book. I know it wasn't what the Bush Foundation expected when they gave me a generous fellowship, but it's what came out. I want to first thank all the great people at the Bush Foundation, especially Martha Lee, for giving me the space in my life to begin writing.

Steve Pett, my good friend, handler and editor, thanks for all your time, hard work and patience. My ego caused me to ignore some of your suggestions and I hope readers overlook any resulting mistakes. Mikesch Muecke of Culicidae Press, thank you for agreeing to publish this book. You and Steve are like the great back-up band that makes even a tired old singer look and sound good. I hope enough people read it so you at least break even on the deal.

Now here I am, again staring at my computer, trying to think of all the other people to thank, that helped to make this book possible. Seriously, the book's about to go to print and I don't know where to start. So how about this, if you're reading it now, at the very least you bought, or borrowed a copy. So thank you. After reading it maybe you'll feel inspired. Here's my hope for you, that when you put this book down you go outside. Find an adventure of your own, fall in love again with your natural home. Maybe that love affair will cause you to fight to protect that place that you love, and that place you love will keep calling you back.

Prologue

March 18th, 2013

"What am I going to do with these boots?" After wearing them straight for three days and 350 miles, they were still in plastic bags where I put them, holding in all the damp stench from the Beargrease Trail. "I bet they've got 10,000 miles on em, at least."

They looked it too. The seams had split and the shoe glue that I'd patched them with several times was all peeling off.

"Why don't you just get a new pair?" Sherri had asked several times over the last two years, even though she really knew why. I'm not only a tightwad but crazy sentimental. I thought about the late December day I bought those boots and my old parka at Reeds in Walker, Minnesota.

"Must have been 2007…maybe 2006. Was I wearing them the night Acorn saved my life?" I wondered out loud.

Those boots had been on my feet for all the Beargreases, UP 200s, every race, hundreds of training runs, even the dog sled trip to Saint Paul. How many nights had I unlaced them in front of the wood stove, pulling out the liners, watching them steam out the footfalls of another night on the trail?

Lately they were hurting my feet. Maybe they were wearing out, or my feet were just getting bigger as I approached fifty. I needed to let them go but how could I just throw them away? Too many memories. I pulled the boots from the bags. Outside I gathered some wood and grabbed some paper out of the garbage can. Soon I had a roaring fire going in a barrel behind our shed. Again I looked at the boots, thought about my feet in them, running next to the dog team up to the Capitol steps, up the last hill of the Beargrease trail before we turned into the finish at Billy's in Duluth, smelling dog pee and looking down to watch my leader Wolf lifting his leg on them. They smelled even worse now.

Finally I placed my trusty Rocky pac boots in the fire. Soon they began to steam, then sizzle. After a couple of minutes the liners caught fire. White smoke rose up, and all the days on the training trail, planning for the next race, dogs running silently, me not wanting anything else in the world, drifted up into the trees of the North Woods. Then the soles, black rubber, caught fire and dark smoke rose up, the hard memories that still plague my dreams, the loss of many of my beloved dogs. The pain rose with the dark smoke and mixed with a fresh snow that had begun to fall. A growing wind caught the smoke and carried it away.

For the next half hour I watched my boots turn to ashes. The fire burned down to smoking embers and was eventually covered by the new heavy snow. I remembered the first time I wore them.

Acorn (photo by Sherri Moe)

Chapter 1

"Come on Acorn, let's go home. Let's go."

The temperature was at least 30 below and we were still 40 miles from the road somewhere between Effie and Northome Minnesota, which is about as nowhere as you can get in the lower 48. We were on a training run, on our way to Effie to stop at the Effie Café for dinner. The plan was to then turn around and head back to the truck I'd left in Northome. The trail just west of Effie was blocked off by a new timber sale with slash piles everywhere. After struggling through slash and over downed trees for a half hour in the dark with my ten-dog team I realized I wasn't going to get to Effie to eat my cheeseburger and fries.

The dogs caught the fatty beef scraps I threw to them. All I had for me was a couple of caramels with waxed paper frozen on. When they're that hard you can't tell what's wax and what's caramel. Worse yet I'd worked so hard getting the team unstuck from the slash piles that I'd built up a good sweat. That sweat was now cold running down my body as we headed back to the truck.

When it's that cold the dogs really move. Watching the dogs loping down the trail I started to laugh remembering the night my friend punched out the windows of his own car in January while we were driving down the freeway. He was pissed that I wouldn't let him drive. But tonight there was no Jim Beam to drink or Rolling Stones and heater to crank up. I pedaled on the sides with one foot just to keep my blood moving but the cold kept creeping in. It was a starry moonless night with the northern lights flickering now and then on my right. When you're freezing your butt off it's hard to enjoy the scenery.

Around 9:00, an hour after I turned around, my biggest dog, Bear, started limping hard and pulling back on his neckline. I was going to have to add 70 pounds of dog to my sled bag. You'd think that a hurt dog would welcome getting a free ride but he fought going into the sled bag like I used to fight my older brother trying to put his dirty socks into my mouth. It took me ten minutes with gloves off to get Bear in the bag and on down the trail we went with my hands stiff and almost useless from the cold. At least 30 miles to go and I was already thinking of a snack of frozen beef fat. The caramels, wax paper and all, were long gone.

The one good thing about having Bear in the sled bag, shredding everything inside and somehow slipping his head and a paw or two out every couple of minutes, was that I had to work harder to push the sled. This slowed down how much colder I was getting. It also was going to add at least a half hour to the time it would take to get back.

Again I laughed remembering that my wife Sherri had made me promise to bring my cell phone. Out here, with no service, a rock would do as much good, but I guess it made her feel better.

Thinking about Sherri made me focus again.

"No more mistakes," I thought. "I will get home and crawl into bed with her eventually tonight."

It was after ten and we were still miles from the truck. I'd been on that trail many times but I really couldn't remember where I was. Now and then, with my fading headlamp, I could sometimes see paw prints in front of us from earlier in the day.

"Come on, good girl Acorn, let's go home."

Acorn wasn't the fastest dog in the yard but she was the best leader I'd ever had. She never forgot a trail and looked back impatiently every time I questioned her. It just seemed like she knew that tonight was serious and we had to get home. She was all business. Sherri always tells Acorn to bring me home safe, and I believe she knows it and intends to do it, no matter what.

When your body temperature drops just a couple of degrees you lose the ability to make good decisions. I was shivering and just standing on the back of the sled. I seemed to forget that pushing the sled would keep me warm and get us home faster. Out of this stupor a ring got my attention. Taking my mittens off I squeezed the phone in my hand and answered.

"What, hello!"

The signal died. I looked at the phone number of the call and saw that it was my wife.

"Oh yeah, Sherri, I gotta get home." I focused my attention, realized I was really shivering and tried to start kicking and running behind the sled. Bear was no longer fighting to get out of the sled bag. Soon I drifted off.

A face full of snow gets your attention. I was lying face first in the snow with the sled tipped over in front of me, buried. My light was focused on Acorn's face looking back at me. Her expression followed by her "arr row rowrow" told me to get my butt back on the sled. She was tired, hungry and wanted to get home. It was 11 p.m., we'd been on the trail since two, and the temperature was still dropping. My hands were numb again so I alternated wrapping one wrist around the handle of the sled while the other swung back and forth. As much as I hated the feeling, I was looking for the burning in my fingers that comes with blood returning to warm them up. It wasn't coming so I kept kicking, swinging my hands and shivering.

Adrenaline must have really been pumping through me because I became very aware. My mind got clear enough to know we were less than ten miles, for sure, to the truck. Acorn had already picked up the pace. She knew where we were, that the truck, a straw bed and food were waiting.

A working dog team is very quiet, an occasional clink of their collars on metal snaps but usually just breathing and the barely detectable beat of forty dog feet running through the snow. We surprised a great grey owl that jumped down and then glided without a sound just over the leaders for almost a minute. It was as if it had never seen a dog team before and was just taking it in.

Confidence returned and ever so slowly so did the feeling in my fingers. They burned as the blood came back. The pain passed like it always does and in its absence came a feeling of total gratitude; grateful to be in that place in the world, on the sled behind ten of my best friends and just touching the edge of life. It's the place generations past came to, especially in this part of the country. Voyageurs, Native Americans and homesteaders I'm sure got to this place often. Of course many died, while others were closer to the edge of survival than I was on that night. I had to think, though, that there had been countless adventurers over the years up in that country feeling like I did then. Pushed to the edge, totally awake and loving it.

On that night, tired, hungry and cold, the world was perfect. And I have to believe that my dogs, covered in frost, running as fast then as they were ten hours before, thought so too.

In the midnight darkness I could just make out the truck and trailer and next to it a van. It was Sherri. My answering and then losing her call had sent her into a panic, and she drove up there to look for me. I don't know how she thought she was going to find anything other than the truck but there she was with a cold bag of Burger King, and I loved her then more than ever. She ran up, obviously relieved that I was OK. All I could do was smile. I drove down highway 71 eating a cold fish sandwich, French fries and strawberry shake while listening to the Bemidji rock station.

"But it's all right now, in fact it's a gas."

She followed me home and after putting away and feeding the dogs I showered and fell into bed. It was almost 4:00 a.m. The alarm would go off in two hours but I didn't want the night to be over. The last memory of that day was the dogs howling before they too went into their houses to sleep.

"I know puppies, it was a perfect night."

Cocoa (photo by Vonda Bezat)

Chapter 2

"I'm only going to get one more dog." Sherri often reminds me how many times I said that, including before we got our second dog, Cocoa. Sherri and I have always had a soft spot for unwanted dogs. Our first, Sierra, was a lab/husky mix we adopted from a shelter. Our second, Cocoa, a Border Collie-German Shepherd cross was an unwanted farm dog. We adopted her in the fall of 1997, when we were in the process of moving and didn't even have a place to live ourselves.

"Where are you guys going?" Sherri had that look that she knew I was up to something.

"Mike and I are goin' down to Chambers."

"Frank, we have a dog, two cats, no place to live and you're going to get a puppy." Sherri had also heard on the radio that a farmer down there had some extra puppies.

"Sierra's your dog. I'm just gonna look."

She shook her head, knowing that I wasn't capable of just looking at a puppy.

"Let's go Mike." Our five-year-old nephew followed me out, getting hit with the screen as he looked over his shoulder at his Aunt Sherri, wondering if he was also in trouble.

"Your door's still open. Ya gotta really slam it." Mike opened and this time pulled with all his strength. The noise told me that the door to my 1971 Ford F100 was now closed.

"Put yer seatbelt on." Mike pulled across and buckled the waist belt.

"Are we gonna get a puppy?"

"We'll go look at em. Sounds like they could be good dogs."

Sherri and I were staying at her parents' farmhouse in O'Neill, Nebraska. We had been on the road for two months in my old white Ford pickup looking for the place we were going to call home. She'd had a job in Sacramento and after a few weeks there I couldn't handle the summer heat, traffic, smog, everything city. A stop in Prescott, Arizona to stay with my dad for a while ended with Sierra eating his Malibu lights. After my dad's reaction to losing his twenty-dollar lights Sherri said, "I'm leaving." We'd been regrouping in Nebraska and had decided to head back to Minnesota, where I had never wanted to leave in the first place.

The dry ninety-degree September Nebraska air blew in through the wide-open windows. Bruce Springsteen's *Born in the USA* played loud enough in the cassette player to hear it over the truck and the wind. We were heading south down to Chamber's Corner where we turned right onto a shoulderless county road. Another turn south brought us in front of the farm.

"I think this is it, Mike. Looks like they're waiting for us."

The farmer was out in front of the house sitting next to a large all-black German Shepherd. One puppy leaned against its mom and the other ran up to us, tail wagging, then quickly stopped to pee. I waited for her to finish, then picked her up. Carrying the puppy I walked up to the farmer and shook his hand.

"Hi, I'm Frank, the one who called. I guess I talked to your wife. This is Mike, my nephew from O'Neill."

"That's the mom." The farmer pointed down at the regal looking Shepherd. She was easily one hundred pounds. "The dad's the neighbor's border collie." He chuckled. "Must have hopped the fence." We both smiled at the thought of the dad, being less than half the mom's size.

The puppy in my arms was licking my face. She was thickly built, mostly black with a little brown on her legs and face.

"They're almost two months old. Our boy wants this little one here." He pointed to the pup next to its mom. "That's the only one left," he said, nodding to the puppy in my arms.

"Well I guess she's comin home with us."

"No charge," he said. "She'll be a good dog."

"Thanks. I'll take care of her."

I nodded to him. Mike and I turned and walked back to the truck. I set the puppy up on the bench seat between us. Mike slammed the door, really wanting to make sure he got it closed. I left the radio off. For a while we drove in silence. The puppy sat between us, calm, like she had been expecting us to come get her and was now going home. Mike was reaching over petting her head when I looked over at him.

"What should we name her? Probably something black or brown."

Mike slightly scrunched his face, making it clear that he was thinking very intently. "How about Cocoa?"

"You mean like chocolate cocoa?"

"Yeah."

"Ok. Cocoa it is."

Nothing else was said. Cocoa laid her head on my leg for the first time and went to sleep.

❊

Our third dog, Rocky, was also an unwanted farm pet. With these first three I discovered mushing. We began with the dogs pulling me on my cross-country skis. It's called skijoring. I learned to mush being pulled by three dogs chasing rabbits. Most runs ended when we'd find ourselves wrapped around or crashing into a tree.

In the fall I'd train them pulling my mountain bike. One day I had gotten off and, for just a second, let go of the bike. It disappeared around a corner ahead of me, bouncing like a basketball down the trail. Tracking the bike parts, a seat here, handlebars there and then the front wheel, I finally found the dogs rolling in the mud on the shore of a pond.

Cocoa soon established herself as the lead dog and Rocky was a great second. Sierra really just liked to get dressed up in the harness and, unless chasing rabbits, was not much interested in running. I was thinking I needed another dog. A student of mine was volunteering at the Humane Society. She came in one morning and said I had to go in and see this dog. She said he had been abused and was very timid and thin. That afternoon I went in to meet Jessie. As my student had told me, he was cowering in the back of the kennel, was extremely thin and had lost most of his hair. Yet even in that condition I could see he was a beautiful Alaskan Husky with one blue and one brown eye.

I began walking him daily and after a few days the shelter manager asked me to take him home, "No charge. He just needs to go with you. We're afraid he's going to die here."

Despite Sherri's initial "It's me or another dog," she saw him and agreed I could take him home. For the first year all we did was give him good care and not run him very much. He was too nervous. Eventually, very slowly, he learned to be a sled dog and, over time, a leader. Over the years we acquired many more dogs, all with their own stories. None came as far as Jessie. I fed and took care of him but he adored Sherri and completely ignored me when she was around. But since I had four dogs it gave me a reason to buy my first sled.

"It'll be easier to train four dogs at once," I told Sherri.

Jessie (photo by Vonda Bezat)

Chapter 3

In October, 2002 I got to go to a work conference in Reno, Nevada. Sherri stayed at home and took care of our six dogs. My job was teaching Environmental Studies at Bemidji State University, and I had organized a group of students to go to an Outdoor Education conference. I thought my life's work would be to educate the next generation of environmentalists. Together my students and I had explored wild places in Northern Minnesota, South Dakota, Arizona, Utah, Washington, Iceland, and California. One night at that Reno conference, on October 25, changed the direction of my life.

We'd been camping in the desert at the foot of the Sierra Nevada Mountains and spending the days at the conference, learning from some of the national leaders how to be better outdoor educators. It had felt like the perfect week, a focused time to learn and teach with some of my favorite students. During a break, before dinner, I left to go find a phone to call Sherri. Walking through the lobby of the conference center I looked up to see a headline on the television.

"Senator Paul Wellstone dies in plane crash in Northern Minnesota."

Staring in disbelief I watched the footage of the accident and grieving friends and family, some of whom I knew well. Paul Wellstone had been a very influential professor of mine in college. In my freshman year my brother died, and my mom, who raised us herself, became disabled from an injury at work bartending. My world was falling down around me and Professor Wellstone saw a college kid in need. He spent a lot of time with me that spring. He and a caring football coach kept me in school. Later when he ran for and became our US Senator I celebrated with his many supporters. There was a man, an honest caring man, who represented us, who we knew would always fight for those who couldn't fight for themselves: the poor, the sick, the old, and the natural world which was my home. He was in politics because he honestly cared about people. I had been lucky enough to know that from personal experience.

I ran from the Reno conference hall down the road. It was twilight, just after dusk. The streetlights were on and the sky remained illuminated by the countless neon casino lights. Instinctively I looked for a place with no light, some place with trees and water in that sea of concrete. I found a park by the Truckee River. On the bank of the river, in private, I stared at the water, snowmelt from the Sierras, and cried. My chest heaved, tears poured down my face and my nose ran down my chin.

"What use is it all!" I screamed. I'd spent the last ten years of my life taking people outdoors, teaching them to understand it, hoping they'd make it a part of their lives and ultimately work to protect it.

"Now who will they vote for," I wondered out loud.

Paul Wellstone had pulled ahead in a tough re-election fight. The election was just over a week away and now his opponent, Norm Coleman, would surely win. Coleman represented politics at its worst. He stood for nothing, never spoke from his heart or said anything with meaning. He followed the path of least resistance to the top; a Democrat turned Republican because there was an opening. I thought of all the smart good people I knew. None of them held political office. Paul Wellstone had been the only one.

I looked down at the mountain river, channeled in concrete, casino lights illuminating its surface.

"I've gotta do something else."

Closing my eyes I tried to focus on my breathing, then listened to the faint sound of the water flowing and tried to smell its mountain home. Then out loud I recited the Serenity Prayer. The immediate quiet of the little park returned. I wiped off my face, got up and slowly walked back to the hotel.

In the spring of 2003 I was, for the third time, trying to finish my PhD at the University of Minnesota. Dann Siems—my friend and fellow Environmental Studies teacher at Bemidji State—and I were making the drive from Bemidji to the Minneapolis campus twice a week. Dann was an uncompromising advocate for protecting the natural world, and most of the time I was right there with him. When I wasn't, he'd beat me into submission with his constant unrelenting logic.

"Damn it, Dann. Just SHUT UP! OK? If you don't I'm going to pull over and kick your ass out. I'm serious."

Not one of my finer moments but he was right, and I knew it. We were talking about the threats to Northern Minnesota's environment, primarily mining. Dann said I needed to do something about it.

"Frank, you've got the skills to do it. You're well liked, good looking and don't come off like a radical, like I do. You know that campaigns drive issue discussions. If you really care about the environment, you've got to run for office."

"I can't believe that putz is our State Representative. Someone needs to beat that guy."

I had just walked out of a Legislative Update meeting in Bemidji. It was April, 2003. Doug Fuller had tried to explain his vote of cutting funding for Bemidji State University:

"The students can just borrow more money."

He voted to cut money for the DNR: "Trees are a crop. We just need to harvest more," was his explanation.

Fuming on the sidewalk in front of City Hall where the meeting was, I called Sherri. "I'm running for the Minnesota House of Representatives."

"You're doing what?"

I spent the next eleven months preparing for the campaign, travelling North Central Minnesota, and meeting with everyone I could think of who might be supportive. Doug Fuller was a three-term incumbent Republican who had earned the distinction as a member of the "Toxic Twelve" from the Minnesota Sierra Club for consistently voting against the environment. The Republicans were organized and well-financed. I was a political newcomer, and when I told people what I planned to do I got comments like:

"How are YOU going to beat Doug Fuller?"

"Fuller's a lifer. We'll never get rid of him."

But now and then I'd get a: "I can't stand that guy. Ya know, you might just be the one to beat him."

Most mornings before I'd hit the campaign trail, I'd take the dogs out for a run. On one of those mornings, in February, we were out near Pinewood, Minnesota, and crossed a road. A school busload of kids was stopped at the crossing and all the kids were plastered to the bus windows, watching us pass by. Many of the kids were waving, some pulled down their windows and yelled out at the dogs. Even the driver was excited to see us and honked the bus horn. I smiled and waved back. And there it dawned on me, "Why don't I let the dogs help me campaign? Everyone loves sled dogs."

On Monday morning, March 2, 2004, we formally launched the campaign from King Elementary in Deer River. After a brief talk to the students and teachers, that could hardly be heard over the barking of our six-dog team, I took off on a five-day dog sled trip around the Minnesota House district that I hoped to represent; wearing blue jeans, leather work boots and gloves, and a light jacket. I was pulled by what I could hardly call a dog team. They were more a dog pack. The leaders were Cocoa and Rocky. Jester was behind them along with Peanut, who was barely a year old. She was an Alaskan Husky that we'd just gotten as a puppy the summer before. In wheel were Lola and Bobcat, who were also Alaskans and had each just turned two. My dog sled team was four huskies led by a German Shepherd/Border Collie Mix and a Chow mix. Rocky, the Chow, kept turning around, trying to fight with Jester and Bobcat. Then Cocoa would chew him out. With all that testosterone on the team she was still the boss.

The plan was to leave Deer River on Monday, camp along the way, and on Friday cross Lake Bemidji and finish at a campaign rally at the foot of the statue of Paul Bunyan and Babe the Blue Ox. It was a trip designed to get both media attention and to highlight the campaign theme, "Protecting Our Northern Minnesota Way of Life." To me it meant protecting our environment.

Up to that point I had never run my dog team farther than eight miles at once. The trip would be over ten miles a day for five days. Years later I'd laugh thinking about the relatively short distance we travelled that week. But then, with my little wooden sled, blue jeans and a leader that wasn't even a husky, it seemed barely possible. For most of the trip I had a handling crew of two, James Conley and Jon Schmeling, two recent Bemidji State graduates who had nothing better to do than help me and the dogs cross highways and camp out at night.

We thought the idea for the sled dog trip was brilliant, that all the statewide media would pick it up, maybe even the national news. With all of our press releases and reminder calls, only the *Western Itasca Review*, a weekly newspaper with a circulation of about five hundred, showed up for our departure from Deer River on Monday. After an uneventful run I arrived in Winnie Dam Monday afternoon to find only my dog truck and a note from Jon and James. They'd gone to get something to eat. Nobody else was there.

On Tuesday the plan was to meet Sherri at the end of the day in Bena, population fifty-one. The dog team was running north on the shoulder of County Road 8 when I saw the dog truck.

"Haw, Cocoa, haw."

Cocoa had already seen the truck and, knowing it meant food and a straw bed, headed straight into the parking lot of the Big Winnie Bar. There was only one other car in the parking lot. Disappointed that nobody seemed to care that the dogs and I were running across the district, I quietly hugged Sherri and we went about unhooking and feeding the dogs.

Sherri was doing everything she could to be upbeat. "They have pizza inside. You want to go in and get something to eat?"

"Sure. Let's get the dogs put away first."

Just as I was lifting Bobcat into the truck a minivan drove up, then a pick-up and another car. Three families and all their kids jumped out. The kids' faces looked like it was Christmas morning.

"Are they sled dogs?"

"Can we pet them?"

Immediately we were surrounded. Sherri helped me answer all their questions and I was sure to slip in that it was beginning of my political campaign. Eventually they all left and we went in for our pizza. Other than the bartender, we were the only ones in the place.

"I'll be with you in a minute."

We looked into a doorway behind the bar and could see a woman preparing a whole table full of individual meals. When she finally came out I had to ask:

"What are you doing back there? We're the only ones here."

"Meals On Wheels. We prepare and deliver over thirty meals twice a day. Helps keep the lights on and it's all these people get to eat. Well, it used to help keep the lights on but since they dropped the reimbursement to only two dollars and thirty-five cents a meal, it's hard to break even. But they still gotta eat."

We ordered our pizza and a couple of cokes. Sherri wanted to know all about the day's run.

"It was fine, beautiful trail. The dogs did great." But I was distracted by the bartender scooping portions into the little compartments of the tin foil dinner trays. Here was a business—clinging to its own survival—whose owner found time to make sure that the poor in the area got at least two meals a day.

When she brought our pizza I asked," Are you going to be able to keep doing meals on wheels?"

"I'm going to try. This is the only commercial kitchen in this part of the county. You guys need anything else?"

"No thanks." When I came in the door I was only thinking about the intense hunger I get from being outside all day in the cold on the sled. The desire to quickly devour the pizza in front of me made me feel intensely selfish. I could eat, virtually any time or thing I wanted. I didn't have to wait at home hoping that someone would again bring me my meals. Sherri and I quietly ate our pizza and I debated whether even to tell the woman why we were at her bar that night.

Sherri pulled out one of my small brochures. "You should tell her."

The woman came back out. "Thanks for the pizza. It was exactly what I needed."

I paused awkwardly. "I'm running for the Minnesota House of Representatives, to be your and your customers' representative in Saint Paul." I handed her the brochure.

She looked down at the brochure, then up at me. "No politician's ever been in here."

It was quiet as she stared into my eyes, as if looking into my intentions. A small smile formed on her lips.

"Good luck. Thanks for comin in." She picked up our plates, put them on the pizza pan and carried them back into the kitchen.

The next two days were spent out on the trail, the only public event being a planned arrival at Cass Lake Elementary on Thursday, just as the kids were leaving school to get on the buses. It was mayhem trying to keep the excited kids from overwhelming the dogs. Sherri, James, and Jon were there helping me keep order.

Sherri yelled out, "How about we all get in a line!"

Soon almost a hundred kids were lined up to greet the dogs. It was useless for me to try and say anything. They were only interested in petting our dogs and sharing their stories.

"We've got a dog. His name's Pogo."

"My dog got hit by a car."

"He looks just like my dog!"

Again it wasn't the campaign event I had envisioned. I looked up from my kneeling position, holding onto Cocoa and Rocky, and saw the reporter from the *Cass Lake Times*, taking a picture that would find its way to the cover of the local paper that weekend.

The teachers and bus drivers had been patiently standing behind the children, letting them enjoy the dogs. One of the drivers had decided it was time for the kids to get on the bus.

"OK! Time to go!"

We had our departure planned for that moment, when the kids were loading onto the buses. Sherri grabbed the leaders from me and I walked back and jumped on the sled. James and Jon ran across the school playground making a trail for the dogs to follow and just as they got to the other side of the yard I yelled out, "Let's go!"

Holding onto the sled I turned and waved. All eyes were on us as we ran through the schoolyard, down a sidewalk and out of sight. We only had twenty more miles, in the next twenty-four hours, to make our entry at our campaign kick-off rally in Bemidji.

❋

"Come on, Cocoa. It's OK."

She was hesitating at the bridge. It was a hundred yard span of US 2, outside of Bemidji. Cocoa looked back as if to say, "Are you sure?"

"Good girl, Cocoa. Let's go."

She threw herself into her harness. Rocky barked, then followed suit. With the sounds of trucks and cars roaring below, we made our first ever crossing of a highway bridge. I paused at the top and looked down at the four lanes of sixty-five-mile-an-hour traffic. I'm sure none in the cars noticed a sled dog team up on the bridge above them but I waved just in case.

A half mile past the bridge the trail wound its way through the Bemidji Industrial Park. I was just able to stop the team in time to watch two semis drive right in front of Cocoa and Rocky. We were in the city of Bemidji, on a paved, barely snow-covered bike trail heading for the middle of town. Cocoa, head down, continued to lead the team like we were out in the middle of the woods, paying no attention to the surrounding traffic. We passed the grocery store and our favorite restaurant, Keith's Pizza. Keith's was at the corner of a major intersection that we were going to have to cross. We waited at the light, a six-dog team, me on the sled, waiting for the light to change.

"Whoa, Cocoa. Whoa."

She stood still at the intersection, listening for my next command. The light turned green. I looked to be sure that all traffic had stopped and we easily crossed all four lanes. There we did get some looks. I waved but was more focused on Cocoa hitting the trail on the other side of Bemidji Avenue, which she did easily. Soon we crossed another four lane road, Roosevelt Avenue, then headed down a residential road before we reached an established trailhead, on the south shore of Lake Bemidji. We had travelled two miles through the city, with no assistance, and Cocoa led us like we were all sitting in a minivan. It was completely uneventful.

❈

Getting the dogs to cross Lake Bemidji was going to be a challenge. Our team had always run on established trails. Lake Bemidji was an endless maze of thousands of snowmobile tracks. The dogs were going to have to run straight across the lake, finishing at a rally at the statues of Paul Bunyan and Babe the Blue Ox at exactly one o-clock, the time we told the media I'd be arriving.

"Hey, Mark. I'm going to need your help." I called him the night before.

My friend Mark Morrissey is a cross-country ski racer. We made a plan that he would meet me at the trailhead at 12:30. There we would rest a few minutes and Mark would ski the two miles across the lake and Cocoa would lead the team behind him. Sherri, James, and Jon would be waiting on the other side.

From across Lake Bemidji we could hear the band, Drew's Cruisers, playing at the rally. It was just me, Mark, and our dogs waiting on the opposite shore. There was a quiet moment when Mark and I looked at each other. From this point on, things would change. The outside world would hear about our campaign. Sherri's and my relatively private life would be gone and a public political life lay ahead. In my head I reconfirmed the decision that I made on the edge of the Trukee River seventeen months earlier. After one more pause and a deep breath:

"OK, Cocoa, let's go."

The front page of the *Bemidji Pioneer* the next morning had a photo of us finishing on the shore of Lake Bemidji. Cocoa and Rocky were leading. Sherri, James, and Jon were there to guide the team in. Mark, dressed in his ski clothes, was smiling in the background. It really didn't matter how the story read, the picture was perfect. Every other newspaper in the district also covered our trip.

Finishing on Lake Bemidji (photo by Monte Draper of the *Bemidji Pioneer*)

Our plan to launch the campaign was a success, and it wasn't long before the opposition responded. Their primary intent was to try and label us as extremists. I had once been a, gulp, vegetarian and Sherri, well she was a yoga teacher. That clearly put us outside the mainstream, so they argued.

A chicken-wing-eating contest was being held as a fundraiser for the local wrestling team. Doug Fuller publicly challenged me to participate, thinking that I would decline. He would then show what a big man he was by eating all those nasty greasy chicken wings and then his campaign would ask: "Where was Frank Moe?" Sherri and Pam, my Campaign Manager, both said I should ignore it, not stoop to his level. Mike, my Communications Manager, and I had another plan. I entered the contest.

I had been a vegetarian but was no longer. Still I ate pretty healthily and most of the meat I ate was wild game, fish or organic beef we got from Sherri's parents. The thought of eating even one chicken wing turned my stomach, but I'm pathologically competitive. I'd eat more than him, or die trying.

The contest was covered live on a local radio station and a friend of mine, Johnny Lee Walker, was the DJ. On the stage were twenty men, sports team coaches mostly, but other local personalities as well. I purposely sat next to Doug Fuller. Johnny was at a table right in front of us announcing the competition.

"Five, four, three, two, one, GOOOO!"

I dove in with two hands. Holding the end of the wing I'd bite down and strip everything off the bone by pulling it sideways through my mouth. As I chewed and swallowed I threw each bone at Johnny.

"And Frank Moe finished another wing. He's throwing the bones right at me."

Johnny laughed hysterically on the air every time I hit him with a bone.

I glanced over long enough to catch a terrified look on Fuller's face as he held a wing with both hands and daintily tried to eat only the meat off the wing. Mike was picking up all my bones to be sure we had a count of our victory.

"Time's up! Put down your wings!" The contest was over and I looked down the line. My pile of chicken bones was one of the largest and easily twice as large as Doug Fuller's. The smile on my face covered up that I was seconds from puking. I quickly got up, congratulated one of the football coaches, who was announced as the winner, nodded to Johnny and tried to look casual walking to my truck. The closest private bathroom I knew of was at Leukens grocery store just down the block. A parking spot was open right in front and in seconds I was kneeling at the toilet, where I stayed for the next ten minutes.

The next day was the election primary. Neither Fuller nor I had primary challengers so it wasn't contested but still it was covered in the media and vote totals were given. The timing was perfect for our ad that ran in the paper that day.

Below a picture of Doug Fuller and I at the contest read:

"Moe beats Fuller 27-14. Eating chicken wings that is."

We were running against a three-term incumbent whose party was going to do anything not to lose. They responded to our ad with a barrage of TV, newspaper and radio ads of their own. Again they chose to ignore the issues, and Fuller's record on them, but instead doubled down on their strategy to label me as an extremist.

For years I had been a volunteer EMT and that summer was on my way home from a call. I was the first on the scene of a rollover accident, where a family of five had been unbelted and were all thrown from the car. For ten minutes, which at the time seemed like an eternity, I gave the best care I could. Finally an ambulance showed up and the paramedics took over. After I helped them load all the victims into ambulances, I got in my truck and drove home. I'm usually pretty calm during the incident but once I got in the car, I began to shake. Looking at my hands I saw that they, and my arms and legs, were covered in blood. I took a few deep breaths and started the truck. Commercials were playing on the local Bemidji rock station and my attention was grabbed by hearing my name.

"Did you know that Frank Moe cares more about plants and animals than people? So if you're a tree, a deer or a walleye, vote for

Frank Moe. But if you care about your kids' schools, your families' health care or low property taxes, then vote for State Representative Doug Fuller."

My blood soaked hands gripped the steering wheel. I started to fume. Up to that point I had ignored all the lies and attacks, choosing to just focus on our own campaign, what we hoped to accomplish if elected. This was the last straw for me. Doug Fuller's voting record was exactly opposite to the claims that his radio ads were saying, and it was time for me to point that out.

When I got home I dug out my voice recorder and turned on the radio, waiting to hear the ad again. Sure enough it ran soon after I got home and I recorded it. That night there were two public events that Doug Fuller and I were both scheduled to attend. The first was a public meeting to discuss early childhood education. Fuller had claimed to be an early childhood champion and in spite of his consistent votes to cut early childhood funding, was a member of the Early Childhood Caucus in the Minnesota House of Representatives. Because of this he was invited to sit at the table with the presenters in front of the audience and media. At the end of the presentation Fuller was asked to give his remarks where he professed his unending support for early childhood education. The presenters were the legitimate state advocates for the cause and chose not to challenge Fuller and his clearly dishonest statements. I would not be so polite. After his comments the presenter asked if there were any questions. I quickly stood up.

"Hi my name is Frank Moe. I am an EMT, a teacher and am running for the Minnesota House of Representatives. I was at the scene of a tragic traffic accident today on North Irvine Avenue."

The crowd was hushed as I briefly described the day's events. Many had clearly already heard about the crash.

"Doug Fuller sits in front of you now saying that he supports this important cause yet his actual voting record is one hundred percent in opposition of what you all are working for. It always has been. But he talks a good game here and many of you are probably thinking you might vote for him again. How does he get away with these lies? Here's the ad I heard on the radio on the way home from the traffic accident today."

I played the commercial to the stunned audience. Just as the commercial ended the room erupted. Many were yelling for an explanation. Some were angered that the event had turned so political. The head presenter was especially angry that I had hijacked her event and she tried to get things back on track.

"Please, if any of you are interested in learning more about Early Childhood Education in Minnesota, we will stay here to answer any questions."

She was someone I knew and it was obvious to me that she was very upset. I didn't care. I had hit Fuller hard and the night had just begun. The second event of the night was a televised public debate to be held at a large assisted-living facility in Bemidji. I walked out to my truck and smiled. The trap was set. Fuller was publically embarrassed. We guessed that he'd become reckless. He would not disappoint us.

In the debate I repeatedly called Fuller out on his actual voting record, citing bills, dates and his votes that were on the prevailing side to cut funding for senior programs. Fuller's campaign manager was sitting right in front of me. As my attacks hit home again and again he got redder and redder. The sweat was beading up on both his and Fuller's foreheads. It was time for our closing statements. Fuller was first. He decided now was the time to spring HIS trap, retake control of the campaign. His campaign had done research and found that I had been the Assistant Guide for a Buddhist meditation backpacking trip in 1995 where I served a vegetarian menu. They knew this was their smoking gun. I was clearly not a real Northern Minnesotan and not to be trusted. He launched his attack.

"Well Frank, I didn't want to do this but I have to tell these people who you really are. Folks, we've learned that Frank Moe led a backpacking trip where vegetarian food was served for AN ENTIRE WEEK! We don't need a radical like Frank representing us down in Saint Paul. Please I again ask for your vote to return to the Capitol as your State Representative."

He looked at me as he sat down with a smirk on his face. He had me. I was done. I heard a small laugh from the audience. It was Geri, his wife. She and Fuller's campaign manager high-fived each other. I stood up and walked over to the microphone.

"First I'd like to thank you all for coming out to this debate tonight, to our hosts and all watching from their homes. I hope you've heard some things that will help you decide on which of us you'll be voting for on Election Day. And thanks to my opponent Doug Fuller for a great and spirited debate. I'm sure he's worked hard in this campaign. I know I have. Doug, I think I've talked to about everyone in this district over the past year. Been to every fair, knocked on almost ten thousand doors and ya know what? Everyone I talk to I ask what the most important thing to them is in this election. Many of them tell me it's their kids' schools, or their parents' nursing homes, or their rising property taxes, or clean air and water. But not one person, not one, has said the most important thing to them is what kind of food I served ten years ago on a backpacking trip."

I paused, smiled and shook my head, then looked right at Fuller.

"Doug, are you still sore about me beating you at that chicken wing eating contest? Really it's not that big a deal. Ya gotta get over it."

The place erupted in laughter. I left the mic and walked back to my chair. Fuller's Campaign Manager jumped to his feet and ran up to me with a look in his eye that said he was ready to fight. Sherri led a group that saw him coming and immediately stepped in front of him. I just looked at him and smiled. To my side a group of Fuller's supporters gathered around him shaking their heads in disbelief. I walked into the crowd and shook as many hands as I could before the crowd dispersed. Our campaign all went out to eat at TGI Friday's that night. We were winning and let ourselves celebrate...a little. We knew there was more to come but we couldn't have imagined what.

Three weeks before the election the Beltrami County Republican Party held a press conference in front of Paul Bunyan and Babe the Blue Ox on the waterfront in Bemidji. Lined up in front of a logging truck were several guys who were looking intentionally rough; stern looks on their faces, dressed in hunting clothes, somehow trying to appear like the "Real Northern Minnesotans." One guy, who was the chairman of the local county Republican party, dressed in blaze orange and was wearing a clown wig. He was actually standing behind a church pulpit and made several allegations against me. His rant concluded with waving around a piece of paper that he said was an affidavit saying that I admitted to dressing as a clown and chased deer from deer hunters, or deer hunters from deer. I can't remember which. Now I've done some crazy stuff in my life but putting myself in front of a loaded deer rifle? All the local press was there and so was Mike, from my campaign. He called me from the rally.

"Frank, you're never going to believe this."

At our campaign meeting that night there was panic. They all wanted blood. We needed to expose all the bad things this guy had ever done.

"They want dirt, we'll give it to em," was their cry.

I just listened. After it died down I said, "We've won. We just need to keep doing what we're doing. They're desperate. We're not gonna be."

Three weeks later it was election night. At two in the morning I was sitting in front of a computer at our campaign party at the Hampton Inn in Bemidji. Most of the two hundred supporters had already gone home and would find out in the morning the election results. I kept hitting refresh on the Secretary of State's website to see if the results from the city of Bemidji had come in yet. With eighty percent of the precincts reporting, we were down by a few hundred votes. Fuller won the rural areas and pockets of wealthy lakeshore properties. I had won the cities and Leech Lake Reservation. It was very close. Bemidji would determine the outcome. Refresh. Refresh. Refresh. Then the numbers came up. We won Bemidji by a two to one margin.

"WE WON!!!"

I was standing on a table in the middle of the ballroom, jumping up and down.

"We won."

My eyes opened the next morning and I looked around at our sunlit bedroom for a minute before I remembered the election and party the night before. Sherri was already gone. She had to be at work by eight. I laid my hand down next to the bed and there was Cocoa, my trusted leader. I rubbed her head as she stood up, stretched, licked my face, then lay back down on the floor next to me, where she always slept. For the first time it dawned on me that Cocoa wouldn't be with me at the Capitol in Saint Paul. I'd be going down every week alone. It was the morning after the election. I was missing them already and I wouldn't leave for over a month.

"We won, Cocoa. You'll take care of Sherri, won't you? We'll get some runs in on the weekends. I promise."

I repeated that dog sled trip around the district every winter that I was in office. For me it was the highlight of my political year. I took off on the sled every morning after having breakfast at a coffee shop in one of the towns in the district. After getting to spend the day on the trail with the dogs, I finished every afternoon at a school in another town just as the kids were running out the door heading to the buses. Their parents and the press were always there.

One day while we were in Session at the Capitol, Pat Garofalo, a friend and Republican Representative from Farmington, smiled and shook his head. "We're never going to beat you." he said as he tossed a copy of a news story of our latest dogsled trip onto my desk.

Some had high hopes for my political career but I had other ideas. I'd caught a bug during that first sled dog trip but it wasn't politics. We entered our first sled dog race, the Mid-Minnesota 150, in February of 2006, two years after my election. Out of thirty teams we placed fifth, and my obsession grew.

Our friend Lisa, who was also an obsessive campaign worker for me, loved taking care of the dogs when I was at the Capitol. Pam, who managed my first campaign, blamed Lisa for enabling my growing sled dog addiction.

"If you didn't take care of those dogs when he was in Saint Paul, he wouldn't get so many."

During my second term in the Legislature Sherri helped me find an apartment in Saint Paul that would allow pets.

"Cocoa, you take care of him for me," she said as Cocoa followed me out to the truck every Sunday night for the drive to Saint Paul.

Cocoa retired from mushing the year after the trip across the district. She spent most of her retirement on the couch or next to my bed. Now and then she'd walk around the dog yard to greet the other dogs but Cocoa preferred the warmth of the rug by the fire in the cabin. When the other dogs were being hooked up to run, she would lift her head and let out a half-hearted howl then put her head back down on her crossed front paws.

We lost Cocoa last April just shy of her fifteenth birthday. Sitting in my chair by the fire last winter I had noticed her twitching on the rug at my feet. I watched her legs move. She was running in her sleep. I wondered if she was dreaming of our days together on the trail, when we learned, or she taught me, to run a dog sled...

Winnie (photo by Vonda Bezat)

Chapter 4

Icy trails are about the worst for sled dogs. Feet going every which way can pull and tear muscles, ligaments and tendons. So on days after a thaw or rain in the winter, we all stayed in our houses for the day and dreamed of better days on the trail. I don't know who was worse, me or the dogs. Sherri says I was a caged animal when I couldn't get out and run dogs in the winter. When I'd go outside for any reason the dogs got out of their houses, barked, howled and watched my every move. Acorn never took her eyes off me and sounded the alarm whenever my actions looked promising. Grabbing a harness or sled sent the yard into an uproar.

It was the first week in January, 2007, and it was the second day of rain. I had to leave the next day for Saint Paul and the beginning of the legislative session. We hadn't had any measurable snow that winter and I hadn't hooked up the dogs to a dog sled since the previous March. Our training runs had only been the dogs pulling me on an ATV. Now I was going to be leaving soon, only to come home for short weekends until the session was over in May or June.

By mid-morning I realized it wasn't going to stop raining so I put on a raincoat—in Bemidji, Minnesota, in January—and went out to feed and take care of the dogs. I also needed to cover up the sleds and trailer. The radio said we were going to get a quarter of an inch of ice and that would really make a mess of all the gear. When I went out into the dog yard they looked at me like there was something I could do about the weather.

"Dad, can't you change the channel, we wanna go run."

One dog, Winnie, wouldn't even eat he was so upset. Looking at him just sitting outside of his house in the rain you'd never know what an awesome dog he was. I had two leaders, Acorn and Fly, which were smarter, but Winnie was the heart of the team. He would never quit. The measure of a sled dog is how tight they keep their tugline. Not once in his life had Winnie's been slack. At the end of races I'd found ice chunks the size of golf balls in his paws, and deeply cut pads and sprained wrists that would have put me on crutches. Never did he even alter his gait, to let me know that there was a problem. I got into the habit of checking his feet every time we stopped, just in case.

Like almost all our dogs Winnie was an Alaskan Husky. What that really means is he was a mutt husky. His markings only gave a hint that there was some Siberian Husky somewhere in his distant heritage but his build was somewhere between a German Shorthair Pointer and a Greyhound. Alaskans have been bred for generations to be tough, fast and have unbelievable endurance. Our team when trained could average over 11 miles an hour for over 60 miles and, after resting for just a few hours, turn around and could run that same 60 miles over again.

Good sled dogs can also eat, a lot. An Alaskan Husky can both eat and burn 10,000 calories a day. That's an animal a quarter my size so the equivalent of me eating 40,000 calories a day or about 60 Big Macs. Sled dogs need protein, vitamins and minerals just like we do but over half of those calories are from fat. For our dogs, that meant beef and several hours a week of me picking up, sorting, trimming and bagging butcher shop scraps: hearts, livers, kidneys, excess fat and the bits of meat attached to it. I think my hands permanently smelled like beef fat. I'd long since stopped noticing it but Sherri did. She often said she'd sworn she wouldn't marry a farmer.

After I fed all the dogs their mixture of beef, fat, water and dry dog food, I grabbed a couple of bales of straw out of the shed and went around to each dog house, filling it with fresh dry straw. The freezing rain was still falling and the dogs all quickly curled up in their new beds. I returned to the house to pack for Saint Paul.

❄

It finally snowed six inches on the first Thursday in January. Early in the legislative year I could usually get away from the Capitol in time to be home Friday. I drove home late Friday night and was awake before first light on Saturday morning. It was a perfect day to train, about zero degrees, little wind and some clouds to block the sun. On the flat lake surface, with only a few inches of new snow, the team was flying. Being the first week in January, the lake ice was at least two feet thick. That's strong enough to hold a semi, but like many lakes there is a current in parts of Big Lake. Coming around an island in the middle of the lake I saw steam rising from the ice right in front of the team. The current had opened up a thirty-foot hole and we were a couple of seconds from dropping right into it. Being that close to possible death made me instantly very aware. Everything slowed down and the next few seconds seemed like minutes.

Without thinking I yelled out, "Acorn! Gee!"

The team turned ninety degrees to the right and all of their feet landed only inches from the large steaming hole in the ice. When the sled got to the opening it was so close that the left sled runner was running right next to the hole. The sled then spun to the right from the pull of the dogs and was teetering on the edge of the ice. I was looking straight down into the lake when I screamed, "Let's Go!"

All twelve dogs threw everything into their harnesses. My sled lurched forward, popping it out of the hole in the ice and we sprinted across the lake. I just stood on the runners, heart racing.

We travelled the two miles across the lake before I even thought to give them another command.

I yelled "HAW, Acorn! HAW!" as we approached the edge of the lake. We turned to the left and for the rest of the run we would stay close to the shore, as far away from the opening as possible. The dogs were running fast and the snow was too thin on the ice to slow them down, so I gave up trying and we travelled the remaining 12 miles home in less than an hour.

Being close to death like that makes you think. It's funny, I don't really fear death, often just wonder about it. But rationally thinking about it, not fearing death and facing it out on the ice are two different things. When death presents itself, unplanned, all my defenses come to immediate alert. Everything in my DNA drives me to stay alive, keeps me from freezing to death or falling into a hole in a frozen lake. The adrenalin surge afterwards had my heart racing and mind totally awake. Travelling around the lake that day, having looked straight down into the freezing water, I knew I was lucky to be alive. Saint Paul couldn't have felt further away.

That night, as I took off my boots next to the fire, I tried to explain the day's run to Sherri, how fast the dogs went and how excited I was to be on the sled again.

Her only response was, "What? You almost went through the ice?"

※

A friend once asked me about giving sled dog rides. He looked at me funny when I laughed at him. I explained that I didn't have touring dogs but race dogs. There was a difference. His look told me he still didn't understand, so I told him really why I didn't give sled dog rides.

In December, 2008 my friend and Veterinarian, Jerry Vanek, had convinced me to give rides to a group of doctors and medical residents who were his students at a Wilderness Medicine workshop. I had given a few rides over the years and could use the money. It was less than a week before Christmas.

It was a warm afternoon, thirty-five degrees and foggy. We split the group of twelve into two and the plan was to give rides between the two groups which were stationed five miles from each other. The first nine rides went off as planned. It was getting dark and I had only three rides to give. The tenth rider was a female doctor who was so excited to be on her first dog sled ride. It was the part of the workshop that she was most looking forward to.

Winter thaws are a time when animals who aren't true hibernators get up and walk around, looking for food or whatever the heck else they do. Three miles into the ride we crested a hill and I heard my passenger: "Oh cute, a porcupine."

I had only a second before the team descended on this quill infested disaster. My only hope to stop the freight train was throwing the sled on its side against a tree on the edge of the trail; but I had a passenger whose head would hit the tree at twenty-five miles an hour.

All I could do was scream "WHOAAAAA!!" and try to brake. In the light of my headlamp I watched the porcupine turn his body so his butt faced the dogs and spread his quills out like a Christmas wreath.

Into the porcupine the dogs ran, literally shredding and swallowing half of it. I was able to grab and kick the remaining half into the woods and turned to see seven of the ten dogs tearing at their faces and covered in quills.

They may not always be the smartest creatures but sled dogs are tough. After some soothing and coaching I was able to get the team back on the trail. Every few seconds one of the dogs would stop to dig at the quills in their face or mouth but eventually they'd all start running again. They knew their job, and that was to pull the sled.

My passenger never said another word.

Approaching the group at the end of the trail, I yelled, "Jerry, you got a Leatherman? The dogs ate a porcupine!"

From there it was a blur. The interns were fresh out of med school and turned the trailhead into an ER ward. A heavy wet snow was now falling. Teams of two were soon working on every dog with headlamps, pliers and hemostats.

Within an hour all but three of my best dogs were free of quills. Tina, Ace and Etta had swallowed part of the porcupine and would need anesthesia to get the quills out of their mouths and throats. These dogs were great at whatever they did, including eating porcupines. We loaded the dogs into the truck. Two still enthusiastic interns volunteered to join Jerry and me at my house to continue removing quills. It was after 10:00 p.m..

The snow had turned into a full-blown snowstorm and several inches were already on the ground. While driving to my house I started feeling dizzy and sick to my stomach but didn't think anything of it. I was worried about the dogs and was worked up by the last few hours of excitement.

After getting the other dogs put away I brought Ace, Tina, and Etta into the house, put them in crates and got a fire going in the woodstove. Jerry and the interns arrived and we began working on getting the remaining quills out. Jerry had gone home and gotten his emergency vet kit. His plan was to sedate the dogs to make it easier to get the remaining quills out.

Sticking needles into sled dogs is usually a challenge but for dogs who had had dozens of porcupine quills ripped out of their face and mouths, it was nearly impossible. Each time was a four-on-one wrestling match. Ace is a lean, powerful, sixty-five pound male that didn't want to be stuck. Only after I threw myself on top of Ace was Jerry finally able to get the catheter into Ace's leg.

I was sweating and feeling cold but still paid it no attention. Tina and Ace immediately calmed down and were almost asleep. Etta didn't relax at all. She was barking and trying to bust out of her crate, scratching at her face and barking.

"Jerry, what did you give Etta? She's out of control."

Jerry looked perplexed. "Must be a paradoxical reaction."

Jerry doesn't speak like normal humans.

We had to leave Etta in the crate, hoping that she would settle down while we worked on Ace and Tina.

I was sitting next to the woodstove but was shivering with a cold sweat running down my face. "Jerry, I'm gonna be sick."

One of the interns ran and grabbed the garbage can and handed it to me. There went my lunch and everything that I'd drunk since.

"Frank, you look pale. Are you going into shock?'

"What from, Jerry?" Yaaaaakkkk.

I was an active EMT and had been on the scene of many gruesome car accidents. Seeing blood didn't have much effect on me. I couldn't be in shock just from seeing the dogs bleeding.

After I had emptied all that was in my stomach I dropped the garbage can on the floor and my head fell back in the chair. For the next few hours I was in and out of consciousness while Jerry and the interns worked on the dogs. Their wounds bled freely all over the floor.

Jerry continued to talk, of course, hypothesizing about why Etta was still wide awake and why I was sick and asleep. Occasionally I'd wake up to his questions.

"What did you eat for lunch, Frank?"

"What?" Dry heave.

"For lunch, what did you eat for lunch?"

"I don't know....a turkey sandwich."

"How old was the Turkey?"

"How the heck am I supposed to know that?" Dry heave.

"Maybe a week or so."

I fell back asleep to my good friend and veterinarian Jerry laughing. So Jerry, the veterinarian, was monitoring my vital signs and keeping me from choking on my puke, and the medical interns were pulling quills out of and treating the wounds on the dogs.

The phone rang and one of the interns picked it up.

"Let me give you to Jerry, he can explain it better than I can."

"Jerry, Frank's wife's on the phone."

"Hi Sherri, Frank's acquired Staphylococcus Aureus"

If it weren't for a plane crash in Antarctica that almost took his life, Jerry would have completed his PhD in Parasitology to add to his DVM. He's the only guy I know who gets off on looking at dog crap under a magnifying glass and honestly spent one night showing us the differences between male, female, and nymph deer ticks while we were eating dinner.

"Jerry, speak English. How's Frank?"

Eventually Sherri got the story. It was almost Christmas and she was working late at the flower shop we owned in Walker, and now had to drive the thirty miles home in a snowstorm. It took her an hour and a half to get there. It was almost 1 a.m. when she walked in on the scene. The smell of blood on the floor and my puke almost made her sick. In spite of the dropping temperature and snowstorm, Sherri threw open all the windows and began scrubbing the floors.

Jerry and the interns finished with Ace and Tina. Etta didn't calm down enough to remove any more of her quills that night. She'd need to go into Bemidji Veterinary Hospital in the morning. All three dogs spent the night in their crates in the house. After a week off Ace and Tina were able to return to training and raced on our ninth-place White Oak team in January. Etta didn't run again the whole season. Porcupine quills had been pushed up through the roof of her mouth and several came out the top of her nose over the next two months. A few quills even came out her eye sockets. Etta eventually recovered completely and ran with us in every race the following year. She liked being in the house too. Eventually she'll probably spend every night there.

I spent Christmas in bed. To this day I can't even stand the smell of deli turkey or the sight of a porcupine.

Sherri's Team (photo by Jerry Szymaniak)

Chapter 5

It was January, 2009, and Sherri was running in the six-dog recreational class of the White Oak Classic. The White Oak was a great regional race with almost a hundred teams participating in four different classes. Hundreds of people had shown up in Deer River, Minnesota, to experience the feel of a sled dog race and be a part of Minnesota's past.

"She'll be fine," I thought as I watched 400 pounds of jumping, barking adolescent dogs in front of Sherri. What we didn't know, but Sherri was about to find out, was that one of them was in heat. As Sherri left the chute, sled runners hardly touching the snow, I had a vision of a skateboard behind an eighteen-wheeler truck. She left my sight; I said a prayer and did my best to let her go. Sherri had run that race the year before and even placed fifth in her class.

I returned to the truck with our handlers Lisa and Teri, to get my team ready for the ten-dog 130-mile race that was going to start in about an hour. We were going through our standard pre-race routine and were beginning to take the dogs out of their boxes and tether them around the truck when Lisa's phone rang.

❈

Sherri and her team left the chute cleanly. Soon after the start the race trail took several sharp turns. One of those turns directed the teams into the ditch next to a road. I've always had trouble convincing the dogs that running in the deep snow in the ditch was better than the wide hard fast surface on the road above. The temptation was just too much for Sherri's team and up onto the road it went.

Sleds have three brakes but all three together have no chance against 400 pounds of dog on pavement. Sherri won't say but I can only imagine what was coming out of her mouth as she was trying to slow six hard driving, spitting, excited dogs, beginning a race, running 20 miles an hour on pavement.

Down the road the race trail again crossed the road and with a little help Sherri's team could have gotten back on the trail. As she got closer to where she would have needed to make the turn she even relaxed a bit. There was a police car and the cop was standing at the intersection directing traffic. Sure, he was going to grab the leaders and help her make the turn back onto the trail, right?

We're all grateful for all the volunteers who help with races. We wouldn't have races otherwise but I doubt this cop had ever been to a race before because his car was parked blocking the trail, making it easier for dogs to hop on or stay on the road. And he may not have spoken English either. When Sherri asked, then pleaded with him to grab the leaders and guide them onto the trail, he looked at her like she was speaking another language.

Buck, a seventy-pound hormone-crazed male, seeing a police car blocking the road and trail, broke his neckline, pulled out of his harness and took off down the road. Sherri glanced at the cop again hoping for some kind of help and his blank stare was the last thing she saw before she turned the remaining five dogs down the road after Buck. She had to catch him before he reached the highway.

Sherri still beats herself up about not finishing the race that day, but chasing a loose dog down a paved road with a sled dog team is pretty damn gutsy. When they got to Highway 6, Buck was running down the middle of it, in traffic. Sherri and her remaining five-dog team followed Buck down Highway 6, waving one arm over her head and yelling to keep the cars from running into the dog. So that part may be more insane than gutsy.

I can just see it now, a minivan full of kids watching a dog sled pass them on the road and saying "Mom, can we get one of those?"

I still don't know how she did it but Sherri was able to catch Buck, in traffic, and pull the whole team over to the side of the highway where they all immediately began either licking her face or trying to get to Kimi, whose heat was behind this male hormone explosion. Tank, an aptly named seventy-five-pound male, was determined to have Kimi. Sherri, who was being licked by five other dogs and tangled up in all their lines trying to keep them off the highway, began to lose the battle protecting Kimi from Tank. Just then, a couple of cars stopped to help. One driver offered to take Tank back to our truck and another handed Sherri a cell phone.

❀

It was forty-five minutes before my start time when the phone rang. I don't remember her words, I just remember thinking "I gotta get my butt there as fast as possible."

My race team was already tethered to our truck so it wasn't an option.

"Teri! Can I take your car?"

It was both tough and a relief to find Sherri at the side of the road. Sherri had been so excited to race, and I knew how upset she would be, but she was safe and so were the dogs. A truck soon stopped and offered to take the team back to our truck at the race start. We loaded up and arrived at our truck fifteen minutes before my starting chute time. I don't know how but Sherri sucked it up and she, Teri and Lisa all got Sherri's team put away and mine up to the starting chute in time.

After hugging and kissing her I said, "Thanks for saving our dogs, I love you." She just held my hand and then began helping Lisa and Teri take care of my team.

My ten-dog team was scheduled to start the pro class 130-mile race in just ten minutes. Dogs respond to and often reflect their owner's emotions. This is especially true of sled dogs before a race. If starting my race without my hat, mittens and food is any indication, I was not as calm as I'd have liked to be…and the dogs knew it.

To be safe I put my best command leader, Acorn, in lead with Winnie, who would drive the team off a cliff if that's what it would take to get to the finish line. Acorn guided us through all the twists and turns of traveling through the town of Deer River but once we settled into the trail to Squaw Lake it became obvious that Acorn wasn't herself and I had to move her back into the team. A wrist injury showed up the next day but not until after she'd powered through 130 miles running in point, the row behind the leaders. I tried several others and as my third leader Fly, fourth leader Peanut and fifth leader Woolley all floundered. We sat on the side of the trail watching team after team pass by.

It had been a stressful day with this being the first race of the year, Sherri's ride down the highway with her six-dog team and now my leaders all baulking (probably because I was stressed out and making them nervous). So standing up at the front of the team, holding Winnie and looking back over the dogs, I saw our new yearling, Wolf, jumping up and down barking as if he was saying, "Pick me, pick me, I'm ready."

Every musher can tell you the one, two or three dogs that came along and brought their team up to the next level, the dogs they don't know how they ever got along without. For me Wolf is one of those dogs.

The previous May I was sitting at my desk in the Minnesota House of Representatives. It was already after 9:00 p.m. and some of the other representatives seemed to think everyone in the State of Minnesota really gave a damn what they thought about every little detail of the bill we were debating.

"Then just vote no!" I yelled.

The other reps looked at me and I could tell that most agreed with me. I could see from the glance by the Speaker that she didn't. So I sat back and pulled up Sled Dog Central on my computer and scrolled through the classifieds.

The add read: "Too many puppies. Two litters of ten and I need to split them with another musher." Quickly looking through the bloodlines showed that these were pups I wanted on my team. I looked up at the clock. It was 9:30.

"Hmmmm…Michigan is Central Time right? Or is it Eastern Time? I can't stand to listen to another minute of this crap. I'm gonna call him." Michigan is Eastern Time.

Another sled dog junkie, Brian was up at 10:30 reading and dreaming about the next season when I called. He told me about the dogs and somehow I convinced him to sell four to me for really not much money. He seemed to believe that I took good care of my dogs but I later found out from him that the main reason he agreed to sell them to me was that I didn't live in Michigan, and he wouldn't have to race against them very often. After the session was over at the end of May I drove to Calumet, Michigan, and picked up Behr, Kola, Kimi and Beowulf who I quickly began calling Wolf or Wolfie.

Behr, Kola, and Kimi all contributed to our kennel but Wolf changed it. Seven years ago Acorn and Winnie raised our team from a recreational touring team to a mid-level pro team. With Wolf joining Winnie and Acorn as lead dogs, I started leaving races with a check in my hand. Mushing was still a big money loser but not quite as bad.

We repassed many teams and eventually placed ninth in the 2009 White Oak. With a couple miles to go in the race, with Winnie and Wolf in the lead I was really in shock of how well the team was still running. One hundred and twenty miles into the race and they're still trotting at over 10 mph. Rounding a corner I saw in front of us another team. The dogs knew we were gaining on it for miles because of the smell and were intent on catching it. The chase was on with not much trail left. Getting closer I saw that it was Mike Bestgen, a musher who we had never come close to beating. We soon passed him and he yelled out to me as we went by. "Team looks good, Frank. Yeah, I'm not really racing this race. Just using it as a training run for the Beargrease."

"Right," I thought, "Why were you just kicking so hard up that hill?"

After passing him, the dreams started flowing through my head of future victories. Just after we passed Mike, two snowmobiles passed me. Instead of making the turn for the finish line we followed the snowmobiles across the road. Mike made the correct turn, of course, and finished seventeen seconds ahead of us. We both laughed at the finish line, but I wasn't laughing as hard when he got his check for placing eighth and I got mine for ninth place. In my mind my dogs were heroes and just driver errors kept us from placing higher.

One dog in particular stuck out. From the time I put him in lead, Wolf didn't stop driving and not once was his tugline loose. That's from a dog that was only 15 months old running next to a large fast five-year-old male, Winnie, who up to that point had been the best sled dog I'd ever had.

※

After the White Oak, Sherri was a little hesitant about training and running our dogs in a race, something about them being "out of control." Teri, on the other hand, was learning to be a musher and didn't know any better. She and I had decided that she would run our second team in the next race. It was just a short six miler so really an easy, safe way to get started, or so I thought. Teri had been out a few times with a team of four of our older dogs and had even driven a larger team with me sitting in the basket. She really had a way with the dogs too. You know how some people are. Animals are just calm around them. I assumed that this meant our dogs would listen to Teri and somehow she'd have no problems running them. Teri had one little habit that we hadn't worked on yet, though. She leaned to the outside when the sled went around corners.

The week of the race came and we needed to get Teri out with the team a couple more times to get them and her ready. We thought it would be best if she could practice on the racecourse itself so we met at the trailhead in Walker. Walking out on the trail I noticed how hard and fast it looked but didn't worry much about it.

"I'll be in the sled with her," I said to myself. "It'll be no problem."

The dogs seemed wild and we took off like there was a bunch of rabbits running in front of the team, but with me sitting in the sled, I thought no problem. Less than a mile from the start the trail came to a T.

Teri asked, "Which way do we go...Oh, it seems the dogs know."

As we made a sharp turn to the left the sled started to tip and I put my right arm out to keep us from flipping all the way to the right. The sled almost tipped but then turned upright and on down the trail we went.

"That was close," I said. Nothing.

"Teri!"

No response. I looked back and about 50 yards behind me Terri was face down on the trail. As I yelled "Whoa!" I grabbed the snow hook and stuck it into the trail.

"Come here Buddha," our command to turn the team around on the trail. The team did a 180 and ran back to Teri where they all stopped and started licking her face.

"They really like you, Teri." But she didn't move. Another 30 seconds passed as I hooked the sled down and tied the dogs off. As I turned back to Teri she began to stir.

"Teri, can you just be still?"

She didn't appear to hear me, got up and walked over to the dogs and started petting and praising them.

"Good dogs, good Buddha." Pause. "Where the fuck am I? How the fuck did I get here." She then proceeded to take off her hat, gloves and jacket.

I'd only met Teri last year but I'd never even heard her say damn. We'd become good friends even though she's a Christian Conservative and I'm definitely not. Her swearing like that and deciding that she had too many clothes on made one thing clear.

"Teri, you've hit your head and have a concussion. Now put your jacket, hat and gloves back on."

She continued, "Fuck! What's going on? Where the fuck are we? Shit!"

"Teri, get in the sled. You need to go to the hospital."

She finally got in the sled after taking off her hat, gloves, jacket and starting to take off her sweater. "Teri! Put your clothes on. It's cold and you have to go to the hospital. Please listen to me. You've hit your head and have a concussion."

"What? How the fuck did we get here?"

Once we got on the sled I called Sherri on my cell phone and told her what happened (OK, Sherri's right about the cell phone thing, we did have coverage there). She said she'd meet us at the trailhead. Soon after we got back Sherri came running up, ready to take over.

"Teri, give me your keys. I'm going to drive you to see a doctor."

Teri wandered her way over to her car, "How the fuck did I get here?"

Sherri unlocked the door and Teri just looked down in confusion at the car that she'd bought just a month ago.

"This isn't my car."

"Yes it is, get in, Teri. You gave me the keys. It's your car."

She reluctantly got in. "This isn't my fucking car." Looking in the back seat, she asked, "What the fuck are my clothes doing in this car?"

I stayed behind to take care of the dogs as Sherri took Teri to the clinic and rode with her in the ambulance to the hospital where she stayed the night. I would have loved to have seen her husband Dave's reaction to Teri's f this and f that before they got her up to her hospital room. There's some of us who could swear in public without people really thinking much of it (me) but the Gapinskis aren't in that group.

Teri didn't race that weekend, or the next, but two weeks later she was following me down the trail with her own five-dog team. Every time I turned around to check on her, her whole body looked like she was smiling. Two years later Teri had her own team of ten dogs, and Buddha was one of her leaders.

Driving the dogs home that afternoon I got a call from our friend Lisa. She had been helping us with our dogs for years and had also recently taken out a small four-dog team of our old retired dogs.

"Frank, can you teach me to run that second team?"

Mocha and Flash (photo by Vonda Bezat)

Chapter 6

The John Beargrease Sled Dog Marathon, at 390 miles, is the longest sled dog race in the lower 48 states. It travels up the North Shore of Lake Superior beginning in Duluth in front of a large roaring crowd. There are big pre-race galas, media, and thousands of fans milling around to mostly see the dogs. For a musher who lives to talk about their dogs and glows whenever anyone pays them the slightest compliment, it's paradise. But eventually you have to put the show behind you, pull the snow hook and start the race. That's where the booties really meet the trail. All the posturing and talk are just that and you, your dogs, their training and the rest are put to the test for the mushing world to see.

For two years we were the new team at the race. Sherri and I had tried to just be nice, ask questions and focus on getting our team through the shorter, one hundred thirty mile, mid-distance race. It was funny to watch some of the egos strut around that race. Our first Beargrease had us parked at the start next to a team that had won the marathon a few years before. Me, being the hick that I am, just walked up to the musher and put out my hand to introduce myself. All I got from him was: "Don't drop your dogs until I get mine back in the truck," as if to imply that somehow our dogs were going to make his sick, bite them or pollute them in some way. I just smiled and walked away. Later I watched him bark out commands to his volunteers who dutifully went about their business getting the team ready. After he and his team left, we pulled our team out of the trailer and began getting them ready for the race, trying to keep the dogs out of the diarrhea left behind by a couple of his dogs.

Sherri and I both loved up and encouraged our dogs as we readied them for our first Beargrease mid-distance race. As a musher, I need to stay focused on the tasks at hand, taking care of the dogs, getting the gear ready, getting updates on the trail and weather, and hopefully staying calm. We ended up finishing in the top half of the field but by the end of the race that diarrhea had started working its way through our team and later that week through the kennel at home. Bugs like that are pretty common, and all the dogs were fine after a week or so. I have to admit that it didn't bother me much when I heard that the team with the big ego musher next to us at the Beargrease start scratched early in the race.

"Better luck next year." I thought.

Before I knew it, next year arrived and there we were back at the Beargrease start in Duluth. And that year I barely made it, and without Sherri. On Wednesday I had driven her down to Minneapolis for a biopsy. The hope was that she would be able to leave the hospital that afternoon and stay the night at my parents' house in nearby Burnsville. We would then drive back to Bemidji on Thursday, giving me a day to pack up all my gear and drive to Duluth for the Beargrease vet check and mushers' banquet. In spite of the minor surgery Sherri was planning to come along and organize the handling with help from Lisa and our friend Ted, a last minute stand in for Teri...who was still having headaches and couldn't remember buying her new car.

The surgery went well and we were just driving into my Mom's driveway when my phone rang. I saw it was Lisa who was probably just calling to let us know the dogs were OK and see how Sherri's surgery went.

I answered the phone, "Hi Lisa."

All I heard was "AAAAWAAAWAAAAWAA.....Puppies."

"What Lisa, I can't understand a thing you just said."

"AAAAAWAAAAWAAAAWAA...PUPPIES!"

We had nine four-month old puppies at home in a pen and I was getting the idea that something was wrong with them.

"Lisa, calm down so I can understand what you're saying."

"The puppies gahgahgaaaah gone. They got outta the pen. They're gone. I wanna DIE."

After a few minutes we figured out that puppies had opened the door of the pen and had been missing for several hours. We walked into my Mom's house. She had prepared a bedroom for Sherri to convalesce in and what smelled like a mouth-watering lunch for me. As I was telling her about the puppies I caught Sherri out of the corner of my eye opening her new prescription of Perkaset and popping a couple with a can of Coke. "We gotta go find those puppies." So much for convalescing.

We drove home talking on the phone to everyone we knew in the Bemidji area that we thought might help us look for the puppies. The next twenty-four hours were a frantic search of our rural township near Bemidji. Sherri, Lisa, and I had help from several friends, the radio stations and the Sheriff's office. Honestly I was so grateful to our community, and by the next afternoon we had seven of the nine at home.

The smallest two, Mocha and Flash were still missing. Sherri had slept little, Lisa and I not at all, but we were still looking with Sherri manning the phone at home. She called me around 5:00 p.m. to tell me a woman had seen Flash on a county road near our house. I was close to there and quickly found him running in the road, clearly terrified.

When I got him into the truck he was shaking and cold. It hadn't been above minus ten in two days and was supposed to drop to 30 below again that night. The sun was setting and Mocha was still out there. All I could think about was that little four-month-old girl afraid and alone. Of course the woods were full of wolves, mountain lions and even packs of wild dogs.

At about four in the morning on the second night of looking I had driven by Lisa walking down the middle of the road, looking down at the pavement, crying, muttering, "Puppies, puppies, come here puppies."

Lisa is like family to us and treats all our dogs like her own. Even though the dogs getting out was mostly my fault for not securing the latch to their pen better, to Lisa it was her fault. It was time for her to find a couch before she got hit by a logging truck.

I brought Lisa to our couch at home and went upstairs to bed for a couple of hours myself. It was Friday morning. I needed to leave for Duluth in four hours to make my Beargrease vet check time. Somehow between now and tomorrow morning I also needed to find a handler for the race, that is, if I was still going.

I lay in bed, just dozing now and then, thinking about Mocha. How could I go, not knowing if she was OK? Then I started thinking about the dogs that were the chosen team for this year's race. There were many young dogs on the team but Acorn was four and Winnie five. Here were the two best dogs I may ever have in the prime of their lives. This was the biggest race of the season and they deserved to race. We were going to Duluth, and I got up after lying down for a couple of hours and began to pack. I could get some sleep that night in Duluth and be ready on Saturday, no problem. Then just one more all-nighter on Sunday.

Having never really handled before, our friend Ted agreed to help and, after hearing my story of missing puppies, our friend and former musher Matt agreed to handle for me. I just needed to suck it up and race.

On the drive to Duluth I went in my head through the improvements we'd made and lessons we'd hopefully learned since last year.

Big dogs aren't as likely to be able to go fast for 120 miles. In 2008 Peanut could barely keep up and Buck had to be put in the sled for the last hills with his 70 pounds in the sled bag. That was a lot of extra work for me and the remaining dogs. In their place this year were two smaller, faster dogs, Woolley and Etta.

Dogs need to be trained to do what their expected to do in a race. For the Beargrease Mid-Distance that means dogs need to be prepared to run 120 miles in less than 24 hours. Not enough training miles before a race and your dogs will be tired, slow and, worst of all, may get injured. We had upped our training miles and all our dogs had run 1200 miles already that year.

I also learned that I needed to take better care of my dogs' feet so that they weren't sore during the race. Dog booties should be used whenever the conditions warrant and, to be safe, whenever in doubt. Each dog also needs to have foot ointment put on between their pads after every run. That can be tough when it's four in the morning, thirty below and you're trying to get at least a couple of hours of sleep but that's when it's most important.

It was January 25, 2009 and as my team was getting brought up to the starting line of our second Beargrease Half-Marathon, the adrenaline and excitement drove out any thought of missing puppies or how little sleep I'd had. The intercom announced, "Frank Moe from Bemidji, Minnesota."

Then the countdown: "Ten, nine, eight, seven, six, five, four, three, two, one, goooo!" and we were off through the streets of Duluth.

The first checkpoint of the race is at Billy's, a bar and restaurant on the outskirts of Duluth. By the time we arrived there, my best command leaders, Acorn and Fly, were both getting overtaken by the rest of the team and Acorn was already limping.

What the heck. The biggest race of the year has just started and two of my best dogs were already having trouble.

I always try and remember that dogs don't make mistakes, mushers do, and if my dogs were having trouble I'd screwed up somewhere. New leaders, Woolley and Winnie, came up front and I rubbed down Acorn's ankle and replaced her bootie. Looking closer I found a good-sized split between her pads.

"How did I miss that?"

I couldn't find a thing wrong with Fly. Last year he was my best dog in this race and now he just wasn't putting much into it. Something was very wrong and it would be a month before I would figure it out.

Acorn limped into the next checkpoint near Two Harbors and while I knew she wanted to keep going, I had to leave her behind. That was the first time in three years that I was in a race without her. It felt like I had left my best friend at the checkpoint. Without Acorn I felt tired and alone. I did my best to focus on the race but even though six dogs were still running hard, we lost ground to the race leaders during the second stage.

We needed something, a boost to finish the last forty miles. As we pulled into the checkpoint at Finland, Ted met us and led the team back to our camp. We had four hours of scheduled rest ahead. I was looking at the team while they were eating and then curling up on their straw I found myself crying. Not out of frustration or exhaustion but from total gratitude. Here was a team with a schedule that had been totally disrupted for almost a week while we were all searching for lost puppies, their main leader was no longer with them and they were still giving every bit of energy their bodies could muster. They could do nothing else. Thousands of years of their ancestors were calling them on. Their next meal would be found at the end of each run where they could feed, curl up and rest to again take up the journey. I was just along for the ride. I kneeled down and began messaging their joints and treating their feet.

Matt showed up. "Frank, ya hungry?"

I was so hungry I could only manage a grunt and a half smile.

"You gotta get warm and dry. Come sit in the truck, I got ya a couple of bacon cheeseburgers."

Within seconds of closing the door to his truck I had half a cheeseburger in my mouth. I looked over at Matt in the driver's seat and could barely make him out through the steam coming off of my cold wet parka.

"They found Mocha. She's fine."

"What? How do you know?"

"Sherri called when I was down in town. I didn't have great reception but got the idea that she was home fine. Slow down on that last cheeseburger, yer gonna choke."

I sat in the truck eating every last edible thing I could find, changed my shirt, which was wet from running behind the sled up the North Shore hills, and went out to check on Ted, Matt, and the dogs. The radio said it was thirty below and would get colder before the sun came up. We readied the team for the final leg. Mocha was home safe, I still had almost a full team in harness and we were running the Beargrease. We'd spent months, 1200 miles and many long cold nights preparing for this moment. Not the start of the race, but for now, the final leg.

There are moments on the trail that are difficult to describe. All the events leading up to them are specific to that time and place. In the twilight of that January morning we were making our way to our next meal, turning back the miles, and noiseless. Winnie and Wolf were leading a team, a pack, on the final leg of our journey. There was food ahead and teams to catch.

We placed a respectable thirteenth out of forty teams and, given the events leading up to the race, I was very happy with our performance. It would be our last Beargrease Half Marathon, and I'd thought, hoped, that we'd learned enough to run the full marathon next year. And the season wasn't even half over yet. The Mid-Minnesota 150, The Midnight Run and the Red River Dog Derby were still ahead of us.

Acorn's sore foot continued to bother her for the next couple of weeks. She missed the Mid-Minnesota and only made it halfway in the Midnight Run in Michigan. I discovered after the Beargrease that Fly had a bad case of worms. Once treated he soon bounced back and led us to a second-place finish at the Mid-Minnesota. He also led the whole way in the Midnight Run, but with only seven dogs we finished fifteenth. The dogs were giving it their all in races but I knew this team was better than we were showing.

I was relatively new to racing, a fact that had been lost on me. My ego told me that we could just step into competitive sled dog racing and be at the top. I was learning that there was a lot more to this sport than I had imagined. Assembling a good team of dogs was far from enough. One at a time the lessons of the trail were sinking in, and my attention to the details grew more focused. Our foot care improved and, not surprisingly, the dogs ran faster. I had also noticed that our dogs were heavier than the teams that were placing ahead of us.

"Your dogs are fat." Three time Beargrease champion Jamie Nelson's words from years ago echoed in my head. I reduced the amount of fat in their diets. They ran faster still. Our best race was yet to come.

✳

There's the golden spot that you sometime reach in a race. Some call it "the magic carpet ride," where you, your training and dogs all come together at one time. For me it was like the perfect buzz. Once I had it I committed everything in my life to get it again. My first magic carpet ride was at the Red River Dog Derby, between Fargo and Grand Forks, North Dakota, in March, 2009. Being the last race of the season in the Upper Midwest, it attracted a field of twenty competitive teams. It was also a twelve-dog race. That meant we would have to take all twelve of our racing dogs, including our yearlings Wolf and his sisters Kimi and Kola. It was the girls' first race.

Leaving the last checkpoint in the dark just after 5:00 a.m., we were in fifth place. Sherri and I were both giddy that our team was running with the leaders. When we left that last checkpoint, with 120 miles under our belt and 40 left to go, I felt like I was riding on a cushion of air. Winnie and Wolf were leading and they ran like starving wolves on the trail of a deer. Their prey were the teams ahead. Within an hour we had passed the first, Tim Caloun's, much faster than he passed us early in the race. Then in fourth the dogs loped after the third-place team.

Matt Rossi and his family have a professional kennel in Northern Wisconsin. Matt's team had taken first place the week before at Ely and had beaten us by a full two hours when he won the White Oak in January. But that was a different day.

Winding our way south on the Red River in the morning twilight, the dogs' heads and ears dropped and our speed increased. The next team was close. Just ahead as we rounded a bend, in the shadows, I could barely make out the team that my dogs had known was there for hours. Each bend in the river brought the team closer and as the sun rose on the bluffs of the Red River of the North we drew up next to Matt. With so many accomplished teams behind us, his obvious surprise at seeing my team driving past his, made me laugh.

"Morning Matt. Who's still up ahead?"

"Just Mike Bestgen and Don Galloway."

He had to yell his answer because we had already moved well ahead of him. Within minutes he was no longer in view and I was looking forward. Mike had passed me earlier in the year at the end of the White Oak, again driver error (mine), and I was looking for redemption. I didn't know how far ahead he was but the team was still driving like they were on a hunt so I kicked and poled as hard as I could. I figured we had about ten miles to go.

"I can do anything for an hour," I told myself. "This is the last race of the year and I've got months to rest."

Just then Tina had to poop. Most dogs learn to do it on the run but not Tina. She's Acorn and Winnie's daughter and was a young star but when she had to go she'd stop dead until she was done. Because she was so fast she was running in point, right behind the leaders. The whole team piled into her. By the time I got the mess untangled and gave the team the "let's go," Matt was again only a hundred yards behind me. We never again shook him and every time I turned around I could see him working his butt off to catch us. It was his last race of the year too.

One minute travelling on a winding prairie river you'll have the wind at your back and the next it'll be thirty miles an hour in your face. Standing up into that wind will slow your team to a crawl. We rounded a bend into the wind and I squatted behind my sled to reduce the drag. As I sat back my ski pole jammed into the snow in front of me and the grip end hit me right in the teeth, bending the ski pole into a U. Everything went dark and then I was seeing stars. Somehow I held on. When my head cleared I turned around and could see the canine teeth of Matt's leaders. We were now being hunted. I felt my own teeth. They were lose but all still there. Porcelain is pretty hard stuff. I turned to my dogs.

"Sorry guys, I won't screw up again. Come on Winnie, Wolfie, let's go."

After running 155 miles they somehow found another gear. Looking up at my team I was stirred with a mixture of awe and gratitude. They didn't know how to give up or to be tired, and to this team I was the leader. I bent the ski pole over my head, close to straight, and did my best to measure up. The team drove up the steep river dike before the race finish outside of Fargo at a lope. We could see and hear the crowd at the finish line from the top of the dike. Looking back I saw that Matt's team was too far back to catch us. We dropped down the other side of the dike and as we sprinted across an open field to the finish I could hear Sherri's "Come on Winnie!"

I rode the magic carpet into the crowd, hugging and kissing Sherri and shaking people's hands. I looked over at my team and began to cry. This was their time. The season was over and we'd come so far. That exact group would never again race together but on that day they were great, and we were one. Dreaming of and planning for next year would begin on the drive home.

❀

Letting dogs go that you've raised from puppies is the hardest thing for me to do as a musher. Later that March, 2009, I drove

Peanut, Buck, and Tank over to the Outward Bound School in Ely. For months afterwards they were the last thing on my mind when I went to sleep at night and the first thought in my mind when I woke up. From their first hook up they had given everything they had to me whenever I asked.

Peanut was a big five-year-old female and for her first two years of racing had run in almost every race I'd entered. Buck and Tank were two-and-a-half and were the strongest dogs in the yard. Tank was huge for an Alaskan Husky, seventy-five pounds, and a total love. If you let him put his paws on your shoulders he'd kiss your whole face. Buck was always close to making the team and even ran in our first Beargrease Half-Marathon.

In distance races big strong dogs usually can't keep up as the miles roll on and I had to carry Buck in the sled bag the last twenty miles. I don't know what was harder, getting a kicking, thrashing Buck in the sled bag or pushing the sled with his seventy pounds in it up the endless Heartbreak Hill on the North Shore Trail. He hated being carried.

If we were in the business of giving rides, those three would have been perfect. But we are a race kennel and that means we have to choose dogs that can run 11 miles an hour for two hundred or more miles. Seventy and eighty pound dogs that can do that are very rare. Buck, Tank, and Peanut were not making the team and we had to leave them all behind when we left for races. Looking at them you could see that they knew that they were not getting to run, but they didn't understand why. It's really not fair to dogs to have them in a kennel where they're not among the best dogs. Selfishly I've wanted to keep all three but I knew they deserved to be in a kennel where they'd make the team. At the Outward Bound School they'd be top dogs, the dogs that the guides looked to when they needed strong fast dogs to get them through a tough spot or to take a group deep into the Boundary Waters Canoe Area Wilderness.

I named Buck after the dog in *Call of the Wild* who was on the edge between being a sled dog and a dog who was living with the wolves who he was descended from. Our Buck would be out in the wilderness, running, howling and sleeping out under the northern lights. That was what he was born and named to do.

Photo by Kathleen Kimball-Parker

Chapter 7

In May 2009 we moved from Bemidji, Minnesota to the North Shore of Lake Superior, about 15 miles northeast of Grand Marais, only a few miles from the Canadian border. There're cooler summers, warmer winters, more snow (usually), trails galore and real hills.

Fall training usually begins around the first of September. That's when the temperature in the early morning drops into the forties. We were in a new place and I was anxious to get started. The first few runs of the season are always chaos. The dogs are worked up,

I'm excited, and the gear usually has some kinks to work out. Add the excitement of a new trail and the gasoline of a dozen females just going in heat and well...my worst ideas usually come at times like these. "To keep the males away from the females," I thought, "I'll just run all ten males first, then the females."

As I hooked up the last dog Sherri had a look like our car was about to fly off a cliff.

"Are you sure this is a good idea?"

I couldn't hear her over the jumping, screaming, fighting, not-having-run-in-six-months, slobber spewing, hormone-crazed dogs, but guessed what she said.

"Ah, it'll be fine," as I wrestled Winnie to a draw and got him hooked up to his tugline.

Just then the whole steel cable gangline, that attaches all the dogs to the ATV, snapped. One hand holding onto ten dogs, I let go of the ATV with the other, and was airborne.

Somewhere behind me I heard a scream, "Fraaaaaank." I managed to hold on for about a quarter of a mile. Then picking up my face out of the gravel I could just make the dogs out through the dust. The team was around the corner and gone. Sherri couldn't believe the distance between my footprints.

This is a musher's nightmare. On their own running they'd be fine but tied up to a gangline one could get dragged, or worse, strangled. These visions were flashing through my head as I ran spitting out blood and what I hoped was just gravel.

Through the pain, blood and spitting gravel I was thinking: "Frank keep running. You gotta catch em."

Running around a corner in the road I almost tripped over the team. They were all stopped and barking at a couple of huge horses. Our neighbors picked the perfect time to bring in a couple of Belgians to haul out some logs from the woods. The dogs had never seen horses and I bet were thinking, "Now those are big dogs."

It gave me just enough time to get the dogs tied to a tree and untangle a couple of the smaller ones. They had some abrasions but nothing serious. Mine were worse.

"Oh my God. Oh my God." Sherri ran up, dropped to her knees and grabbed a hold of Socks who had some blood on his shins. I was wondering if it was his or mine.

I jogged back home to get the dog truck. Before I could leave the driveway I had to cut up and drag off a birch tree that was hit by the ATV when the gangline broke. Before breaking the line the dogs jolted the ATV hard enough to crash it into the tree knocking it across the driveway. A post-terror-stricken Sherri described the tree crashing to the ground almost in my footsteps. She wasn't as amused as I was about having another story to tell.

Two days later, learning from my mistakes, I alternated rows of males and females hoping to keep them separated as we ran down the road. This time we didn't even make the road. Winnie didn't bother with the girls behind him but took the whole team into the dog yard where the remaining females were. The ATV stopped on a crushed doghouse. Sherri wasn't there to help me separate the males and females who were all so happy to see each other.

Sled dogs are such simple animals. I envy their focus. They are motivated by only a few things: their order in the pack, who they can kick the crap out of, and who can kick the crap outta them; sex, really with anything when hormones are in the air; eating, the more meat the better; and some basic comforts, water, warmth, shelter, a scratch under the chin and some trust: Are you going to be the big dog and take care of them?

Their economy is perfect, no waste. Hell they even eat their crap and get every last damn calorie out of it. No courtships either. They just stick their butt in each other's faces and then bam. Ten weeks later here come the puppies. I had a friend like that in college. He'd just ask women at the bar if they wanted to have sex. He said it usually only took three or four asks, never more than ten. I prefer being married. It's sometimes challenging but I love my wife, and she makes a perfect cherry pie.

Sled dog tracks are close to wolf tracks. If you were to follow the average housedog, all full of Alpo, piss and vinegar, you would see irregular tracks that wander side to side. Sled dogs, like wolves that they are genetically very close to, match their footsteps front to back. This saves energy and leaves footprints that are generally in line and regular, again very efficient.

They are first and foremost a member of a pack. Sled dogs fight or get close to fighting to figure out who's ahead of who. For you to have their trust they have to believe that you are at the top of the pecking order, the big dog. That means that no one in the dog yard fights, and the musher needs to make that rule very clear. A good shaking will put an exclamation point on that rule when needed. Acorn is an alpha female, no question, and she'll take my role as big dog if I'm not around. Females who challenge her quickly pay the price. Once even her own daughter, Tina, needed several stitches after getting too bold.

Once Jester, a big but older male, got off his leash and decided to pay Acorn a visit. Now I don't know this for sure because I wasn't there when it happened, but I'm guessing he just came into her circle and she kicked the crap outta him for getting into her space. Acorn got a cut on the chin, lost two lower teeth and has a broken canine tooth. Again I wasn't there but it looks like Jester was just trying to get away from Acorn, she had her teeth sunk into him and his frantically pulling away caused her to hit her mouth on the post her leash was tied to.

I showed up not much after and found Jester limping around the yard, looking like a tko'd boxer. It took me a half an hour to figure out who he was in a fight with. Finally I looked over at Acorn and she was clearly smiling, showing off her two missing teeth. Later at the vet, a place where I spend a lot of time and money, Acorn didn't even flinch at getting three staples in her chin. She kept busy watching and trying to eat the vet's pet parrot.

Pain? I don't think Acorn knows it, definitely not in the way we wimpy humans do. I'll limp if I have a blister on my big toe and she's run fifty miles with a deep cut on her foot. Only when the swelling got too big for the joint to work properly did her gait change and I noticed. It still was a fight getting her into the sled bag for the rest of the run. She chewed the line I had clipped to her collar and tore through the sled bag by the time I pulled the hook to get started again.

"OK, Acorn. Have it your way."

I put a bandage on her foot, put a dog bootie on top of it and put her back in lead. The only place she was happy.

🔱

So yes, I'm a guy and I think that guys (maybe women, too, but I don't claim to understand or know what's best for them) need to learn to be tough. I don't see a therapist because my brother and I used to kick the crap outta each other or because my Dad and I had a few goes either. For how many hundreds or thousands of years have boys been fighting with their dads? Is this a crime? What are dads supposed to teach their sons anyway? This world we live in isn't a cakewalk. No one owes me a living and sometimes I just have to suck it up and fight on.

My dad and I talked once a week for all of my adult life but getting along was always a struggle. When I was a kid he was a violent drunk, and he and my Mom split up. We argued or would fight every time we were together. My brother Paul was crazy enough to jump between us a couple of times. Once, after my brother died, my dad and I really got into it. Of course he was drinking and all I remember was my step mom screaming as I was dodging my dad's punches.

I grabbed him, "Don't you ever try and hit me again!" and threw him to the ground.

I picked up some of my stuff and ran down the stairs. All I had was a bike, some clothes and a sleeping bag. It was after midnight. I had stopped at his place trying to ride from Minneapolis to my uncle's house in Southern California. That night I rode from Omaha to Lincoln, Nebraska. Riding through the bluffs outside of Lincoln I watched the sun lighting the clouds on the horizon. I'd been riding straight all night through the demons and the fog. The sun was rising. I was done fighting my dad.

Several years passed before I visited him again. During that time I got sober myself and learned to forgive him. I had to for my own sake. I also began to see that in spite of his alcoholism, he never gave up. Even after three failed marriages, bankruptcies and several failed businesses, he always picked himself up to fight another day.

My mom is even more of a fighter. She waited tables at night when we were kids, after she left my dad so she could be with us during the day and weekends. I remember her getting home from work in the middle of the night, packing up the car and getting us up first thing in the morning to go camping for the weekend. She'd sleep during the day while my brother and I fished and would get up in time to fry up our catch for dinner.

My mom's job raising us alone got harder as both my brother and I got heavily into drinking and drugs at a very early age. I was busted smoking pot for the first time when I was eleven. My brother Paul got into cocaine in high school and repeated trips to treatment didn't work. It took his life before he was twenty-two. Mom held her head high through it all and even picked herself up and went back to college after my brother died. She was fifty.

❁

Sled dogs don't fear tomorrow or regret the past. They are only afraid of immediate danger, another bigger dog, thin ice, wolves or a bear. You'd think that thirty-six dogs would keep away most animals but living up in the Northern Minnesota middle-of-nowhere we get visits from all kinds of wildlife. Finding remnants of smaller animals is a daily occurrence in the dog yard.

One fall night we had one of those windstorms that comes with blowing out an Indian summer and in the first front of winter. Fifty mile-per-hour gusts were dropping nearby trees and large branches into the yard. The dogs always get pretty worked up when there's severe weather, so I didn't pay much attention to their noise. When their barks didn't die down by midnight I had had enough. Barking doesn't bother me much unless I'm trying to sleep. Running out the door in only my sandals and underwear I was going to put an end to whatever was behind me not sleeping for the last two hours.

"Enough. Stop it. Go to bed."

Dogs don't understand most of what we say to them but they are very attuned to our tone and manner. The sternest warning I could give standing there in my underwear went nowhere. The dogs were still in an uproar. I stopped and realized they were barking at something, and it wasn't their nearly naked boss in sandals.

My eyes were beginning to adjust to the darkness and something moved at the edge of my vision. Walking to the end of the driveway I noticed that the dogs down at this end of the yard were in a panic. There was something at the edge of the woods. What I was thinking there in my underwear and sandals running after something that had the whole dog yard in an uproar, I'll never know. To the edge of the woods I went. Standing next to huge yellow birch with a diameter of almost four feet I suddenly knew that whatever the dogs were barking at was on the other side of this tree. A proper functioning brain would tell someone to return to the house or at least get a shotgun but I, armed with underpants, looked around the tree.

As I looked to one side a bear's head mirrored my stare from the other side of the tree. For an instant we captured each other's eyes. Then from somewhere sanity crept back in and I yelled, "Get outta here, bear!"

Simultaneous to my scream the bear jumped up as if to climb the tree then lunged back into the woods with a deep "woof." I'd been told that bears barked but had never heard it before, and here I could actually smell the exhale of that bark. I yelled a few more times before I walked back up the driveway. Almost to the house I started to shiver. It could have been the 30 degrees and wind. At least that's what I told my wife when I got back in bed. After I mentioned the visiting bear she sat up, "What? You were just out there in your underwear? How big was it? We need to put the shotgun by the bed."

"Yeah, that's a great idea. I'll trip over it getting outta bed and blow my foot off."

The dogs didn't worry about the bear coming back. They just returned to their houses. I lay in bed now not so interested in sleep, and thought about our dogs, listening to the wind.

The storm blew and for a time the dogs were quiet, then over the wails of wind I heard their song. It started with just Acorn, then Ajax and a couple others. On the third howl it was all thirty-six dogs at once, carrying again and again, then trailing off. We'd like to put human emotions on their songs but I don't think it works that way. It wasn't relief, happiness or some single expression. Their chorus seemed to just capture the moment. This was their place and their sense of being there.

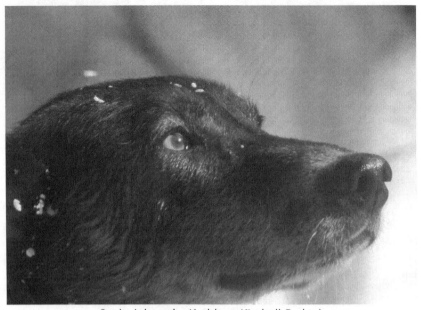
Socks (photo by Kathleen Kimball-Parker)

Chapter 8

Harry Lambirth, a long time musher from Blackduck, Minnesota, gave me some advice at the end of the 2009 season. We had just placed third in the Red River Sled Dog Derby.

Harry asked me, "How many miles you have on those dogs? That's the best they've looked."

"About fifteen or sixteen hundred."

"You need to have that many going into your first race of the year, not your last."

"How am I supposed to do that when we don't have good snow until sometime in December?"

"A lot of fall miles on the ATV."

Now there are competing schools of thought on how many miles and how fast to train sled dogs for mid and distance races.

One group, led by Jamie Nelson here in Minnesota, would have at least two thousand training miles on your dogs by the Beargrease at the end of January. They will train their dogs to march and get used to hard work. Jamie knows what she's doing, too. She's won the Beargrease several times and had some good Iditarod showings. She finished thirty-third only a few years ago and I know she was well into her 60s. So it works for her, Harry, and a lot of other mushers.

Another group of mushers likes to go fast, train not as many miles and take longer rests in races. The risk to this strategy is it's easy to push your team too fast too early, ultimately having to scratch from the race. You and your dogs get too hyped up at the beginning of a race and after forty or fifty miles of speed you think, "Damn this could be the year." You start writing your victory speech. Then it happens. Your dogs start to slow down, a couple begin to limp and you crawl into the next checkpoint. Your best dog refuses to eat and your victory has turned into a scratch.

I've come to believe that there are as many ways to train a dog team as there are mushers. Nobody knows my dog team as well as I do, assuming I'm paying close attention to them. Watching your dogs will tell you a lot: when they're tired, nervous about the dog next to them, thirsty or sore. All sports have a subtlety to them. Mushing has as many subtleties as you have dogs. A fourteen-dog team has fifteen egos, fifty-eight feet and endless possible screw-ups… which are ALL the musher's fault.

Of course you can learn from other mushers, if they'll share with you their secrets and you'll listen. Jamie Nelson will tell you, "You need to get a lot more miles on those dogs, run them at night when it's cold, don't let the dogs train you." That's all hard and takes a lot of time. It's easier to just run the same easy trail every day, stay at home in front of the fire when it's cold, and not worry if the dogs don't follow your commands.

Scratching is usually done in the best interest of the dogs. It's usually driver error, though, that's behind the scratch: running the dogs too fast, not enough training or maybe poor food and hydration.

In the end your race performance will show how well you've been training. There's no hiding there.

✳

The only ones I know who obsess as much about the weather at I do are other mushers and farmers. If one weather service doesn't predict snow, I'll check another then another. If none do, I just get depressed and go cut wood or do dog chores. Hanging around the dogs usually picks me up. They are great teachers. The weather forecast? Last year's or next year's races? They mean nothing to the dogs. It's just right now that counts. Am I harnessing them up for a run, coming around with a bucket of food or just stopping by to clean up their circle and give them a rub down? They are just so happy to see me, how can I stay depressed? The dogs have this look in their eyes like you are the most important person in the world, and they want you to just sit right down and spend the day with them. If I didn't have thirty more dogs to go visit, I would too.

Acorn was pacing out in the dog yard. Stopped. "Yeoowwow wow wow." Then pacing again. She looked beautiful, in perfect race form and a new winter coat. It was her day off but she wasn't interested in resting. It was almost Thanksgiving and we'd had nothing but cold rain for a month. All the ATV miles were starting to wear on me and them. Their feet were sore along with my hands, lower back and butt. I went to bed that night after checking the long-range weather forecast one more time, hoping that maybe it had changed.

✳

"I'm getting too old for this."

A sharp pain in my right shoulder and a cramp in my left thigh woke me up at 5:30. Eight hundred milligrams of ibuprofen and a half hour later I was fumbling over the stove making coffee and thinking about getting a handler. Every other musher I knew who had as many dogs as I did had at least one other person, usually twenty years younger, doing half the work or more. Running the ATV three hours a day on rocky, uneven trails started out in August being a lot of fun but was, by the middle of December, kickin my butt.

"My collar bone feels broken…what an old wimp I am."

The truck that I was building a box on, to carry the dogs to races, just got hauled off to the shop. I couldn't raise my arms over my head and half the dogs were limping on sore feet from running on hard frozen ground. How on earth was I going to get that whole broken-down mess to the Beargrease starting line in two months?

The night before on the ATV, running a fourteen-dog team, I was thinking about my old life and how much smarter I was than the politicians still down in Saint Paul. Soaking wet, on my ATV, it was thirty-five degrees, raining, and so dark that I couldn't make out the trees on the sides of the three-foot-wide trail…until I hit one. A few minutes later I was back on the trail with a broken headlamp and missing a mitten.

"Yeah, I'm a genius."

My ATV and sled were my soapbox. The dogs didn't listen but it got things off my chest. I was still a Democrat. Sometimes I wondered how. Maybe it was because I still believed we stood up for people who needed it: the homeless, kids in screwed up homes, seniors on Social Security. Instead, we ended up being the party of Trial Lawyers, Teachers' Unions and the protectors of the abortion rights of a woman in the ninth month of pregnancy; especially if one of us is seeking the DFL endorsement for higher office. That's when those special interests really extort commitments out of the candidates. Cynical? Yeah, that's why I was out there on the ATV with fourteen dogs in the rain and not down in Saint Paul.

On December 17 there was still only a dirty couple of inches of snow on the ground. I had hemorrhoids from riding my old four wheeler for hours every day, training the dogs for when we'd finally get snow. That night it was fifteen below and windy. There was no way to keep my old Honda ATV running at those temps. It was like riding in a shopping cart getting pulled over boulders for five hours. I was running out of ibuprofen and not sure which I was more worried about, my butt or my liver.

The dogs were tired of it, too. Winnie wouldn't even come out of his house when it was time to hook up to the ATV. If we had snow and I pulled out the sled he'd go crazy but he wasn't interested in another jerky night pulling me on that big steel-wheeled thing. The others were starting to sour too. Running at night helped some. It was more exciting maybe than during the day but I still needed to rest some dogs, not because they were physically tired but bored.

A light snow was falling…"Oh please, oh please keep coming."

꙾

Eventually it always snows in Northern Minnesota. Whatever you believe about God, I don't think he cares whether it snows or not. But if he does, I'm convinced that instead of giving us six to eight inches when I pray for it, he dumps a huge load of heavy wet cement. It was the day after Christmas, and it had just snowed so much our road wouldn't be open for three days. The storm knocked down hundreds of trees onto the trails. It would take another week of hard trail clearing work before I could safely run the dogs again. Not being able to run the dogs because there's too much snow was worse than not having enough. At least when there was no snow I could train them on the ATV. Every day that passed without training the dogs was torture, not only for me but anyone who had to live with me. So what that it was Christmas. I couldn't care less.

Of course I had to try-run the trail before it was all cleared. It had been over a week since the dogs had run and this was crunch time. They needed to get long hard workouts in or there's no way they were going to be ready for the Beargrease in a month. So off I went with ten dogs breaking trail through twenty inches of snow and Sherri behind on a six-dog team. The dogs were crazy. They had been pulling the ATV without the motor running for five hours a day, six days a week before going cold turkey. Nothing was going to slow them down, not the sled brakes, not the thigh-deep snow nor the hundreds of downed trees and low hanging branches laden with the heavy wet stuff. The branches all hit my face at about fifteen miles an hour. Goggles were worthless, knocked sideways and covered in snow. I couldn't see a thing and just kept getting whacked in the face like a bloodied boxer who had no defense against the next punch. But the dogs needed the training. Every time I looked back to check on Sherri I saw her sitting behind her sled below the handlebar and not getting hit by branches.

"She's obviously much smarter than I am," I thought as I turned back around and, BAM, I got whacked again.

The last time I got whacked before we turned around, knocked me off the sled. The dogs kept running with me holding onto the handlebar, dragging under the snow, as the sled tipped sideways.

"AAAAAAAAHHHHHHH!!!" I'd had enough. Finally turning the teams around, I could feel the warm blood running down my face. Somehow I still felt satisfaction knowing that most of my competition wasn't stupid enough to be out running yet. I had two black eyes and cuts across my nose and cheeks, but we'd gotten a run in. A fair trade, I thought.

After the Christmas blizzard and breaking trail with my face, we started trucking the dogs over to our friend Dennis' house. His trails were open and connected to the snowmobile trail so we could again get some longer training runs in. We'd already missed a key week of training. All those long nights on the ATV would prove to be critical, not in building for some longer runs on the sled later as we had hoped, but as the primary training themselves.

The first major race of the season in the Upper Midwest is the White Oak Classic starting in Deer River, Minnesota on the second weekend in January. There's not a lot of prize money but it's a well-run race that gives teams a chance to see how they measure up and to prepare for the big show later in the month, the Beargrease.

We had time for only two long sled runs and a couple shorter runs the week before the race. Tina and Fly had had a litter of puppies that we suspected would be future super stars but they were only sixteen months old. A few already showed that they were faster and stronger than some of our veteran dogs, but we didn't know how well they'd hold up to a long race. Were they ready mentally and physically to run 130 miles in twelve hours at the White Oak or 380 miles at the Beargrease? The last two long training runs before the White Oak were our chance to see.

Puppies don't all mature at the same speed. Generally the larger the dog the later it matures. Males usually mature later than females. Out of a litter of ten, five showed that they looked ready to race: Socks, a lean and chatty black-and-white 45-pound male; Storm, a quiet sensitive cream colored 45-pound male; Flash, a little 42-pound white fireball; Nita a 42-pound mostly black energizer bunny of a girl; and Esther, a 40-pound brown female full of love, energy and confidence. Two others, Moo and Bart were a little bigger, still growing and would push to make the team the next year. The fifty and sixty mile runs a week before the race blew me away. It wasn't even the first race of the season and the team was running as well as it had at the end of last season. Plus we had young dogs in the mix that were already pushing to make the team. It was going to be tough but we'd have to decide which dogs to race and which to leave home.

When I started to load the dogs onto the truck they all knew it was to go to a race and they barked, whined and pleaded to be picked. The dogs left behind stood and watched as the truck pulled out. I heard from the people left behind to care for the dogs that, within seconds, a mournful howl began in the yard that continued off and on for hours. We left for Deer River with the best ten-dog team we'd ever had.

I always honestly believe that I have the best dogs and have a good chance to win every race we enter. When we don't, I never blame the dogs. They always do their best, with no exceptions. The weak link is always me; how I train, feed, care for or race them.

Sherri and I have learned so much about mushing since we started with our two housedogs fifteen years ago. It makes me crazy to think that in fifteen more years I'll look back on how I run dogs today and laugh at the mistakes I made, just like I now look back at my first years of mushing. I used to feed generic dog food from the feed store and wondered why everyone else's dogs had more energy than mine. I started training the dogs by having them pull me on my mountain bike, until I fell off and saw it break into pieces being dragged down the trail at twenty miles per hour.

From there I progressed to a three-wheeled cart with a brake that only worked when you were standing on it. When the dogs would get tangled I had to get off and run up to fix the tangle before the dogs figured out I'd taken my foot off the brake. It didn't take long for them to know that when I was off the cart, the brake was also off. I learned to catch the handlebar and jump on as the cart rolled by. One night I slipped on the ice after I grabbed the handlebar and dislocated my shoulder as I fell on my face. I was thinking, "Don't let go of your dogs!" That old adage is no good when your arm is out of its socket. Again off they went around the corner going at least twenty miles an hour, while I lay on the ground with a face full of dirt, gravel and blood. Making a sling out of my jacket I hobbled about five miles before finding them tangled in the trees, all in better condition than I was.

I was supposed to speak at a political rally that night. After hiking out to the county road and flagging down a truck, I used their phone to call the party Chairman who was MC of the event. I told him what happened and to please explain this to the convention.

"You want me to tell them what?"

Now I train with an ATV.

Acorn and Tina (photo by Vonda Bezat)

Chapter 9

On the way to the White Oak that year I was more nervous than usual. I knew the dogs were fast and well trained. The question was if I was up to the challenge? The best teams from the Upper Midwest and Central Canada were all going to be there. Being the first race of the year, it's always kind of a shakedown, a preview of the year ahead. It was also a return to some of my old training trails. The dogs knew them and we had a lot of history there. Still I decided to go out a little conservative. As good as I thought the team was, we couldn't sprint 130 miles.

Acorn and Ajax would lead the first leg. Both were great command leaders and would set a more moderate pace. The first leg from Deer River to Northolm is over sixty miles and I planned to arrive in about six hours. The dogs had other plans and we pulled into the checkpoint in five and a half hours, so fast that Sherri and Lisa weren't even there to meet us yet. Luckily our friend Teri was waiting for another musher and helped me run the team into town. We picked up a couple of high school kids on the way and together we wandered the streets of Northolm looking for Sherri, Lisa, and the dog truck. Finally I saw them and, leaving the team with the high school kids, ran over and yelled, "Hey Sherri, can you guys help us bring the team over to the truck?"

"What are you doing here; you're not supposed to be here yet." She was obviously surprised.

"Yeah, I know, but the team really cruised. Can you help me bring them over and tie them to the truck? You too, Lisa."

"Wait, I have to get a different pair of gloves." Lisa ran the other direction towards her car.

I turned around to see that the high school kids were clearly overmatched and were all being dragged down the road.

"Would you guys just help me bring the team over!"

"Oh yeah."

"OK." And they both came over and grabbed the dogs.

Within minutes all had eaten, were lying on beds of straw, covered in blankets, booties off, getting massages.

Now Sherri yelled at me, "Go get into some dry clothes, eat and get some rest. Have you drunk any water"

I didn't have a chance to respond.

Handing me two liter bottles, she said, "Here, drink both of these."

Sherri woke me at 12:30 a.m., a half hour before our planned departure. I got up, put on my boots and walked over to the team. They all were up, had fresh booties on and were whining to go. Out of thirty teams we had the fifth fastest first-leg time, just where we wanted to be.

An ATV came over to our team and hooked up to our sled to guide us down to the start. It was a welcome sight because the dogs were more psyched up than at the very beginning of the race. With Winnie and Wolf in lead we took off with me standing both feet on the brake. My GPS said we were still going fourteen miles per hour. Soon after leaving we passed the fourth-place team, Mike Bestgen. I didn't see another team until Effie, the next checkpoint.

There's nothing like coming into sled dog race checkpoint at night. Usually you can see the bonfire a mile away. Then you smell the smoke and can make out figures in front of the fire. The dogs speed up, knowing that food and attention from Sherri and Lisa are waiting. The checkpoint trail is lined with handlers hoping that you are their team. Your handlers are so excited to see you but the rest just give a polite clap. Their looks give away their true feelings, disappointment that you are not their musher. We ran past them all to a place Sherri had set up for the dogs to have a quick snack and get their feet checked.

I could see that the third-place team, Jerry Papke's, was still there. We could leave in twenty minutes, just a few minutes after Jerry. I knew Winnie and Wolf would catch him. Before we left, Mike showed up, along with the sixth-place team, Kirk Aily. With four teams so close together, there would be quite a race to the finish in Marcell, about thirty miles away.

We brought the team up to the starting line a couple of minutes early. In spite of already running the fastest one hundred miles they ever had, the dogs were barking and lunging to go.

I said to Dan, the Race Marshall, "They don't understand why you won't let them go chase that next team."

"They're pretty excited there, Frank."

I smiled. "They're just showing off," just as Tina lunged and pulled the snow hook out. We barely got the team stopped again at the starting line.

The same group of about fifty handlers was still lining the trail and clearly not amused by our team's antics. Paula, Matt Rossi's wife, came over to us with a huge smile on her face. "Do you have good leaders?"

"Yeah, I think so. I haven't even called them up yet"

"Well, now's the time. You go have fun."

Sherri gave me a big hug and kiss. "I'm so proud of you."

"Five, four, three, two, one," and we were off.

Every musher has a handful of runs that they'll remember forever. The sights, sounds and smells become part of us. That night there was no doubt in my mind why I spent the thousands of hours training this team, thousands of dollars caring for it, and was taking four times the recommended daily doses of several pain relievers to just keep it all going. All ten dogs we started with would finish: Winnie, Wolf, Acorn, Ajax, Fly, Tina, Ace, Kimi and, in their first race, Storm and Socks.

Our dogs loped all the way to the finish in Marcell, not stopping once for anything. We soon passed Jerry and were in third place. That was the last team we saw until the end, where Ryan Anderson and Nathan Schroeder had already come in first and second. They went on to be the two dominant teams in the lower 48 states for the 2010 season.

Sherri and I grabbed onto each other at the finish. We stopped for just a few seconds at the finish line, looked into each other's eyes, and saw that the other had started to cry. We had had our best race ever, and it was only the first one of the year.

〰

The morning after the White Oak Sherri had to drive down to the Twin Cities for work. She'd be gone until Thursday. Being the head handler, she'd gotten even less sleep than I had over the weekend. I was worried about her making the six-hour drive to Minneapolis. Leaving at 5:30 in the morning she said: "Don't worry, I'll drink coffee, and the memories of the weekend will keep me awake."

There was an uneasiness in my stomach as she drove down the drive, through the dog yard, in the early morning darkness. It was twenty-five below zero, calm and the dogs were quiet. Acorn came out of her house and sat, watching Sherri's truck drive out of sight. She then turned and looked at me before we both went back into our houses.

Mornings after races are spent sorting, cleaning and putting away gear. Unpacking all the bags and boxes gives me a chance to relive the race. Dog booties and a half eaten sandwich were exactly as I left them when I stuffed them into a bag out on the race trail. The smell of that moment spills out of the bag when it's opened.

Closing my eyes I'm standing on the runners, on the trail between Big Fork and Marcell. There are no sounds but the quiet rhythm of dogs breathing and feet falling on the trail.

Sherri had handed me that sandwich in Effie two nights before. "You need to eat something too."

I had taken a few bites on the trail and it made me smile thinking about her making and packing that sandwich knowing that she'd probably have to force me eat it. I thought about our partnership, a team that came together so perfectly on the trail, with me and Sherri and the dogs...

"I can't eat anymore. I'll save it for later." I stuffed the sandwich back into my sled bag.

The memory faded and I was back in the house with the contents of a stuff sack spread out over the floor. I took a bite of the mashed cold sandwich, thinking about and missing Sherri.

I heard a noise from the computer. We live too far off the road to have a phone and, because of all the hills, don't have cell coverage. The only way someone can contact us is by satellite internet either by email or Skype, an internet phone service.

The computer was ringing. Our parents were the only ones who ever called us this way. I walked over to the computer and pressed Enter to answer.

"Hello"

"Frank, this is Jim." My stepdad. "Do you have a pen?"

"Yeah, why?"

"Take down this number. It's for the Two Harbors hospital. Sherri's been in a bad car accident and you need to call them immediately. They won't tell me anything."

My mind raced. "OK." I took down the number and hung up. Throwing on a coat and putting on my boots, I grabbed my phone, wallet and truck keys. I put Cocoa in the house, Shiva in the kennel, Gus in the truck with me and drove down our windy snow-covered road as fast as our top-heavy dog truck could go.

"Ok, Frank, just breathe. Oh, please God. Oh please. No."

It was a half hour drive to where I could make a cell phone call.

"Why wouldn't they tell Jim anything? Oh God, please take care of her."

That morning was the longest our road had ever been. "What will I do without her? So many people love her so much. I'm going to have to call her parents. Oh Peggy."

Our truck bounced down the road. My heart was beating up into my throat. "Oh, no, this just can't be happening. I don't want to live without her. What will I do with all the dogs? How can I even look at them?"

I finally got to US 61. "Just another five minutes or so and I can call."

On the highway my hands shaking caused the truck to swerve. "Dang it, Frank. Keep your act together. You gotta get to her."

Rounding the corner about five miles from Grand Marais I knew I'd get a cell signal and pulled over on the shoulder. Staring across the bay towards town, I paused for just a few seconds.

"Please, God, take care of Sherri." And I dialed the number.

"Two Harbors ER."

"This is Frank Moe, Sherri's husband. How is she?"

"Um, I'm not in there with her. Ah, I don't know, let me get someone who is."

"What?" I waited and waited…

"Hello, is this Mr. Moe?"

"Yes, what happened?"

"Well, I don't know for sure. It was some kind of accident…I think—"

"Is my wife OK?"

A pause, "Yes, she will be." The tone in her voice revealed that she now understood my panic and needed to assure me that my wife was alive.

"Oh my God, thank you. How is she?" I started sobbing.

The nurse began to describe Sherri coming in and out of consciousness due to a severe concussion and whiplash, and then stopped.

"Are you OK?"

"I didn't know if she was alive. For a half hour I thought my wife might be…dead." The sobs went on.

"Yes, she's alive and is here asking for you when she's awake. Now you need to take your time and get here safely. We may send her to Duluth but come to the Two Harbors hospital ER first. Do you know where that is?"

"Yes, can you just call me if you transfer her to Duluth?"

I hung up. "Gussy, she's going to be OK."

The tears eventually slowed and my hands stopped shaking enough to start the truck.

"God, thank you. Thank you."

✳

"Where's my wife? Sherri Moe." I was running into the emergency room wearing my dog-crap-covered boots and Carhartt jacket, still unshaven and not bathed from the weekend's race. From the look of the nurses behind the registration counter they must have thought I was straight out of the movie *Deliverance*.

A woman, who I later learned was the supervisor, stepped out from behind the counter. "Mr. Moe. Sherri will be fine. She's down the hall in room 207 and has been asking for you."

I walked into the room to find Sherri lying on her side, sleeping. From the sunlight shining in I saw a few pieces of broken glass from her shattered windshield reflecting in her hair, and then the subtle rise and fall of her chest. Here was my little angel and I had never been so grateful for anything in my whole life. The only sound in the room was the rhythmic beeping of her heart monitor. Sitting down next to her I gently grabbed her hand and kissed her forehead. Her face was swollen, with cuts around her eyes and nose. Slowly Sherri's eyes opened half way and I could barely make out an attempted smile.

"You're here."

"I came as fast as I could."

She grimaced. "I'm thirsty. Can you get me some water?"

I got her some ice to suck on. As she fell back asleep I put my face up next to hers, "I'm here to take care of you, sweetie. You're going to be OK." My tears fell on her cheek. "I love you Sherri."

Just after 9:00 that morning Sherri had been stopped at a light on Hwy 61 in front of Superior Shores just outside of Two Harbors. A line of four cars and trucks was in front of her as the front car was waiting to turn left. The Deputy Sherriff said the SUV that hit her from behind never even slowed down.

"No signs of braking at all. Must have hit her at fifty."

Her Chevrolet Colorado was driven into the Toyota Tundra in front of her, whose driver was also in the Two Harbors Hospital. The eighty-year-old driver and passenger of the SUV that hit Sherri were both airlifted to Duluth.

Sherri had a severe concussion and whiplash. She still hasn't fully recovered. Later that day I tracked down Sherri's truck. The impact caused the whole truck to bow upwards like an upside-down V. Looking in the shattered windows I saw that the airbags had deployed, obviously saving her life. The cab was covered in shattered glass and Sherri's scattered belongings. I noticed a strong strawberry smell and then saw that some kind of strawberry yogurt had covered the interior. Sherri had stopped at the Coho Café in Tofte for coffee and breakfast to go. She never even got to eat it.

The vision of her driving down the highway, minding her own business, thinking about where to stop to eat her breakfast and then getting so violently hit again made me cry, and it just kept coming. My chest heaved as I held my stomach, bending over right there in the car lot. Pent up tears poured out. All the time we'd been away from each other, the fear and anger over the struggles we'd had, all came up and out as meaningless; they meant nothing when compared to losing her. This truck that had been mine—the only new car I'd ever bought—had no value except how it protected Sherri.

*

Sherri's gasps and grimaces, on our way home two days later, told how bumpy our road and driveway was. I tried to miss what I could but always seemed to find another bump for everyone I drove around. Finally we passed through the dog yard and up to the house. The dogs were crazy that we were home.

"Oh, the babies, I missed them so much," were Sherri's first words since we'd left Two Harbors.

Sherri spent the next several days either in her easy chair or in bed rotating a dozen bags of frozen peas between her head, neck, and the freezer. By the end of the week the fight with the insurance company had begun. The crash had broken and scattered Sherri's stuff all over the truck and road. State Farm, the insurance company for the driver of the SUV that hit Sherri, was already disputing her medical costs and wanted receipts and pictures of everything that she hoped to have replaced.

"How the heck is she supposed to come up with all that?"

After a couple of weeks of fighting with them we were literally forced to hire an attorney. Sherri couldn't work, had huge medical bills and wanted her truck and other possessions replaced. For someone who was experiencing intense head-and-neck pain, depression and despair, this could really put her over the edge.

"These insurance adjusters' job is just to pay out as little as possible," I said. "I bet they get bonuses the more difficult they make it for people."

It was less than two weeks before the Beargrease, by far the longest race we'd ever attempted. Sherri struggled just to get out of bed and I was trying, poorly, to be a good nurse and husband. Finally, after I grew too tense for her to deal with she yelled, "Just get outta the house and train those dogs. You're driving me crazy."

"Really?" I was dressed and out the door before she could change her mind. We had missed a week of training, and I took this as permission to run dogs twelve hours a day for the next week. Half way through Sherri asked if I would just take her to a hotel in town. As hard as it was to admit, it was the best thing for both of us. Sherri needed to relax and take a long hot bath.

I'd been trying to take care of her; cooking, cleaning, asking repeatedly, "Is there anything else I can do for you, Sweetie?" Then I'd run out the door for another sixty-mile training run.

There comes a point before a race when it's no longer possible to improve your dogs' endurance by running long hard runs. Just like humans training for a marathon, you wouldn't go out a few days before the race and run twenty-six miles. By ten days before the race the dogs were as trained as they were going to get. After that it was just shorter tune-up runs; forty, thirty, twenty, then just ten miles two days before the race.

Even though this was my rookie year at running the Marathon, I had been optimistic on our chances to place. Our last three races had been a second and two third-place finishes. Now, after missing so many critical training runs, I was just focused on getting to the finish line. That would be quite an accomplishment, too, given that only six teams finished the year before.

A few of the training runs before a long race like the Beargrease need to be campouts where we travel thirty to fifty miles, camp for a few hours, then return home. Two weeks before the race we made our halfway stop at my friend Dennis' place. The dogs and I ate and afterwards I tried to get the team to settle down and rest for a while. No chance. They were barking, fighting, playing, chewing the gangline; it was time to pack up and head for home. Ajax and Wolf were in lead and just nuts to go.

"Let's go, guys." And we tore back across the parking area that was below Dennis' house. For just a second I looked down to put on my glove and when I looked up we weren't on the trail but on the hard packed driveway into an area where Dennis parks his work trucks. Between the trucks we went at a lope, over the plowed snow berm behind the trucks and down a twenty-foot drop into a dense woods.

"Whoa, whoa, Ajax!"

All twelve of the dogs were instantly wrapped and tangled around trees but were still trying to pull, especially Ajax. Maybe he just figured he needed to pull harder and the team would start going again. I blew a gasket.

"Damn it, Ajax, you know better. When I say whoa, I mean WHOA!"

Ajax saw his boss screaming things, and all he understood was that I was mad. Grabbing his and Wolf's collars I crawled up the hill, dragging the team back up the through the snow we had just tumbled down. I had to stop more times than I can remember to untangle dogs from trees, each other and my legs. If I hadn't been so mad, I don't know if I'd have found the strength to get the team back up to the parking area. Hooking the team to a truck bumper, I finished untangling all the lines and shook out as much snow as I could from my coat and bibs. All my clothes were soaked with sweat and snow. It was going to make it a cold trip home.

Giving the dogs a strong "Haw," we made the sharp left onto and back down the trail.

"What the heck has gotten into you guys? Ajax, you're just going to go forward no matter what, aren't you?"

After six years not once had he listened to whoa. I couldn't remember Ajax ever wanting to stop, not once.

We made the thirty-mile trip home in less than three hours… and I was standing on the brake the whole way. I didn't say another word until I got into the house after tying out and feeding all the dogs. It had been a long time since I had gotten that mad with them. It does absolutely no good and I knew it. In fact you can blow all the trust they have in you with an episode like that. Luckily they didn't seem fazed at all. I hoped they weren't and was disappointed in myself.

So much had gone on in the last two weeks. My nerves were raw and I let it get the better of me. Before I went into the house I walked back over to Ajax's house. He came out with his usual whole body wag, still glad to see me.

"I'm sorry, Ajax, you're a prince. How about starting in lead at the Beargrease?"

After scratching behind his ears and under his chin, I walked to the woodpile, grabbed an armload, and carried it to the house. Sherri opened the door for me.

"How'd it go?"

"I think we're ready."

Flash (photo by Kathleen Kimball-Parker)

Chapter 10

"Who's going to handle for you, Frank? Sherri's not going to, is she?"

Betsy had asked a great question. Betsy and Odin are friends and mushers nearby. For a large long race like the Beargrease you need a handler team with a head handler. It's like a pit crew for a Nascar race. I had three other handlers for the Beargrease but we'd be in trouble without Sherri running the show, and I knew it.

"I don't think I'll be able to keep her from doing it, Betsy."

It was less than a week before the race and Sherri and I hadn't even talked about if she was up to handling or not. I was just trying to control what I could, and we were barely keeping it all together with her recovery and my obsessive training. Sherri was still plagued with headaches and was under strict doctor's orders to get lots of sleep. Handling for the race would mean she would have to stay awake for virtually four days straight.

On Wednesday of race week we were on the way back from Sherri's doctor appointment in Duluth. She pulled out a pad of paper and asked, "Have you thought about what you're going to want to eat on the trail?"

"Are you sure you're going to be up to it? You're not going to be able to sleep much for days."

"Well, who else is going to do it?"

The race started at 1:00 p.m. on Sunday, January 31st. Our vet check was on Saturday at noon. The three days before were a blur of fixing and packing gear, chopping meat, cooking and bagging food and getting those last few tune-up runs in. We also had to decide which fourteen dogs were going to race. All ten of our race veterans were going: Acorn, Winnie, Fly, Ajax, Woolley, Etta, Ace, Tina, Wolf and Kimi. Five of Tina's pups, who were now sixteen months old, had been training with the veterans. Socks and Storm had raced well in the White Oak. Nita was an obvious choice too. She had never once had a slack tugline since we started training back in September. The choice was between Esther and Flash for the fourteenth spot. Both were fast and had the habit of jumping and barking whenever the team slowed down. Flash was a little bigger but Esther was already a leader and with 380 miles to go, I'd need every one I could get. Esther would go.

Pulling out on Saturday morning, all loaded up, I stopped the truck, got out and walked over to Flash's circle. He sat and licked my face. We'd run over 1500 miles together already this season.

"You almost made the team, Flash. I know you coudda done it too. You'll get your chance. I promise."

I drove away to the howl of the dogs left behind.

Finally being on the road, driving to our first Beargrease Marathon, was more than anything a relief. For years we had planned, trained, sweated and bled to be where we were now, driving to and ready for the Beargrease. Taking a deep breath all I could do now was drive and try to listen to the radio. But in my head I ran through my equipment list one more time. There ended up being additional things we would need but none that I could think of right then.

Canal Park in Duluth will always mean the staging of the Beargrease to me. I can't go there without walking around envisioning the dog trucks, barking dogs and excitement of the race to come. Driving in and finding a parking spot was familiar but different this year. Now we were part of the big show, the full marathon.

It was warm for January 30th, maybe ten degrees and not much wind. For most mushers that's jacket-and-baseball-cap weather. Races are already a big social event for people whose weekends are usually spent on the trail with their dogs. The relatively warm sunny parking lot made that day a carnival of dogs, friends and rivals. As a musher it can get overwhelming, seeing old friends, answering questions from the race fans, trying to get your dogs dropped (take them out of their boxes), and as usual I also had to pee.

"I drink too much coffee."

Getting sucked into the carnival, I took at least an hour to get to and from the bathroom in Grandma's Sports Garden. Walking back to the truck I saw that Lisa was there. She and Sherri had the dogs dropped and watered already. I love having handlers. Lisa has become family but honestly I think she comes to the races for the dogs and not us. She greets every dog like a long lost child and they jump on her, lick her face, knock off her glasses, pee on her shoes, and none of it bothers her.

"Hey, Frank."

I looked down the parking lot to see Steve Pett walking towards us. Steve and I had met the previous summer in a coffee shop in Grand Marais. Finding any excuse possible to not write my PhD dissertation, I was studying the last year's Beargrease race times when I looked up and saw his Beargrease hat.

"What's with the Beargrease hat?"

He said he was, "Just a fan. I went and watched the start once."

Soon I was answering all his questions about our sled dogs and, after learning that he was an English professor at Iowa State, telling him how pointless my own PhD research was, I confessed: "All I really want to do is run dogs."

"Sounds awesome. I'm writing a novel about a musher and would love to come out and visit your kennel."

He visited the kennel the next week and volunteered to be a handler for the Beargrease before he left. Now at the race he was anxious to get started but I really didn't have anything for him to do, so I said: "You've got to get to know the dogs before you can help take care of em. Spend some time petting and scratching all of them."

Steve didn't question me a bit, just dropped to his knees and started petting the nearest dog.

"When you're done with that, open up all the storage compartments and see what all is in them. You'll need to use all of it some time over the next few days." Before he was done he had emptied out every box and bag in the truck. Later when I wanted him to practice putting jackets on the dogs, I found him digging through the glove box.

My main concern for the race was not going too fast at the start. The dogs were going to need to run 380 miles so we needed to pace ourselves. Sherri had bought me a GPS for my birthday to monitor my speed and I'd be using it in the race to keep the dogs below ten miles an hour. In past races we'd been shooting for between eleven and twelve miles an hour and those teams were smaller, eight, ten or twelve dogs. I wondered how I was going to keep fourteen amped up well-rested crazy dogs going ten miles an hour. I was getting a lot of advice from the race veterans.

"Frank, you should carry an extra hundred pounds in your sled."

"Put twenty two-inch bolts on your drag pad and stand on it the whole time."

"Good luck!"

I called my friend Matt. "Relax Frank, you'll be fine. Just use your brake and don't carry a bunch of extra weight. Do you wanna tire em out pulling that weight up all those hills?"

Good point. I quit worrying about it and it turned out to not be a problem at all.

The hardest time for me is waiting for the race to start. I'm sure the ceremony of the Beargrease is interesting and meaningful to many of the organizers, volunteers and fans of the race, but for me it's just something I have to wait through before we can hit the trail. My body was standing in Grandma's Sports Garden with the beating drums, the crowd, slideshow and announcer, but my head was in the dog truck and out on the trail. Not really worrying, just thinking and wishing I was there. The beginning of the bib draw snapped me back.

Beargrease 2010 was being hyped as a battle between several returning champions. Father and son John and Jason Barron were both returning two-time Beargrease champions. Jason had won the last two. Like all sports, mushing has its egos, and some of them need to grab the microphone and enlighten the rest of us. Last year's champ took ten minutes before he gave the mike back. I caught a couple of other mushers' eyes rolling.

Four-time champion Jamie Nelson from Togo, Minnesota, was also getting a lot of attention. She'd been focusing on the Iditarod for the last ten years and even though she was well into her sixties was still very competitive. Jamie has a long mushing history and a reputation for long slow steady runs. She'd be in the back or middle of the pack for most of the race and usually end up at or near the front as the rabbits dropped out or slowed to a crawl.

Jamie can be both gruff and generous. Many mushers, including me, have spent time training up at her place in Togo. Usually in exchange for some work she'll let you sleep in her bunkhouse and train with her. There will be no doubt what she thinks about you and your team:

"That dog's fat."

"You call that a pass?"

"You need to find a dog that can lead."

There were two other returning champions that were both from Northern Minnesota. Blake Freking from Finland, Minnesota, was racing the Beargrease again before he headed to the Iditarod. Mark Black of Hovland, Minnesota, said to the press, "I've raced more Beargreases than anyone…and this may be my last."

We didn't often lose to Blake, Mark or Jamie, but we'd never raced this far before. The longest race we'd ever raced was the 2009 Red River Dog Derby and that was only 165 miles. The Beargrease Marathon is 380 miles, so much longer that it's a totally different race. We were underdogs to all the champions and a few other contenders.

My friend and neighbor, Odin Jorgenson, comes from a mushing family and was attempting the Beargrease for the third time. During training for the Beargrease Odin, his wife Betsy and I saw each other on the trail often. They were always travelling a steady speed, around eight or nine miles an hour, and I'd go blowing by them at eleven or twelve mph.

"You got a hot team there," he said one day but underneath we both questioned the other's strategy.

Several more mushers went up to get their bibs before my number was called, number fifteen out of thirty. That was fine. The trail would be well tracked before I got there but I wouldn't be so far back that I'd spend the first hundred miles passing teams.

There was noticeable applause when I walked up on the stage. Geoff, the Race Director said, "You've got some fans here, Frank."

Sheepishly I replied, "Aw, I just bought em all drinks."

Finally all the bibs were drawn and we could get out of there. Sherri and Lisa got to the hotel ahead of me. Sherri called me from the Fairfield Inn.

"They've rented our room to someone else."

"What? We already paid for the thing."

"They're trying to find us another room. Everything in town is booked, though. The guy says he'll keep looking."

"He'd darn well better. Call me back."

There I was, driving a dog truck around Duluth the night before the Beargrease with no place to stay. The race used to find host families for the mushers. They didn't seem to do that anymore or maybe it was just that there were not any families who wanted to host fourteen dogs and a group of people that smelled like dog crap. We had called all over before we found the room at the Fairfield Inn for $150. Now we were out the $150 and had no place to stay.

After another hour Sherri called back. "They've found us a room at a budget hotel by the mall. The guy says they'll pay for it and refund the difference."

They gave us the cash for the room but we never were refunded the difference. At that point I didn't care. I needed to drop the dogs and get to bed.

I love being out on the road with the dogs. It's great to have handlers to help take care of them but whenever I can, I try to go drop them on my own. It was after midnight, the night before the race and even though I was pretty tired, I spent some extra time with each of them.

"Acorn, this is what we've been working on for five years. You're going to lead out with Ajax tomorrow."

She responded by quickly licking my face a few times and then an "Ow wow wowwow." Acorn was beautiful. Her defined muscles were clearly visible beneath her shiny black coat. I looked at her and Winnie, who were both now six years old, and wondered how many more years they would be my best dogs. Racing without them was not something I could even think about. After so many miles, near misses and races, here was our biggest challenge yet.

I walked around the truck one more time, bringing each dog's head near mine, scratching under the chins. I relaxed. This was my team and there was not another one in the world that I would rather stand on the runners behind tomorrow. We might not have another moment alone together until we were well out onto the trail. I squatted down, sitting on my heels, and looked up and down the truck. What amazing animals they were and I was the one who was lucky enough to ride out with them. All the thousands of people involved in this race and I get to be the one on the runners behind this team. There was no more fortunate man in the whole world.

I thought of a night during the last week of college. It was after three in the morning. Looking around the room, I saw most of my friends sleeping on the floor. I drained the last of the Jim Beam and lit another cigarette. *A Whiter Shade of Pale* was playing on the stereo. College was over and when I woke up, the rest of my life would start. If I just stayed up, the night and my youth would never end.

I would never be a rookie again.

The gap between the drapes showed the first light of race day. Pausing for a minute after my morning prayer, I listened to Sherri breathing next to me. Maybe I could get up without waking her. She'd be the one responsible for taking care of the dogs at the checkpoints for three days; I could feed them myself this morning.

The morning showed that we weren't the only team staying at the motel. I dropped the dogs, fed, watered and cleaned up after them. Other mushers and handlers were busying themselves around the parking lot. A few I recognized, most I didn't. Chopping fifty pounds of frozen meat was all that needed to still be done that morning. While chopping I met Lyle, a sixty-plus-year-old insurance agent from Iowa who had just taken up mushing.

After I finished and was about to get into the truck to drive over to the start I asked him, "Whattaya doing for the next three days?"

"Well, ahhhh, I gotta work tomorrow."

"Ah come on, you should come help handle for three days."

After taking a few pictures, he said, "Let me think about it. I'll probably see you there." Then he drove away.

Our parking spot at the race staging area was right next to the port-a-johns which meant a constant stream of spectators, well wishers and questions:

"Why don't your dogs look like sled dogs?" (Most people expect to see Siberian Huskies or Malamutes)

"Why don't you feed them more? They sure look skinny." (The average housedog is fat)

"Do you put shoes on after you put those socks on their feet?" (That lady's socks must look like dog booties)

Sherri had to step in and tell people to leave me alone so I could get the sled packed and gear ready. As organized as we were, it still seemed crazy; thousands of people, loud rock and roll music, the exact opposite of what I normally experienced when mushing. The race veterans were fine, just another race to them. Winnie and Wolf were howling to go an hour before the start. The young dogs—Storm, Socks, Esther and Nita—were obviously nervous; more commotion than they had ever experienced. We kept them in their boxes as much as we could, and I knew once we got out on the trail they'd be fine.

Lyle from Iowa showed up but I could tell by how he was dressed that he was just there to watch. Teri, our friend with the memory problem, was at the start too, and she was ready to work. A few hugs and pleasantries and she got down to work treating and bootieing the dogs' feet.

Our start time was 1:30 and we needed to be in line by 1:26. At 1:20 we started hooking up the dogs to the gangline starting with the leaders, Acorn and Ajax. We worked our way back skipping the places where Ace, Winnie and Wolf would be. They'd get hooked up last. They were nuts and the whole team went crazy when they got hooked up. That meant it was time to go.

Volunteers showed up to help us run the dogs up to the starting line. I picked the two largest guys to hold onto Ace and Winnie. They still were dragging these guys around. Steve stood on the back of the sled with me to give it more weight but flew off onto his butt when we rounded the corner into the starting chute.

Two minutes before my time to go, the team in front of me left. We were then signaled to bring our team up. I let up on the brake just a hair and the team dragged ten volunteers, Sherri, Teri, Lisa, Steve and me all up to the starting line where four other guys grabbed my sled and another took my snow hook and hooked it to a tire. For the next minute or so I was safe to check on all the dogs, look for tangles, thank the volunteers and share a just a couple of seconds with Sherri.

She looked beautiful even in her parka, fur hat and huge pac boots. "I'm so proud of you. Acorn will take care of you, just take your time and we'll see you in Two Harbors."

"Thank you, Sherri, I wouldn't be here without you."

I hugged and kissed her before I kneeled down between Ajax and Acorn. I didn't say anything, just grabbed each of their heads and held them close to my face. Acorn pulled away just enough to give me a few quick licks. I got up and walked down the gangline giving each dog a scratch on the head and stepped back onto the runners of the sled.

"Fifteen seconds"

I took a deep breath and broke into a huge smile.

"Ten seconds, nine, eight, seven, six, five, four, three, two, GO!"

The starting chute was like being shot out of a gun, a long barrel of race fans that went on and on. The leaders and other veteran dogs paid no attention to all the yelling from the crowd. They were already on the hunt for the team ahead. The younger dogs got a bit nervous. One guy let out a scream when we went by and Esther, who was in point, almost jumped over the gangline.

"It's OK, Esther, good girl. It's OK." She regained focus and drove again into her harness.

The Beargrease Trail winds through the outskirts of Duluth before heading northeast to the next checkpoint near Two Harbors, thirty-five miles from the start. The highlight of this leg is all the fans along the trail. Some are alone taking pictures. Others are with their kids playing in the snow and waving as you go by. My favorites are the large groups of snowmobilers hanging out around campfires cheering and offering brats, water, pop and beer to any musher who can grab them as he goes by. Cleaning out my sled bag at the end of the race I found an empty Coke can and a ketchup-stained napkin from one of those brats.

Our plan was to stay just under ten miles an hour for as long as the team could maintain that speed. For the first leg that meant that I stood on the drag pad (piece of snowmobile track with bolts drilled through it) and the main brake on all but the steepest uphill sections of trail. The dogs looked awesome and I felt sure that they were going to keep up this pace for the entire 380 miles. The hills were constant but with the dogs fresh and travelling so well, I hardly noticed them. We passed three other teams and were passed by one.

The checkpoints meant we got to see Sherri. When we got close I caught myself letting off the brake. Looking down at the GPS I saw that we were going twelve miles an hour.

"Easy, easy guys." And I again stepped on the brake. Still a long 345 miles to go.

After being on the trail for about three and half hours we turned into the first checkpoint. Just under ten miles an hour, perfect. I caught sight of Sherri but none of our handlers. Immediately I knew something was wrong. I stopped, signed in and stood on the drag pad as Sherri and a couple of race volunteers ran the dogs up to our truck.

Lisa came running up as we got to the truck tripping and falling across the gangline. Sherri was steaming mad.

"This is ridiculous. I can't do this whole thing myself. Where are the handlers?"

Steve showed up with the water and I stayed out of her way busying myself getting the food ready to feed the dogs. Lisa had her head down and was grabbing and scattering straw on the ground. Only some of it was landing in the right places.

We were squeezed in between two other trucks with another in front. Two of them were running and exhaust was surrounding us and the team. The lot had been plowed free of snow so there was nothing to put a hook in to anchor the team. Sherri got the OK to hook the sled to the bumper of the truck behind us. Other mushers who had just come in were barking orders to handlers. Being so early in the race all the dogs were wound up, barking, some fighting. It was chaos. Sherri was trying to pull out the dog bootie bag from the truck and was again yelling. I walked over to her.

"I have a job to do. Where's Teri? Lisa and Steve just got here!"

I grabbed her hand and attempted to walk her away from the dogs. She jerked it away.

"Please, Sherri, can we get away from the dogs?"

I had visions of having to scratch and thought, "Here goes my Beargrease luck again and it's only Two Harbors."

The look on Sherri's face told that my mentioning the dogs sunk in. She loved them every bit as much as I did and realized the effect her rant was having on our team. She took a breath.

"I can't do this alone. They all had to drive their own cars. Lisa stopped at the yarn store. Steve was waiting at Holiday for Teri. I don't know where she is."

Teri had just walked up and got to work on the dogs' feet. She'd obviously heard Sherri but never said a thing about it.

In 2009 only six teams even finished the Beargrease Marathon. All of the finishers took a minimum of two hours at the first Two Harbors checkpoint so I was determined that we would take at least two hours there. It proved to be a waste of an hour of our total minimum 28 hours of rest, an hour that we would desperately need later.

After an hour the dogs were fed, massaged and rebooted. Then they fidgeted, barked, fought and chewed off booties.

"Oh the heck with it. Let's roll."

We turned the team around and made for the checkpoint starting line. We had rested for one hour and fifty-three minutes. Since it was 7:00 and dark, the leaders wore flashing lights and I had my headlamp on. Both are mandatory after sundown. Fly and Woolley, brother and sister, were now leading. They were both excellent command leaders. Woolley was a step slower than Fly and I figured she'd keep the team under the planned ten miles an hour.

It was the third time we had been on that stretch of trail and the dogs obviously knew where we were going. The moon had yet to come up and the sky was cloudless. After a few miles the trail climbed up to a long plateau with views of Lake Superior to the South. The starlit sky and the great lake melted together on the horizon. The night was quiet with no wind.

Except for a couple of teams we passed on the forty-two mile run to Beaver Bay, we were alone on the trail. There was an occasional smoldering campfire but it was Sunday night, and the snowmobilers had long since left the trail. After only an hour, the energy from the Subway sandwich Sherri brought me at Two Harbors was long gone. Digging in my sled I pulled out my snack bag. Cookies, Pop Tarts, deer jerky were the staples. Health was no consideration; just get as many calories in as possible. Plus it had to be stuff I really liked because I didn't always get hungry when I needed to eat. I tore open the cookie bag. Three cookies and a thermos of Russian Tea and I was feeling back to full strength.

Watching the team's effortless running I thought of how far we'd come. It was only six years ago that we'd made our first trip by dog sled.

Thirty miles into the run the Beargrease race trail turned south to the Beaver Bay checkpoint. It was over ten miles down to this lakeside town and the conditions changed dramatically as I got closer to the lake. The trail above had a groomed two-foot snow base and the further we descended towards the lake, the thinner the snow became.

Three miles from Beaver Bay the trail took a sharp right turn off an old railroad grade and dropped into the valley that becomes Beaver Bay. Mushers must have often missed the turn because there was a guy a few hundred yards before the turn yelling and waving his arms. Some guy on the side of the trail yelled something. I had no idea what he said and just raised a mitten. You know you're not on the race trail anymore when you look down and there aren't any dog tracks in the snow. It dawned on me that the guy yelling back there was probably trying to tell me something about the trail turning, and I'd missed it.

The trick to turning your team around on the trail is to do it quickly. Running up to the front, I grabbed the neckline between Fly and Woolley and ran them back past the sled. It went perfectly; before each row of dogs knew we were turning around the dogs in front of them were next to them and going the opposite direction. Gloating to myself about my brilliant dog handling skills I almost missed the trail on the way back. The sharpness of the corner and steepness of the drop caught me by surprise and I flipped the sled. Driver error again. A few seconds dragging on my face on the frozen hard snow slowed the team enough for me to stand up and get back on the runners.

Two mistakes, bumped and bruised a bit but most importantly not more than a minute lost. I looked at the GPS. It read 12 mph.

Standing on the drag pad I gave a, "Whooaaaaa, easssyy."

The trail now paralleled the road down the steep valley into Beaver Bay. Close to the lake the trail had turned to ice and the GPS now read 14 mph. I was standing on the claw brake with both feet, but we were still gaining speed running in the road ditch down to the checkpoint. Sparks were flying up from the claw brake digging into the pavement under the thin layer of ice.

The Beaver Bay checkpoint was essentially a junkyard opposite Lake Superior on Highway 61. I had visions of flying across the highway at the bottom of the trail and right into the partly frozen lake. I was prepared to throw the sled over on its side and hope for the best. Just then we rounded a slight corner and I saw a group of people around the trail, like a big catcher's mitt.

Sherri, bless her heart, called out: "Here Fly, here Woolley." Like they needed any encouragement to run.

Somehow Sherri, Lisa, Teri, Steve and a half dozen volunteers grabbed the team as they went by, keeping us from crossing the highway and plunging into the lake.

"Come on, let's go," Sherri commanded as everyone immediately ran the team up a hill and into the middle of the junkyard-turned checkpoint. Stumbling over junk, rocks and other dog teams I tried to follow along as best I could.

I thought I heard Steve say something about rocks, just as a large one took my legs out and my face hit the sled handlebar.

"Dang it, can we slow down for a second?"

Sherri yelled back: "Steve's supposed to tell you if there's any rocks."

I stepped off the sled and walked away as they brought the team to a stop. I found a piece of junk to sit on and tried to calm down. Checkpoints are supposed to be where we refuel and relax. All I wanted to do was hop back on the sled and hit the trail. Taking a few deep breaths I began the serenity prayer:

"God grant me the serenity to accept the things I cannot change, courage to change the things I can and the wisdom to know the difference."

Again and again I said it. My breath began to slow. I felt my face. My nose and upper lip were tender but no blood. Sherri and our handlers were doing everything they could for me. The dogs were awesome. Our team was running with the race leaders. The only problem was me. I needed to calm down and go feed my dogs. Walking back to the team I saw that Lisa already had them bedded down, Teri was working on their feet, Steve was getting some food for me, and Sherri had the cooker ready with hot water for the dogs' food.

"Hi, sweetie." She kissed me. "The water is ready for you to feed the dogs. I don't know how much you want to feed them here."

I looked at Sherri. When the steam from her breath cleared I saw the frost on her eyelashes. Her expression let me know that everything was fine. Looking again to the dogs I saw Fly rolling on his back in the straw. He already knew what Sherri was trying to tell me.

I sat down on my heels and dumped equal parts kibble and beef into a bucket. Then I added a few scoops of ground-beef fat and poured the hot water over the top. Immediately I was surrounded by the steam and I began to stir until the beef was thawed and the mixture was lukewarm. Each dog got a full two-quart bowl to start. Once they all received their ration I went around the bucket and gave seconds. The biggest and thinnest dogs got the most. The five-gallon bucket had about a gallon of the stew left. I poured this into a cooler for later and put the lid on it.

Lisa picked up the bowls as Teri covered all the dogs with blankets. Wolf and Ace wouldn't lie down and they wore theirs standing up. I walked up and down the gangline petting each dog's head and saying a little something. They were running a perfect race and had such trust in me. I was the weak link. Sitting back I said another prayer asking to be more their equal. Leaving them in Lisa, Teri, and Sherri's hands I walked over to Steve's heated van for a two-hour nap. It was midnight on the first night of the Beargrease.

It's tough for me to sleep at a race. The dogs were being cared for, I knew that, but my mind was still running down the trail, thinking about each dog, how they were doing and which ones should be leading when we left Beaver Bay. Soon I was sweating in the heat of the van and asked Steve to turn off the heat. He did as I asked, and eventually I dozed off.

Less than an hour later I woke up shivering. My sweat had turned cold and frost was covering my snowsuit. My watch showed 2:10 a.m.. I looked up at the outside thermometer on the van and it read nine degrees.

"Nine degrees? I'm turning into an old wimp."

Steve stirred up front. "Yeah, it's been that temperature since we arrived. Feels colder though."

We later figured out that the van thermometer was broken and the reported temperature that night was seventeen below.

"Steve, I'm kinda chilled. I'm going to go for a walk and warm up a bit."

Walking back towards the dogs I was digging in my pocket for some cookies that I had remembered sticking in there. My hand landed on something else and I pulled out a red felt pouch that was tied closed at the top with yarn. It was filled with tobacco. All the mushers had received one at the opening ceremony to give as an offering at the grave of John Beargrease, there in Beaver Bay. I had put it in the pocket of my snowsuit so hopefully I wouldn't forget.

The Beaver Bay checkpoint felt like a train station at rush hour, seemingly chaotic but everyone efficiently got to where they were going. Prior to the race there had been discussion about why we were going all the way down to Beaver Bay, to a checkpoint that was basically a junkyard, just to drop off this token at John Beargrease's grave. The argument was that the trail was icy and dangerous and the checkpoint was, well, a junkyard. I had stayed out of the discussion being a rookie but also had my doubts. Now I had the pouch in my hand and more than an hour before I needed to worry about getting the dogs up and ready for our planned departure time at 4:00 a.m. Wandering through the maze of sleeping dogs, alcohol cooking stoves and roving headlamps I found a race judge and asked him where to find the gravesite.

"Oh, let's see…I think it's across the road over there. There should be a trail up the hill to it."

"Thanks."

I found the trail quickly and the snow showed that there had already been a few visitors. Climbing the snow-covered stairs I came to a small clearing in the woods with a modest square monument, a couple of feet high, in the middle. At the base of it were three other tobacco pouches. After reading some of the text I kneeled and placed my pouch at the base, said a simple "Thank you" and stood up.

Even as sounds of dogs barking, a banging pot, traffic in the distance rose up, the place where I stood felt quiet. I turned off my headlamp and let my eyes adjust. Soon I could make out the trees surrounding the gravesite. The clearing was small, maybe thirty feet across. It was only a couple of hundred yards from the scene below but there was just me, this monument and four pouches of tobacco.

The cold soon got my attention and I turned to leave. As I approached the stairs, I stopped, turned and again said, "Thank you;" then I found my way back down to our dog team.

The dogs were just starting to stir when I arrived. Lisa and Teri were getting ready to reboot them.

Sherri walked up to me smiling, "There you are. You should eat." And she quickly put a bag of cookies, pop tarts and deer jerky into my gloved hands.

"Here, drink this." She handed me a liter bottle full of warm water. Staying hydrated is always a challenge when it's that cold but it's just as important as calories to stay warm.

"I also made you some coffee. It's over next to the cooker."

The cooler was still full of dog food from when we fed them earlier. I poured it into the bucket, added some hot water from the cooker, stirred it and the steam rose around me. After filling fourteen bowls of the watery mixture I ran them all up to the dogs. They all went to work and in seconds I heard the sound of empty bowls banging against the rocks as the dogs licked to get every last drop. Picking up the bowls, I returned to the cooker and my coffee. I looked at my watch. It was 3:45. I had fifteen minutes before we planned to leave. From Beaver Bay, the dogs and I were on our own for the next hundred miles.

"Sherri, remember I won't see you again until Trail Center at around 8:00 p.m. tonight."

"I know, we've been through this already. We're going to get a bath and some sleep."

Four a.m. found us at the starting line and no sooner did I get there than they started the clock.

"Just a second, we aren't ready yet."

"Sorry" was all I got in response.

So I yelled, "Let's go!" and I wasn't even on the sled yet. Grabbing the handlebar as the sled flew by, I flipped it on its side and dragged behind if for a few seconds before righting it. We were on the trail again towards the Sawbill trail over fifty miles away. Another fifty plus miles later was Trail Center where I'd again see Sherri, Lisa, Teri and Steve. That would be at least seventeen hours and over 100 miles from now. For this quarter of the race it was just me and my fourteen dogs. It was the part of the race that I was most looking forward to. The dogs and I would settle in to a rhythm heading into the halfway point of the race. Hopefully we would maintain a comfortable pace and arrive in Trail Center in position to challenge the top teams. Fly and Woolley, brother and sister, were in lead. They weren't our fasted dogs but both were crack leaders and would set a comfortable pace. We still had 300 miles to go and I was in no hurry.

It was cold, about twenty below and I was tired, having hardly slept and getting chilled trying. After only a half an hour I was struggling to stay awake. The team was still too fresh for me to do any kicking so I alternated between snacking on cookies and drinking coffee from my thermos. Still my head was bobbing. It was more than that night's lack of sleep. It was all the previous nights of lying awake thinking about the race, who would run where and how well we would do. Those sleepless nights now had added up.

A portion of this trail ran next to a power line with typical wood power poles holding up the line. Pretty soon those power poles began to move closer and closer to the trail until one jumped right in front of the sled. I yelled, threw the sled on its side and dragged on my face down the trail until we stopped. I looked up with a face full of snow to see all the dogs staring back at me. They all had a look that said, "What was that about?" I looked over at the power line and the nearest pole was fifty feet from the trail. We hadn't hit any and none were in the middle of the trail.

Getting back on the sled I said, "Let's go," and kept an eye on those power poles in case they moved again. In minutes my head started to bob when again one of those poles jumped right in front of the sled.

"Aaaaahhhh," I screamed as I threw the sled over and braced for impact. We slid to a stop. I looked up. The power poles were now not even alongside the trail but had angled off into the woods some time back. The dogs were clearly irritated and didn't wait for me to yell "Let's go" before they took off again.

My falling asleep was getting in the way of their race. As always I was the weak link in the team. I began alternating between running and drinking coffee. I could manage maybe running ten seconds at the speed we were travelling before I stumbled back onto the runners. Soon the need to pee was keeping me awake.

"If I can just hold it until the sun starts to rise." But the need grew too great and I knew I'd have to go soon. Holding onto the handlebar with one hand, standing with both feet on one runner, I unzipped my snowsuit and opened up all the layers. Peeing off the side of your sled at twenty below travelling at ten miles an hour is sure to keep anyone awake but it's not something you want to take any longer than it has to. It's bad enough to have that temperature blowing on your face.

After getting zipped up I looked to the eastern horizon and saw that the starlight had faded. Dawn was coming and I thought, "This is only the first night. How am I going to get through two more without falling completely asleep and running this sled straight into a tree?"

The trail turned to the north and, staring at the fading North Star, I knew we had made the turn towards Sawbill. The sun lit up the sky on our right and we wound our way up the Temperance River Valley. I felt the first rays of warmth on my cheek. The sunrise was bringing to life the landscape around us and the first long cold night was over. Standing on the runners, watching my fourteen teammates perfectly running as they were born and trained to, for the first time it dawned on me that here we were, on the John Beargrease Trail. Several teams were ahead but the majority were behind us. We deserved to be in this race.

Ace (photo by Rhonda Silence/*Cook County News-Herald*)

Chapter 11

We came into Sawbill with about ten teams already there. Several teams hadn't rested at Two Harbors so their race clocks and ours were different. Race strategy was just starting to become apparent. Some teams chose to rest at both Two Harbors and Beaver Bay. Others were choosing to run a bit slower and longer, only stopping at Beaver Bay and leaving more of the mandatory minimum twenty-eight hours of rest for later. The twenty-eight hours is a minimum and teams are free to take more and many do.

The full daylight of morning combined with all the activity of the checkpoint kept me fairly awake and lively. But the dogs needed a big meal, feet attended to and some sleep. I got their needs met in a half hour, which meant they could sleep for almost four hours. We planned to stay there for five hours. I went off to find something to eat. The checkpoint had a small mobile home that was hauled in for the race. The hosts provided pancakes, sausage, coffee, and juice. I scarfed down a plateful sitting next to Jason Barron and Colleen

Wallin. We hardly talked, focusing on getting our food eaten so we could return to our teams.

With the first full stomach I'd had in days, I filled my thermos with coffee, thanked the hosts and walked back to stretch out next to the dogs. It was a relatively warm, sunny, ten-degree day and I was feeling sleepy. The checkpoint at Sawbill is set up to allow for spectators to walk around and see the camping mushers and their dogs. After talking to a few spectators and Rhonda from the *Cook County Herald*, I lay down in the straw next to Tina and Ace. Dogs don't tell you they like or approve of something but I knew the dogs were glad I was there with them. Tina got up and circled, making a new bed right next to my sleeping bag. Ace moved his head over and laid it on top of my leg.

The sounds of the checkpoint faded in and out as I dozed intermittently over the next two hours. By noon it was time to get up and start readying the team for our planned 1:30 departure. Sawbill was an unassisted checkpoint and since I was on my own I wanted to give myself plenty of time. I got the alcohol cooker going so I could warm up another light meal for the dogs, trying to be as quiet as possible so they could get every last minute of sleep. But as soon as I began filling bowls, all eyes were on me. Everybody ate well again and Ace started eating his dish when it was empty.

"Hey, Frank, that dog's eating his dish. Ya know if you fed him some better food, he wouldn't be doin that."

It was Matt Rossi, whose team was in the woods the next campsite over from mine. He was sponsored by Native, a rival brand to our dog food sponsor, NutriSource.

"Yeah, that dog food's been doin' great for you the last couple of races."

After just beating him at Red River we placed well ahead of Matt's team at White Oak, and he hadn't forgotten. We talked as we readied our teams to leave. Without at first realizing it, we were racing getting our teams bootied.

"Pretty fast for an old guy, Matt. Who blows your nose for you when your handlers aren't here?"

"Good luck catching me, Frank, if I get outta here ahead of you." Matt did leave a few minutes ahead of us and we didn't catch him...that is until this same checkpoint down-bound 200 miles later.

The dogs had had a long five-hour rest at Sawbill, eaten two meals and were again acting like it was the beginning of the race, banging into their harnesses, barking to go. Winnie and Wolf were in lead and we quickly got into a nine mile per hour pace that we could keep up for the fifty-plus miles to Trail Center.

Just as I was marveling at the sunset, the perfect trail and our dogs' flawless performance so far, I noticed that Woolly's tugline was loose. She had led the two previous legs and must have burned herself out. Soon not only was her tugline loose but she was pulling back on her neckline. When a dog starts to neckline, not only is it not contributing to the team but it cancels out another dog. I stopped the sled, checked her feet, legs and shoulders for any problems. Finding nothing I moved her to the other side of the gangline and pulled the hook to start again. Moving her and my encouragement kept Woolly off her neckline but her tugline was still slack. She'd have to be left at the next checkpoint.

"So no big deal, I still have thirteen strong dogs in harness. We'll be fine."

Just then Tina stopped dead, dragging herself and the rest of us to a stop around her. She had to poop and still refused to do it on the run. Really I don't think I could poop on the run either so I didn't blame her but after we started running again, Tina was favoring her right leg.

"What? Tina, you're limping now because you had to stop the team to poop?"

Her limp only got worse and Tina would also have to stay behind when we left Trail Center, the next checkpoint. In three years of racing Tina had never been injured. She was an awesome dog that I always counted on, never even considering that she wouldn't finish a race. Now we would be without her too.

It's hard not to let your mind spiral down when you're sleep deprived and a couple of things go wrong. Just an hour before I had been thinking the hype about this race being so hard was a joke, now the thought began to creep into my head: "Maybe we won't even finish this thing."

It was time for a snack and some coffee. I couldn't let my mind go down that road. We weren't even halfway into the race yet. Looking at the rest of the dogs I saw twelve athletes perfectly in sync. There was no quit in them and even Tina was powering through her limp. I knew better than to try and put her in the sled bag to carry her to the checkpoint. She'd tear it to shreds trying to get out. Again I settled into the run, the magic of the trail and the stars that again owned the sky. Of the thousands of people involved in this race I was again so grateful to be the one out there, on that sled, behind that team of dogs, fourteen of my best friends in the world. My only sadness was that two would have to be left at Trail Center.

Trail Center is both a place—a collection of businesses and cabins halfway down the Gunflint Trail—and a historic store/restaurant: old logs, big burgers, mugs of beer and walls adorned with memorabilia of Beargreases past. Arriving there at night feels like a part of history. The place was buzzing with handlers, spectators, and arriving dog teams. We hadn't seen another dog team in five hours but there were a few in already and more arriving behind us. The race was on; the main competitors were all on their games now and we were right in the middle of it.

Sherri seemed to always know when we were arriving at a checkpoint. Out of the distance from across the lake we heard, "Come on, Winnie, here Wolfie," causing the team to break into a sprint. Sherri, Lisa, Teri, and Steve led the team up to the truck and were about to quickly go into their roles of getting me and the team ready for a rest. I hadn't talked to anyone since my banter with Matt Rossi at the last checkpoint and felt the need to download to these guys what had been going on for the last hundred miles.

"Can we wait just a minute before we start taking care of the dogs? I just have to let you all know that I am having one of the greatest experiences of my life." I went on to describe the last hundred miles as best I could, trying to get the point across of how they were making it possible for me, how grateful I was to them and how incredible our dog team was. Maybe they were listening, I don't know, but being the great handler team they were, they seemed more anxious to get to work on me and the dogs. We had less than five hours before leaving on the longest leg of the race, the seventy mile "Trail to Nowhere." My pep talk may have just been for me but they let me make it.

I walked around the truck with Sherri, talking about all the dogs, giving her the news about Tina and Wooly. She then stuck me in the cab of the truck with two cold pizzas from My Sisters Place in Grand Marais. When hungry I can eat a whole large myself, but with the excitement of the race and the pizza being cold, I could only stomach a couple of pieces. Dozing for about an hour after eating, I woke up wet and cold.

"I need to get outta these wet clothes."

Getting out of the truck, I stepped over a dog tied to the side of the truck. It was Ajax. He opened his eyes, looked up at me, rolled over to his side and picked up his front paw, the signal for me to scratch his chest.

While I was scratching his chest, Ajax and I stared into each other's eyes. He was so relaxed, just doing what he was supposed to, resting. Ajax had raced almost every race we'd done since we bought him as a yearling in 2005 from sprint racers Gary and Jane McCollum. They were selling some dogs and put him up for sale to bring attention to all the other dogs they were trying to sell. I jumped at the chance to buy Ajax and all he'd done for us since then was run; he never once stopped in a race or had to be dropped. We call him the Prince because of how regal he looks with his proud stance, tail high in the air, tall graceful build, red and white coloring and piercing blue eyes. He looks like a champion.

Sitting on my heels I ran my hand across his head. "You keep resting, Ajax. You've still got a couple of more hours to sleep. What a prince you are." I knew if I had asked him to get up right there and lead our team out onto the trail he'd have done it and been barking, tail wagging to go.

Most of the rest of the dogs were sleeping, except Tina, who was going to be staying there at Trail Center and was getting a massage from Sherri. Smiling at Sherri, I leaned over, held Tina's head next to mine. "Thank you, Tina, you are such a good girl." She'd be staying here, but four of her pups would be running with the team when we left Trail Center.

Standing up I saw Woolly already in the truck with the mark from the vet signaling that she was "marked out" or no longer able to race. This little white forty pound girl had given everything she had leading a fourteen-dog team for a hundred miles. She'd done her part and now could rest. Opening the door I put my head next to hers.

"Good girl, Woolly, you can rest now."

Sherri was now massaging Sock's wrist. One of Tina's pups, he was only a yearling who was already a star. "The vet said his wrist was a bit swollen. You may want to drop him too."

"Really, he wasn't favoring it at all. Where's the vet?"

"He's inside, you may want to go talk to him."

I turned and walked towards Trail Center.

Inside I found a raucous crowd. As I walked in, the leader board was straight in front of me. Of course I had to walk over and look at it. One team was clearly leading, Nathan Schroeder's, and then another ten of us were all bunched up pretty close, all averaging between nine and ten miles an hour. With varied run/rest schedules places didn't matter much at that point, except it was clear that Nathan's team was well ahead of the rest of us, averaging eleven miles an hour. I looked over and standing next to me was Ben Tande, a musher friend of ours from Walker who was handling for Nathan.

"Hey, Ben, he's going pretty fast. Ya think he can keep up that pace?" I obviously didn't think so.

"They looked good coming in. I guess we'll see. Your guys are looking good too. Gonna have to drop any dogs here?"

"Yeah, two, maybe three. You seen the vet?"

Just then I looked over and saw Gregg Phillips, the vet who had looked at Sock's wrist.

"It's a little tender. Can you get along without him?" he asked.

"I suppose I could but he seemed fine coming in."

"If you're going to keep him in the team, you'll need to be careful to bag him if he starts to favor it."

"Of course I will. Thanks."

In my head I thought: "There's no chance that Socks is going to need to be carried. He's a rising star and never even has had a limp. He'll be fine." But I'd never been on the next section of trail. I'd heard it had some steep hills. Trying to describe how steep the hills were between Trail Center and Devil's Track to someone who hasn't been on them would be like trying get someone who's never left Florida to understand what forty below feels like. While the temperature was only twenty below, we were about to learn what steep meant and regrettably so were the dogs.

We ran the dogs up to the starting line on Poplar Lake and Jason Barron was already there getting ready to go. We lined up behind him.

"Three, two, one" and his team slowly left with a spray of snow blowing up behind his sled. He was standing full on his drag pad.

The thought of leaving Trail Center, almost halfway into the race, right behind last year's champion immediately clouded my mind. I don't remember saying goodbye to Sherri or the crowd lining the trail. I was solely focused on keeping up with Jason, which should have been no trouble at all with him braking as hard as he was.

Not even a mile from Trail Center we pulled up next to Jason. We told each other that we thought the other's team looked good before he let me pass.

"I could win this thing, in my rookie year," I told myself. I had planned to let the dogs run around this loop and back to Devil's Track, not slow them anymore with the drag pad, on the longest and toughest section of the whole trail. Now we were there, after I'd held the dogs back for almost half the race, and now it was time to race.

Pulling ahead of Jason, I soon lost sight of him. I wondered if he was still braking or if my team was really that fast. I was alone on the trail. After leaving Poplar Lake the trail crossed the Gunflint Trail where the landscape opened up around me. A full moon illuminated a landscape of steep granite domes spiked with the charred trunks of red pines which had been burned off five years ago in the Ham Lake Fire. It was so bright I could barely make out the beam of my headlamp.

The dogs were attacking the steep trail up and down the granite domes. A new trail, the full moon, and after slowing them up for the first half of the race, I was finally letting them run. It was two in the morning on the second night of the Beargrease. And after fighting sleep the previous night, on that night I was wide awake, in awe of the landscape, the night, the dogs, the whole experience. We were just present, all right there in the moment, for the next two hours, twenty miles of brilliant solitude, singleness of purpose. We weren't racing, just running at night. It was perfect.

When a team is moving like that, the gangline flows in a uniform steady rhythm. Everything's in sync. You feel like you could travel forever, wish you could. But it always ends.

The trail narrowed for about a quarter mile, turned ninety degrees to the left and dropped down so steeply that it felt like I was falling off a cliff. The brake was only keeping the sled from hitting the wheel dogs. Then we were spit out onto Gunflint Lake and I was able to slow the team down to a sane speed. Looking over the dogs, I saw the Socks was favoring his left wrist, the one that the vet had warned me about at Trail Center. Setting the hook, precariously, on the lake, I walked up the gangline greeting every dog and when I got to Socks he was chattering, barking to go.

"Hold on there, Socks, let me check out that wrist of yours." He kept pulling it away from me but I could see that it was clearly swollen.

"Looks like you're going to be riding for the next thirty miles, buddy." I unhooked Socks and carried him back to the sled.

I'd seen other mushers pull dogs out of their sled bags that seemed like they'd been sleeping in there, enjoying the ride. Never, not once, had I had a dog willingly go in the sled bag. The fight to get Socks in brought me to a sweat.

"You're not even fifty pounds." You can't be mad at them either.

They just want to run, be a member of their team. That's all they know.

I still had eleven dogs in harness when I pulled the hook on Gunflint Lake.

"Let's go Winnie, Wolfie. Let's go."

The team worked at getting back into a rhythm, but the magic was broken.

Exiting the lake, the trail crossed a road and then climbed another hill too steep to walk up, so steep that if I wasn't holding onto the sled, I'd be on all fours. Right at the entrance to the trail on the other side of the road was a team blocking the trail. The dogs couldn't get around it and Winnie didn't like to wait. Pacing, right then left, he was about to take the team down the gravel road when I set the hook on a small tree and ran up to grab the leaders.

Yelling, "Why did you have to stop right there?"

"Sorry, got a loose dog. I'll try to get over."

Peter was as calm as I was worked up, and he was the one with the loose dog. I didn't say another word but ran my team up past his. The right thing to do would have been to tie my team off and try to help Peter get his dog, or at least just wait for him, but I was racing. Those were precious seconds I was wasting. The fact that minutes and hours separated teams at the finish of this four-day race hadn't dawned on me. I had to go now. Passing his team I let the leaders go and grabbed the sled as it came by doing my best to hold on as the dogs dug in, not running but climbing up the trail.

Without realizing it I was pushing my team. There were a hundred and fifty miles left to race and I was acting like we were in the last thirty. Not understanding why he wasn't in the team, Socks was kicking and doing all he could to stick his nose out of the bag.

The crazy steep hills continued and just when I thought that we were getting into some kind of rhythm, the grand daddy of them dropped us out onto Loon Lake.

"How on Earth do they get a snowmobile up that thing?"

We were out of the nonstop roller coaster of a trail but coming out onto the lake felt like we'd run into quicksand. We sank into the soft snow that had drifted over the new trail. I was kicking with everything I had to keep the dogs moving at the speed I thought they should be travelling. We were barely going eight miles an hour.

Soon there was a light at my back. Turning I saw a team had caught us and was looking to pass…and another right behind them? "What?" We'd been flying before we hit the lake. How could they have caught us?

"Hey, Frank." Is was Jason. I just nodded my disbelief. Then Peter, with all fourteen dogs in harness, also passed. He didn't say anything, just went on by.

Without even thinking I gave chase. "This is temporary," I thought. We'd again catch and pass those teams. I had Winnie and Wolf in lead. They could catch any team.

"Let's go. Let's go!" I tried to kick even harder. The sweat ran down my forehead and back.

Up the gravel road on the other side of Loon Lake we all ran. I was poling and running, like the finish was in sight. Switching sides of the sled I looked down to avoid stepping on the runners. Before I knew what happened we had taken a sharp left.

"What the …." We were now off the trail, headed downhill on another trail, in the wrong direction.

"Winnie, where are you goin?"

Braking was no good. He was on a mission. The trail quickly ended and we plowed into the trees, tangling every dog and the sled in the underbrush, buried in the snow. Not slowing down to think about what happened or why, I was a crazed man trying to free his team and get us turned around. Somehow I still thought we could win this race, seconds mattered.

I had crossed the line, driven my dogs, even my great leaders too hard. Winnie had never balked in his life and I had driven him to the point where he looked for an out, taken the team off the trail. It took me months to realize this.

Clothes soaked with sweat, exhausted, I drove the team back up the trail and, turning left, gave chase to Jason and Peter. We would never catch either of them and would be passed by two more teams before we slowly crept across Devil's Track Lake on Tuesday morning. The last five miles on the lake into the wind seemed endless. Even then, as slow as we were going, I thought we could still regroup and give chase out of Devil's Track. There were over a hundred miles to go, plenty of time to catch up.

Coming into Devil's Track Landing we passed a team coming the other direction.

"Where are you going?"

"Sawbill." It was Nathan Schroeder. Jason wasn't leading this race. Nathan was and he was four hours ahead of all of us. My delusion of winning as a rookie finally cracked.

"Come on, Winnie. Come on, Wolfie." Sherri yelled from the landing. Those words sounded like heaven and woke us out of our stupor. The gathered crowd cheered us in as we trotted up the landing. We had completed what I thought would be the hardest run of the race. Time for a rest, a change of clothes and breakfast.

After being on such a remote section of trail all night, coming into a resort area close to the city of Grand Marais seemed very strange. It was only eight in the morning and there were already buses with kids everywhere coming to see the dogs. Race fans crowded around asking questions but I was in a daze and having trouble answering. I remember staring at one woman and not having a clue what she was talking about, like she was speaking to me in a foreign language. She eventually just walked away.

After getting the dogs fed and bedded down, I went into Devil's Track Landing for breakfast. We sat in a nice bar restaurant with CNN playing on the television. Sherri and I didn't have television and seeing it here, after having been out on the trail for the second night, seemed like such an interruption. The news of war and celebrities was meaningless to me. My mind was on my dogs and the trail ahead. While we were all pretty tired, I was sure that the dogs and I still had the remaining 130 miles in us.

Getting up to go to the bathroom, I checked out the leader board. It showed that we were in twelfth place, but that didn't mean a lot because the run rest schedules still weren't equalized. While I was up, Steve got a call from Lyle. He said the results page on the internet had us in fifth place. I didn't believe that either.

After a meal of eggs and pancakes, which I couldn't finish, I went back to the truck before I'd try to sleep. It was late morning and the checkpoint was crawling with spectators, school kids and well-wishers. All the dogs were sleeping with their blankets on, except for Wolfie. He just sat there with his blanket draped over his back looking over at me as I walked up. Walking over to him I kneeled and rubbed the sides of his head, holding it close to mine. I couldn't believe he was only two. He was the strongest dog coming into Devil's Track and here he was, not even wanting to sleep. The excitement of the event, the fans, getting to run again soon, I don't know what it was but he wasn't interested in sleeping.

Looking over I saw that Ace was half sitting up. His blanket was draped over his shoulders and his head was bobbing up and down. As tired as he must have been, he still was trying to stay awake. Getting up and kneeling next to Ace, I held his head next to mine then took off the wrist wraps that he was wearing to keep down the swelling. He tolerated wearing them but wouldn't lay down with them on.

"It's OK, Ace. You can sleep now. I won't leave without you. I promise."

I laid him down on his straw and re-covered him with his blanket. He stretched and closed his eyes.

We would try to leave here in three hours with Wolf and Winnie again in lead. I needed to get some sleep. Having only two hours in the last two days was catching up with me. Crawling into the back of the van I looked out at the dogs still sleeping, except for Wolf and Ace who were both now sitting with their heads bobbing up and down. Closing my eyes made me feel like I was back on the sled. Part sleeping, part gliding down the trail, I passed the next two hours. A fitful sleep but the best I had gotten in three days.

"What?" I sat up with a start. "I gotta go."

I jumped out of my sleeping bag and quickly looked at my watch. It was 11:30 a.m.. I had only slept for an hour. We weren't planning on leaving until 12:20. Looking out of the van I saw that

Teri and Sherri were starting to wake and bootie the dogs. I put on my boots and jumped out. The dogs needed another light meal and I always insisted on doing that myself. Maybe it was that I thought it made them more willing to work for me, the one that fed them, but I really think it was my ego.

"Nobody else knows them like I do or feeds them the right amount."

Mixing up their light meal, the second in four hours, got all of their attention. Wolfie started barking. How interested dogs are in their food is an indication of how the dogs are doing in a long race. Lunging at you when you're bringing the bowl means they're ready to go now. Sniffing toward you, then eating the food when it's put in front of them is still pretty good. If a dog turns its nose up and won't eat, then there may be trouble. Almost all the dogs were lunging for their food. Etta didn't get up when I put down her bowl, just sniffed it and put her head back down on her paws. I kneeled next to her and petted her sweet black head. She left her eyes closed. This sweet little girl had given all she had to get us to Devil's Track.

"Good girl, Etta. You can rest now. Thank you for working so hard." I held her head next to mine for a few seconds then got up and went to get a vet. She would need to be marked out to join Socks, Woolly and Tina in the truck. Sherri would feed them after we left for Sawbill.

Our plan was to go through the Sawbill checkpoint, saving our remaining mandatory rest for Finland over seventy miles from Devil's Track. We had never run through a checkpoint without stopping but looking at the run/rest schedules from the previous year, I'd seen that's what the leaders did. We were there to compete and would do the same.

"Train like you want them to race." I was about to learn what that meant.

The excitement of the checkpoint added to the dogs' energy. They were jumping and barking when we hooked them up and ran them down to the lake to start the next leg. We were leaving in fifth place, pretty good for a rookie, and that was still going to my head. Winnie and Wolf would lead us out again.

"Five, four, three, two, one."

"Let's go, Winnie. Let's go, Wolfie."

They ran out onto the lake but with so many snowmobile tracks going everywhere they wandered a bit and then Winnie did something I never thought possible. He sat down. First I just stood there and stared in disbelief. How could my super leader not want to lead?

"Put Acorn in lead." I heard Sherri yell from behind me. I switched Acorn and Winnie. "Let's go, Acorn. Let's go, Wolfie."

Acorn lunged and got the team going in the right direction. The team sluggishly made their way back across Devil's Track Lake. Acorn always puts us right on the trail. At that point in the race she wasn't too fast but at least we were making progress towards Duluth, still over one hundred and forty miles away.

A light snow was falling and it was a relatively warm ten degrees. I figured that I'd be running up all the many hills in the next seventy miles so I was dressed lightly, gore-tex shell and pants, couple of fleece layers, gloves and hat. No warm boots either, just light mukluks. The wind across the lake felt cold but I figured once we got off the lake the wind would be less in the woods and I'd be warmer.

Once we got off the lake I switched Winnie and Acorn again. Now he seemed to want to lead and our speed picked up a bit, still less than nine miles an hour but better. The team settled into a new rhythm and I was giving everything I had to getting us up all the hills. Sweating, I took off my jacket. But no matter how much I ran or kicked, we didn't speed up; in fact an hour after we left we seemed to be slowing down.

"Your dogs will go slow too" is what I got when I asked other mushers how come they were only going seven miles an hour or less in the last hundred miles of the Beargrease.

"Maybe your dogs but not mine."

Now we were travelling about eight miles an hour, with a hundred and twenty miles to go when we came to the hills before

Sawbill. I remembered some hills on this trail on the way up but not like this. In my sleep deprived state I was wondering if somehow they had gotten bigger. They must have or maybe we were on the wrong trail.

"Trail."

I didn't even know he was there and Rick Larson from Montana passed me going uphill, standing on his sled, with a cigarette in his mouth.

Now we were in sixth place. "Shit, maybe if I push a bit harder we can tail him into Sawbill." Within fifteen minutes Rick was lost from sight, beyond the next hill. I kept pushing.

Four hours after leaving Devil's Track we came down the hill into the Sawbill checkpoint.

"Come on Winnie, Wolfie." There was Sherri waiting. She, Teri, Lisa, and Steve grabbed the team and ran us through the checkpoint to the starting line for the trail to Finland. At the line the dogs were looking around, obviously confused. There were their handlers but where was their food? Their beds? Their massages? Sherri shoved a sandwich, a thermos of coffee and a new water bottle in my sled bag.

"Good job. Keep it going. See you in Finland." She gave me a kiss.

"Let's go, Winnie. Let's go, Wolfie."

After a pause, they slowly began to trot down the trail and across the Temperance River bridge and then stopped. I set the hook, looked back behind me at the people, including Sherri lining the trail, turned and opened the sled bag and pulled out a bag of snacks for the dogs. Handing a couple to each dog, I made my way to the front. After giving Winnie and Wolfie theirs, I gave both leaders a vigorous petting.

"You guys can do it. You're such good boys."

I ran back to the sled and pulled the hook.

"Come on, Winnie. Let's go, Wolfie."

Again we started to move slowly up the long trail to Heartbreak Hill. I was both very thirsty and hungry. The dogs were working so much harder than I was. Somehow this was lost on me. They needed more food and water if we were to keep making progress down the trail.

We were at least moving and I remembered the sandwich that Sherri had given me at the checkpoint. I pulled out the white paper bag. Inside was a bag of gourmet potato chips, a turkey-and-Swiss sandwich with lettuce and tomato on some kind of fancy bun (later Sherri told me it was ciabatta). I would have been happy with a sausage, cheese and egg biscuit from Holiday gas station but Sherri wanted me to have something healthy. For the last four hours I had been snacking on deer jerky covered in dog hair and crushed chocolate chip cookies.

After removing the gold foil tab, I pulled the sandwich out of the stiff clear plastic wrapper and tried to take a bite. The bread was the kind with a tough outside, really more designed for dining in at the Coho Café in Tofte where Sherri had bought it. I gave it another shot and was able to tear off a bite but it was dry. Then a thought occurred to me and I started laughing. Digging in the bag again, I pulled out what I suspected would be in there, packets of Dijon mustard and mayonnaise. So there I was trying to kick and run up this hill with a dog team running on fumes, one of my hands on the handlebar of the sled, a sandwich barely balanced on the top of the sled bag, tearing open these packets of mustard and mayonnaise with my teeth and trying to squeeze them onto the sandwich. After squeezing one packet onto the sled and the other onto the snow, I gave up and grabbed the sandwich and squished it up into a ball. I was gnawing on this gourmet sandwich ball when a team pulled up next to me. It was Mark Black.

"Hey, Mark, I'm kinda slowing down here."

"Yeah, me too. I wish I had more dogs left."

I stopped running with the sled to let him by. "See you down the trail."

He waved his reply. Here was the same guy who had scolded me to keep my dogs away from his at our very first Beargrease. I thought, "Maybe he's not that bad of a guy after all."

Mark's team slowly pulled away from us. I was hoping that my team would pick up the pace a bit and tail Mark up the long uphill but they kept turning their heads, glancing back down the trail toward the last checkpoint. At that point I knew I should have stopped at Sawbill at least long enough to give the dogs a light meal. To turn around now and go back could be a disaster. After we left again the dogs would keep wanting to turn back and might refuse to go past the spot where they had turned around the first time. No, we had to go on. I stopped and gave them all another snack. They were all still eating them, a good sign.

"Let's go, Winnie, Wolfie. Let's go." And we crept further up Heartbreak Hill.

When sled dogs get tired they look for reasons to stop. If one of them has to pee, then they all stop. The males find reasons to mark the side of the trail, leaves blow across the trail, anything becomes an excuse to stop. Getting them started again gets harder and harder.

The dogs were stopping, often. I hadn't remembered them ever stopping on the trail, EVER, even in training.

Sledding through the hills behind Lutsen Mountain is travelling through country that is so beautiful that people come from all over the nation, the world, to see it but it meant nothing to me. I could describe what it looks like from seeing it at other times but not by memory from that day. On that late afternoon I couldn't see the country around me at all. I was focused on the dogs, racing, just getting my own cold wet tired body to Duluth, and was beyond tired. I had been tired twenty-four hours and a hundred and fifty miles ago. Most mushers I saw from the beginning of the race were either sitting or standing while I was kicking or running. My legs were constantly cramping so I'd have to switch which side I was kicking on. Sometimes they both were cramping and I'd just stand on the back of the sled using ski poles to help the dogs. Knowing that I had shorted them rest made me all the more determined to do all I physically could to help move the sled forward. Getting so depleted myself was proving to be my biggest mistake of all.

Finally we were at the top of Heartbreak Hill. It's only five miles from Sawbill and we'd been on the trail already for over an hour. At least we had a big downhill to get the dogs going again. Cresting the top I could see Mark Black ahead.

"Ok, guys, let's go, we can catch him."

But we didn't. He continued to pull away. The dogs made OK time going downhill but at the bottom we crossed another bridge. These scenic bridges became nightmares that meant a long uphill climb was coming, often a mile long and rising 1000 feet or more, a twenty percent grade.

The dogs had learned to know what bridges meant too. Seeing the next bridge and long uphill ahead, the dogs stopped.

"Hey, puppies, do you want another snack?" I gave them one and they perked up a bit and began up the hill...before they stopped again. Winnie had to pee. This time I had to go to the front of the sled to encourage them. Nothing worked, they wouldn't go. I sang and jumped around.

"Isn't this fun?" Still nothing.

I looked back in the team. Maybe Acorn wanted to lead? I brought Winnie back into the team and brought up Acorn.

"That's the answer, Acorn will always pull."

Acorn pulled a bit and slowly again the team made some progress up the hill, maybe a couple of hundred yards, then stopped. No amount of encouragement would get them moving. Standing next to the team, pretending I was happy and giving them praise, pets and hugs, I began to wonder, for the first time in the race, in my life, "Maybe we're not going to make it."

"Is that you, Frank?"

I jumped. It was Rita Wheseler passing me on the trail. Dropping another place in the standings didn't even enter my mind. Here was help. No matter how tired the dogs were, they would chase another team.

"Hi, Rita. Mind if I follow you up the hill?"

"No problem. Hope it'll help."

It did. With Acorn and Wolf in lead, we climbed the next hill. We didn't keep up with Rita but seeing and smelling her team was enough. Soon we crested another hill and descended into the next valley...where the team stopped, wouldn't go. No dancing, singing or snacking would help. Then, one by one, they started to sit. A couple began digging in the snow to make beds. If they lay down we were done. They would go to sleep and I would lapse into hypothermia, maybe freeze to death. I was soaked with sweat, without my warmest clothes, and it was over twenty below zero. My mind raced. "Who was behind us? Would they come along soon?"

And then behind me I saw a headlamp and the flashing light on a leader.

"Who's that?" The next musher pulled up next to me.

"Hi, Colleen. It's Frank."

"Are you OK?"

"Not really. My team doesn't want to go. "

"See if they'll follow me."

Colleen called up her team. My dogs had stood up when she arrived obviously interested in seeing other dogs. When she left my team began to barely trot, following Colleen and we slowly made the climb up out of the valley. Pushing and kicking with all that I had, we still weren't able keep up with Colleen, but we got to the top of another hill and down the other side. At the bottom Colleen was no longer in sight and as I'd feared the team stopped soon after crossing the next bridge. Quickly I grabbed the remainder of the snacks and handed them out. Most of the team wouldn't take them so I dropped the treats in the snow in front of each dog.

Esther, Kimi then Storm and Acorn sat down without eating. Then they started to lie down.

Quickly I began grabbing every dog and bringing each one to the front to see if they'd lead us up the hill. Acorn, Winnie, Nita, Esther, Storm, Ace, Fly, none of them would go.

I was shivering and began to get very anxious. My mind flashed back to Two Harbors.

"How many hours or days ago was that?"

I'd talked to Ryan Anderson, who wasn't racing the Beargrease this year so he could focus on the UP 200.

"Frank, you know you have fast dogs. Try and slow them down. The race is on the last day not the first."

He then told me about how in 2006 his team stopped on the trail between Finland and Two Harbors. They all lay down and wouldn't get up. He spent many hours there on a very cold night, becoming hypothermic, until he and his dogs were finally rescued by a volunteer group of snowmobilers.

I looked at my team lying down and then at the dense woods around us. The full moonlight illuminated the mature forest. There were some pines and fir trees but none with low branches to cut off for beds for the dogs. No easy wood to get for a fire either. It would be a long cold night here.

Again I looked back to the team. Ace, Winnie, Wolf and Ajax were still standing and every dog was watching me, looking for some sign of what was next. I sank to my knees in front of the leaders, Acorn and Wolf.

"Come on, guys. We can't stay here."

I held their faces next to mine, scratching behind their ears. This would be it for the year, maybe beyond, and worse if we didn't get rescued. I got up and continued down the team, giving them all hugs, thanking them for working so hard, so much harder than they ever had. I was cold, tired, delirious, shivering, and I sat down in the snow to wait for whatever our fate would be.

There was no sound, just stillness and cold, hard moonlight.

"I'm so sorry, puppies. What have I gotten us all into?"

There was nothing left and I just sat.

Ajax (photo by Kathleen Kimball-Parker)

Chapter 12

Out of the quiet and despair I heard a bark, then another, and another. I struggled to my feet to see Ajax, who had been running in wheel, barking and wagging his tail.

For a moment I just stared, dumbfounded. Here was the dog who had taken the team over the embankment on our last long training run. I had cussed him out and then had to try and make it up to him when we got home. Yes, Ajax had never quit, never stopped even when I wanted him to. I had held our last training run against him, didn't even consider having him in lead now when it mattered most.

"Do you want to lead, Ajax?" He barked again, now wagging his whole backside.

I stumbled to the back of the team, unhooked Ajax and brought him to the front. I carried Acorn to the back, then quickly walked through the team giving them all encouraging rubs.

"Come on, puppies, we can do it."

Yanking the hook I yelled out, "Let's go, Ajax. Let's go, Wolfie!"

Ajax pulled into his harness, pulling Fly and Winnie who were behind him. Wolf began to pull too, then slowly, haltingly, the whole team started moving. I tried to push and kick as best I could. My legs felt like Jell-O.

We had twenty miles to go to Finland, at this speed another three hours. Ajax and Wolf stopped some to mark the side of the trail but each time, with an encouraging "Let's Go," they'd start trotting again, leaving their mark behind.

I kept reminding myself that I could always take one more step. When we got to hills I didn't even look up at them. My eyes were focused on the dogs and the ground in front of me. "Just one more step. One more. One more."

Two hours of this passed and I was in a trancelike state when out of nowhere we were crossing a gravel road. Then from under a headlamp I heard, "Looking good, Frank. Just a few miles to Finland."

"What? Oh, thanks."

Struggling to keep my balance on the sled, I turned to see it was Curt LaBoda. He'd come out in the middle of the night to cheer us on.

"Yeah, right," I said to myself but it was then I knew we were going to make it. The dogs and I were all on vapors but that little encouragement, just a few words from a friend who had driven out deep into the Superior National Forest, in the middle of the night, were enough to wake up my confidence. The dogs had run this trail several times before, and their confidence grew too. There were no more pee stops. The end to this march was in sight, less than an hour away.

The lights from the small town of Finland were visible from the trail as it descended into the Baptism River Valley. The last two miles were a gradual downhill. My legs were shot and all I could do was stand on the sled and hold on.

Finally, rounding a corner, there was a campfire, the checkpoint. Immediately several people jumped up and out of them I heard Sherri: "Come here, Winnie. Here, Wolfie."

Sherri grabbed the leaders. "It's Ajax."

It wasn't Winnie who brought us in, but Ajax who had stood up when the rest of us gave in to exhaustion. Here was the former sprint dog that I had doubted would make the team, that had taken us over the embankment two weeks before. It was Ajax who would never stop, who brought us into to Finland on that long, cold night.

Sherri, Lisa, Teri, and Steve grabbed the team and ran them to the truck. The dogs all stopped there on their own. I looked over and saw Curt who had shown up to help Sherri. I wanted to greet him, tell him how much just a few words meant but when I stepped off the sled, I fell to the ground. My legs were too cramped to walk. He and Sherri grabbed my shoulders and helped me to Steve's van.

"Are you OK? How are the dogs?" Sherri's face showed her fear and fatigue.

"We gotta shut it down here, honey...Can you take care of the dogs? I have to get out of these clothes and get some food and water..."

Looking at everyone's faces I saw that they thought I was going to scratch. It had been hours since I'd even thought of the race. It had just been survival, getting to Finland. But the Beargrease was back to Duluth, not just to Finland.

I looked over at the team. Ajax and Wolf looked back at me, proud, mouths wide open. They could go on after a good rest and if they could, so could I.

"We'll go at first light. Wake me up an hour before."

I climbed into Steve's van and began taking off my cold wet clothes. The back door was open, and I heard Sherri.

"Steve, I'm having a rough time. I need to lie down too. Can you take care of Frank? Curt, can you help Teri with the dogs?"

I'd forgotten all about Sherri's car accident, that she wasn't supposed to do anything strenuous for a few more weeks. She was still fighting neck pain, headaches, fatigue, and dizziness. There she was on her third day in the cold with little sleep and paying the price. I was helpless to do anything for her. All I could do was drink the water and juice that were put in the van for me. I was asleep before I had finished them.

"Ahhhhhh."

I woke to my legs spasming. After a half an hour of stretching and massaging, the spasms finally stopped. My watch read 3:30. I had slept for two hours. The most I'd had in days. I looked out into the checkpoint and everything was quiet. The dogs were sleeping and since I couldn't see any of our handlers, I assumed that they were too.

Lying there I was wondering if I should get up and get everyone going. The clock was running and our competition was out on the trail. I looked again out at the dogs. They would probably all get up now and head out into the night if I asked it of them, but should I? They had given more than they ever had, saved me from possibly freezing to death, and they needed a long rest. I said I was going to give them until 5:00 and that's what I was going to do.

It seemed like I'd only just closed my eyes when the tailgate of the van opened and in came Cocoa. Sherri was worried about me and put Cocoa in the back to wake me up. Cocoa, my fourteen-year-old retired leader, lay down next to me. My mind went back to our home, where I would be sleeping in a couple of nights. Cocoa would be sleeping next to me on the floor. But before I could be there, we had a job to do. Duluth was only seventy miles away, two more legs of thirty-five miles each. We'd also be able to rest for another mandatory six hours at Two Harbors. At that moment, lying in the back of the van, barely able to move my legs, the feeling came to me. I knew we were going to finish the Beargrease Marathon in our rookie year.

Looking around the back of the van I found my bottle of ibuprofen and took four more along with a quart of juice. Ten minutes later I'd gotten most of my gear back on, opened the van and stepped out into the cold early morning darkness. Twenty-five below immediately reminded me of the night before.

"Here, Frank." Steve handed me a large travel mug of coffee. "There's more in your sled."

I looked over to see the sled and gangline ready to go and the busy headlamps of Curt, Teri, and Lisa getting the team ready.

Trying to walk, I lost my balance, dizzy, and my legs were numb. A minute of stretching and walking in circles brought back the circulation. My head cleared and Sherri was in front of me.

"I've got their food ready. Do you want to feed them?"

We looked into each other's eyes. Her look and weight of concern was gone. She too knew we would finish. Here was my wife, who should still be on bed rest, running the show. Her job wasn't done either until we got to Duluth. I held her close.

We separated. "Thank you, Sweetie. We're going to be OK."

"I know." She smiled. "Now go, feed the dogs."

The dogs all were getting massages and their booties put on when I brought around their second meal of the checkpoint. Everyone ate. Only Ace, Wolf and Winnie were standing up; but they were all eating and all ten would leave Finland with me that morning.

The Finland checkpoint was now mostly empty. It's often where teams scratch. We had learned why on the trail but would pass through this wall that had stopped so many others. Twelve teams were on the trail ahead of us, several more were still behind. One of those teams moved through the lot. It was Curt Perino, Team New Zealand, on his way to the starting line. We'd catch and pass him on the way to Two Harbors and wouldn't see another dog team on the trail all the way to Duluth.

We walked the team up to the start. Most were still tired but Wolf and Nita were lunging and barking. Their energy rippled through the team. I hooked them down and walked to the front hugging and petting each dog, finishing with the leaders, Ajax and Wolf. Without them I'd still be out on the trail, fighting for my life. I was trying to thank them but their barks and jumps said they just wanted to get back on the trail.

"Five, four, three, two, one." And we were off on our way to Two Harbors and Duluth. Up the hill out of Finland the dogs ran again with purpose. We rounded a corner at the top of the hill and the dogs stopped. Someone had decided to feed just outside the checkpoint and there was dog food scattered all over the trail. Not only was this against the race rules but dirty mushing. My dogs were now stopped, only a half a mile from the checkpoint. The fear again surged up in me.

"Come on, puppies. We can't stop here!"

I raced to the front, grabbed the leaders and ran with them until all the dogs passed the food. My fears were groundless. The team continued running past me and I barely caught the sled on its way by. Dragging behind it, I finally found the runners with my feet. For the next hour I just stood on the runners and let the dogs run, at their pace.

The dogs never stopped again on the trail. The seven hours of rest at Finland had paid off. Ajax and Wolf led the entire rest of the way. Two of Tina's pups, Esther and Storm made it to Two Harbors but were too tired to go all the way to Duluth; still pretty good for only being fifteen months old. Their sister, Nita, on her way to being a superstar, made it the whole three hundred seventy-five miles. She finished with Winnie, Acorn, Fly, Ace, Kimi, Wolf and the hero, the dog that saved our race, that saved us: Ajax.

Fifteen teams out of the thirty that started the 2010 Beargrease Marathon would finish on that Wednesday in February. Nathan Schroeder won handily. We came across the finish line at almost 11 p.m. in thirteenth place. The public celebration at the finish line was sparse with most of the spectators having already gone home. About two dozen race fans, marshals and handlers sat around the bonfire at Billy's Bar, on the outskirts of Duluth.

For us it didn't matter who else was there. We hugged each other, the dogs, laughed, cried and celebrated together for the next two hours. Eventually the dogs and gear were all put in the truck and our caravan left for our hotel in Duluth.

"Hey, Sherri, I'm hungry." It hadn't occurred to me until then that I hadn't had a meal since the morning before at Devil's Track.

"Nothing's open. We have some trail mix. I think I have an apple."

"I gotta find somethin' to eat."

At two in the morning I was leading our caravan around Duluth's deserted streets until I saw a lit up sign. Herbert and Gerbert's.

"What's that place, Sherri?"

"A sub shop."

"Let's eat."

"I'm going to wait in the truck."

My meal to celebrate finishing my first Beargrease Marathon finish was the Comet Candy, a roast beef and ham sandwich, plus a bag of Doritos and a Coke.

Sherri drove so I could eat my sandwich. Steve's van followed. Teri's car didn't move and just sat behind in the parking lot. We turned around, drove back into the parking lot and shined our brights on Teri's car. She and Lisa were sound asleep. Sherri hit the horn and they jumped out of their seats. They didn't think it was very funny.

We still do.

Sherri and Nita (photo by Lisa Boulay)

Chapter 13

After the Beargrease we had only two weeks before heading to Michigan for the UP 200. While the Beargrease is the longest sled dog race in the lower 48, the UP 200 (actually 240 miles) has the biggest crowds of any distance race outside of the Iditarod. The city of Marquette shuts down the main street of town, hauls in snow and hosts a nighttime start that draws over seven thousand race fans. We had a healthy team after the Beargrease. The only dog that still was bothered by injury was Socks. I should have listened to the race vet at Trail Center and left him there. The habit of kicking myself would only get worse.

You gotta be a sled dog junkie to drive a Chevy truck with over 200,000 miles on it, loaded with fifteen dogs and another five hundred pounds of gear all the way to Marquette, Michigan and back.

"I don't know why they call this only a half-ton truck? I've at least a ton and a half in it and it seems to be going just fine."

The best thing about the truck was the cassette tape player.

"Honey, which tapes do you want me to bring for the trip?"

"Tapes?" Was all the response I got.

"I'll just bring em all." And I stuck four cases behind the driver's seat, after pulling out the Allman Brothers and sticking it in the stereo.

The UP 200 is a twelve-dog race so we brought the same team we did to the Beargrease, without Woolly and Socks. Both were pretty upset to be left behind. Socks ran around his circle with a slight limp. Wooly just barked, to remind us not to forget her. After all the dogs were loaded, I walked over to her.

"You'll race again, Woolly. I promise." I held her close. The UP is a faster race than the Beargrease. Woolly was a great leader but a step slower than the other leaders. She would race again and well, but never again for us. If I'd have known that then, I wouldn't have been able to leave her behind. Later in the year Teri needed a good leader for the little race team she was building and as hard as it was, we knew that Woolly would be perfect. She became Teri's best leader. Every dog deserves to be someone's best dog and Woolly was.

The huge crowd in Marquette was overwhelming. It felt like everyone in the UP was there. Darkness fell and all the streetlights came on to show the mile long starting chute right through downtown, lined with snow fence and seven thousand spectators. We'd known the crowd would be huge and maybe a distraction so I planned to start with our most reliable race veterans, Acorn and Fly, in lead.

Brian Tiura showed up to help finish putting booties on the dogs and so did our friend Troy from Hovland. So without much time to breathe after finishing the biggest race of our lives, we were in downtown Marquette, Michigan, hooking up our best twelve dogs for the UP 200. Again we were rookies and were just looking for a respectable finish.

Hooking down the dogs at the starting line I could barely hear the announcer over the dogs barking. They gave you a minute in the chute while they counted down and read your bio. I looked in amazement at the dogs that only two weeks ago were beyond exhausted. They were jumping, barking, ready to go for another 240 miles. After checking on them all, I quickly thanked everyone and gave Sherri a hug and kiss. Just for a moment we caught each other's eyes. We both were nervous, knowing that we wouldn't see each other until the halfway point in Grand Marais, Michigan. The first checkpoint, in Wetmore, was unassisted, so I'd be by myself with the dogs. She quickly snapped back to her handler role.

"Take it easy for the first half. Remember it's our first time here too. Two hundred forty miles is a long ways."

"I know, Sweetie. See you in Grand Marais. I love you."

"Fifteen seconds."

I jumped back on the runners. Three big volunteers grabbed my sled and handed me my snow hook. Sherri let go of the leaders.

"Five, four, three, two, one, goooooooo."

I had all my weight on the brake trying to slow us down but the snow wasn't deep enough for the brake to bite much. We were flying. At the end of the starting chute was a steep downhill at the edge of Lake Superior with a ninety-degree corner at the bottom. A standing room only outdoor bar sat on the outside corner where all the drunkest, rowdiest spectators waited for the carnage at the bottom of the hill.

Seeing the mass of people at the bottom I had visions of my sled cracking the whip right into them. At least they'd stop me from going into the lake. But at the bottom I had more control than I thought, with plenty of deep snow to make the turn. Not wanting to miss the chance I let the back end of my sled whip around the corner spraying as much snow as possible out into the crowd. Looking back from the sled it reminded me of being on a water ski at a family reunion and cutting inches from the dock where the picnic table was. The spray drenched my family. I think they still love me but I'm not so sure about the fans in Marquette.

The first twenty miles of the trail was along an old railroad-grade snowmobile trail next to Lake Superior, mostly lined with homes and cabins. Many of the homes had bonfires out front and partiers lined the trail. A lot of kids were there trying to hand me candy as I passed by. I high-fived as many as I could. The adults were yelling for us, handing us brats and beers if we wanted them. I could've gotten drunk before I got out of the county, but I just took a brat, some candy and a bottle of water.

Looking back I could see the headlamps of all the teams behind me trailing off like cars at night, spread out to the horizon. I looked ahead into the darkness when Sherri's words came into my head. We were going too fast and I slowed the team down to ten miles an hour. There were about two hundred thirty miles to go and the Beargrease had proved to me that my dogs would in fact slow down in the end.

The trail soon climbed up into the hills which led through Deerton and on to our first checkpoint, Wetmore, sixty miles from Marquette. The trail was exciting, hilly with a lot of curves and, at night, challenging. Coming around an especially sharp corner my leaders, Acorn and Fly, jumped off the side of the trail to miss a sled parked sideways across the trail. I quickly threw in the claw brake and looked at all the former contents of that sled spilled out all over the trail in front of us. The dog tuglines were tied up in knots. The dogs were jumping in all directions trying to free themselves when the yelling musher tripped over one of the lines and fell on his face.

My dogs were still too amped up to stay put long enough to help so I ran up to the leaders and guided them through the woods, getting tangled in the underbrush but finally coming out on the trail in front of the other team. Once on the trail the dogs were ready to go, banging their harnesses, and they popped the snow hook. I jumped on and looked back at the team in the trail. I saw a headlamp still flashing in all directions. The barks of the musher's dogs faded as we wound our way down the trail. I later learned that it was his first distance race and he was trying to use it to qualify for the Iditarod. He didn't qualify.

My team came into the Wetmore checkpoint a little after one in the morning looking strong. A volunteer guided us to our parking spot in what served as a campground in the summer. Our drop box of food, fuel, dog blankets, bowls and dog booties was waiting for us there, along with a bail of straw. After tying off the dogs I opened the bail of straw and made beds for them all. They dug into the straw, some peed on it but none were too interested in sleeping yet, which was a good sign. Next I poured alcohol into the cooker and filled the pot full of snow to melt for the dogs' soup. While the snow was melting, I took off the dog booties and quickly checked for any injuries that I may have missed watching them on the trail. There were none. They were all just interested in what I was cooking.

Soon the dogs were all fed and bedded down. When I was covering them all with blankets, a team pulled up in the campsite next to me. It was Martin Massicotte, from Quebec.

"You have fast dogs."

Martin's English is no better than my French but we talked a bit while I finished taking care of my "fast dogs." It doesn't matter the language, there's nothing a musher likes to hear better than his dogs are fast. I was glowing, looking at them all proudly. Martin'd been mushing for years and won many races. To come in that far ahead of him was a pleasant surprise. Later I learned it was that much because he was having a bad race as it was that I was having a good one.

It's always hard for me to leave my dogs at a checkpoint once they're fed and bedded down. They're my teammates, and I want to just lie down in my sleeping bag next to them and go to sleep, but it was below zero, and I was wet, cold, and hungry. The checkpoint had a small heated building where the race veterinarians, radio operators and officials worked. There was also a volunteer in there that made food for the mushers. As much as I wanted to stay with my dogs, warmth and pancakes were calling.

I returned warmed up and with a full stomach to ten sleeping dogs. Wolf and Ace were both sitting up, looking like they were waiting for me. I laid them both back down, put their blankets over them and got in my sleeping bag on the straw next to them for a nap. I had two hours before I planned to leave and even though I wasn't likely to sleep, getting off my feet would feel good. Wolf and Ace might try and sleep too if I was lying there next to them.

Nothing makes me feel more like one of the pack than lying next to the team while they're sleeping. Lying there under the stars the feeling came to me again:

"Here we are, in the middle of a race. This is what we dream about in the heat of July, what we work for all year." I heard Ace and Wolf's breathing slow before I joined them for a nap.

Later that morning I was back on the sled, as the sun was coming up between the hills of the UP. Standing on the runners, I thought of the mental torment I had put myself through on so many mornings, how different it was than on this one. The past fall was the worst. It usually starts the moment I open my eyes. I wonder if the world will be better or worse off if I get up and be a part of it today.

Eventually I get out of bed because Cocoa has to go out and, being fourteen, she really has to go out. I may go out with her and fire up a smoke, if I haven't quit that week. I sit in the shed and look out at the dogs. I would have decided to pull the plug long ago if it weren't for them.

"My Mom will never again have the son that she can brag about to her friends, and Sherri is stuck living in this shack, on this long horrible road and has to crap outside in an outhouse." And on it goes: "On her own she'd live in the city, a modern normal convenient life. Sherri and my Mom would both be sad for some time if I were gone but that would pass along with the disappointments that they have had with me."

"Quit being such a cry baby and feeling sorry for yourself." And I get up and go back in the house and get the coffee going, where the dialogue continues.

"Maybe the dogs would be better off too. I'd have to try and find homes for them all first. Do I give them all away to the right homes or sell the best ones to get some money for Sherri and to pay my Mom back what I owe her?"

I doubt that I could survive trying to part with the dogs but leaving that brutal task for Sherri would be horrible for her when I'm gone. Then I look out the window and watch them, running, playing, barking, often stopping to look up at the house to see if I'm coming out.

"They're all I have now. What would my life be without them?"

I often wonder about the afterlife, if I'll get to see them all again, us running together, forever. Will I no longer have to worry about paying for their food and care? Worse is feeling worthless when Sherri has to pay for it.

She just says: "They're our babies."

I know she loves them. My mind fixates on whatever tones in her voice might indicate a resentment about the dogs or our lifestyle. Sherri, I'm sure, also wonders how long she can live like this.

I couldn't do it at the house. It would need to be in a place that Sherri wouldn't have to be the one who found me.

"I should put her, all of us, out of our misery ... but would the dogs be better or worse off?"

Wolf stands out in the yard and barks at the house. He just wants to run, has no concept of despair. "I can't leave him, Acorn, Fly, Winnie, all of them. I'm closer to them than any people." My ego tells me I'm that important to them too.

I wouldn't mess around with it either, no cry for help. I'd do it right, the first time, with a gun. My brother had a few failed attempts but when he really wanted to die, he did. A noose is for someone who's made up his mind.

"I don't want anyone to know that I'm considering it either. They'll put me in a locked ward, make me talk to some paid shrink for forty-five minutes a day and pump me full of happy pills. Without the dogs there, it would be 'yes' for sure. No thanks."

The problem with yes is you can't change your mind. Dead's dead. No gives you the chance to later say yes. Each day so far has been no.

"The dogs need to run, then eat. I'll decide after that."

The dialogue continues while I ready the team. Sometime during the run, watching the dogs, I start to think about the first race. I count the days, maybe less than sixty away. I envision which dogs will make up the ten-dog White Oak, fourteen-dog Beargrease and twelve-dog UP 200 teams. Something starts to change. The balance shifts to "not sure." I stop at a water hole, put the ATV in park and walk next to the team, praising them all. Getting to the leaders I look back down the team, at their faces. They look up from their drink and, one at a time, bark, again and again, throwing themselves into their harnesses. I run to the back and grab ahold of the handlebar, as the ATV drags past me, and throw myself up onto the seat.

"OK, let's go." And I let go the brake and the wheels stop dragging and start to roll. I may crack my first smile of the morning. The ride continues and my decision is no, for one more day.

I don't think about the life or death choice when I'm racing the dogs. It's clear.

❧

On that UP morning my life was there with the dogs. I was relaxed and kept reminding myself that it was our first UP 200.

"Just enjoy being out here with your dogs," I said aloud.

More than any race, before or since, I was able to do that. For the next day and a half I let myself be a beginner. On the way to Grand Marais, Michigan, from Wetmore I found myself smiling and just enjoy watching the dogs run. It was maybe five in the morning, just before the morning twilight. The time before sunrise is usually the toughest for me to stay awake and I started nodding off. I remembered that Sherri stuck her iPod into my sled bag.

"Just take it. Put it on when you're tired."

It was small, so I decided not to make a big deal about the weight. I smiled as I dug through the sled bag and put my hand on the iPod. Soon I was bouncing back and forth on the back of the sled to the music of The Band. Sherri had loaded it with all my favorites.

Dogs are so in tune with us and our emotions. When I stopped to fix a tangle and give them a snack, the dogs were all wagging their tails and barking to go. We were all enjoying being out on a long run together. Nothing else in the world mattered.

As we got closer to Grand Marais, the sun rose higher and warmed the air and trail. The snow softened and we slowed down. In past races I would get frustrated, push harder.

"It's OK puppies. It's slow for everyone else too."

The second leg of the UP 200 race trail runs through the hills near Pictured Rocks National Lakeshore before descending through a series of wooded valleys to the shore of Lake Superior and the town of Grand Marais. The team picked up speed as we descended the shaded trail. The halfway-point finish line, right in the middle of town, was lined with hundreds of cheering spectators. Looking at the crowded street ahead I said to the dogs: "I didn't know there were that many people in Grand Marais."

We approached the checkpoint and I saw Sherri in her usual spot waiting for us at the finish line. "Come on, Wolfie. Here, Fly."

I yelled back: "Sherri, this iPod is the best present I ever bought you!" A burst of laughter came from the crowd. I ran up, gave her a hug, and we ran the team over to the truck for their longest rest of the race. It was only me, Sherri and the dogs. Everything was going smoothly and we were having a great time racing. We weren't winning, or even close to it. We were just doing what we were supposed to be doing, spending a winter day with our team. Nothing could have felt more right. After feeding, bedding down, checking feet and massaging all the dogs, Sherri and I sat in lawn chairs next to the team and soaked up the thirty-degree winter sun.

We finished the next day on a warm afternoon in downtown Marquette in front of an enthusiastic crowd and the local media. We arrived in twelfth place out of thirty teams that had started the race.

That finish, along with our finish in the Beargrease qualified us for the Iditarod in only our first year of distance racing. The team and I were tired but healthy. Our little boy Fly led the whole race and Wolf finished in lead with him. A big meal awaited them all. They'd need that and several more to get their strength back. We had one more race to go this year, and it was less than a week away.

Fly (photo by Kathleen Kimball-Parker)

Chapter 14

It was March 12, had been raining for three days and hadn't been below freezing in two weeks. That was early May weather for Northern Minnesota, not early March. Sitting at our kitchen table I was looking out on the dog yard. The dogs were all standing outside their houses in the rain and looking at the house waiting for me to come out and do something. Whether it was out of impatience, boredom, or something I didn't understand, they were all howling every fifteen minutes or so. The dogs were in the best shape of their lives but were essentially done for the season. Sure I'd take them on short runs again if we got more snow, or even do some ATV training before it got really warm, if the trails dried up. But, for now, we just had to sit and wait.

In my mind I went over the season, every training run, each leg of every race and considered what I should have done differently. Did I push the dogs too hard? Not hard enough? Bring the right dogs? Feed them enough? Too much? Occasionally my mind stopped and I just watched them and listened. These incredible animals had carried me through a season I had dreamed about. I just couldn't believe that it was over.

"Wasn't it just the other night that I was going through my equipment list for the first race of the season?" Those two months had passed by in a breath, and now it rained.

It's easy for me to live in the moment when I'm in the middle of racing season. There's just so much to do that it's all I can do to just do the next thing in front of me. Now and then I have a moment that I can pause, usually on the sled, and take in the magic of what I'm doing. Of all the people in the world, in those times, I honestly believe that I am the luckiest. I get to be out there, on that sled, with the dogs pulling me as the sole purpose of their lives. Words can't describe the gratitude I feel.

Being in the moment on that morning was impossible.

On March 6, six days earlier, I was in Ely, Minnesota, the day before the start of the Wolf Tracks Sled Dog Race. "I'm hot. It must be sixty out."

I took off my jacket and was walking down the street in a t-shirt and jeans. The melted snow was running down the street and pouring into the storm drains. All that remained were crusty black piles of ice along the sidewalk.

"They said there's a foot of snow on the trail. That should hold up until tomorrow."

I doubted my own words as they came out of my mouth. Winter in Northern Minnesota reliably lasts into April but the temperature hadn't fallen below freezing in a week. What had been the best snow pack in years was now showing spots of bare ground. Sherri, Lisa and I walked through Ely on what felt like a spring day.

"I'm going to go drop the dogs."

"Frank we just did an hour ago."

"Yeah, I know but it's hot. I wanna check on em."

I walked back to the truck. The shade that we'd parked it in on Sheridan Street, the main drag in Ely, was now only protecting half the truck. The dogs on the other side were panting in their boxes. I got in and drove it to another parking place that had better shade. After I hooked up all the drop chains around the truck, I took each dog out and snapped it to a chain. They were all warm and I made them a baited water mixture. Every dog lapped it up as fast as I put it down. After I picked up all their bowls I walked around to each one giving them pets and scratches. They were all in their best shape of the year, probably their lives. Just beautiful dogs in their prime, with one more race before the long wait for next year.

The Wolf Tracks was a shorter, faster race, only one hundred and twenty miles broken into four thirty-mile runs. This was the type of race that we always did well in. After the Beargrease and UP, I'd needed to get the dogs running fast again, so I only let them run twenty miles two times and then a short fast ten miler on the morning before we left for Ely. They were home in forty minutes, over thirteen miles an hour. The dogs were running fast and ready. Our plan was to go out quick and try and hold the speed for the whole race. Winnie and Wolf were going to lead as long as they could, hopefully the whole way. The fastest teams in the Midwest were there and we planned to give them a race.

That night we fed the dogs in a deep fog caused by the melting snow. The thermometer read forty eight-degrees and it was ten o'clock. I was edgy, not ready for the season to be over yet. Sherri was just trying to give me some space.

"What the heck happened to winter? I'll be training on the wheeler next week."

There was little sleep for me that night. The drip drip drip of winter melting kept reminding me of the season's end. I got up at twilight and fed the dogs in the fog. It was still thirty-nine degrees.

All morning we waited, watched the snow melt and waited. Before the 120 mile ten-dog race was a six-dog thirty-mile race at nine in the morning. They left the starting chute in a spray of water and slush. The fog burned off and the temperature rose to fifty degrees by ten o'clock. A mushers meeting was called for the ten-dog race at eleven o'clock. I looked at the starting chute and it was nothing but wet pavement leaving town.

"We're going to move the start to Tower and cut the race to sixty miles. The trail out of Ely is just too dangerous."

Stan Passananti, the race marshal had the authority and responsibility to make sure the race was run as safely as possible. He said there had been some crashes during the six-dog race. We loaded up the team and drove the thirty miles to Tower. At least we would still have a race.

We arrived in Tower, dropped the dogs and started unloading our gear. From the top of our truck, where I was unhooking the sled, I saw a group of mushers and handlers standing around Stan. Some of them began walking away. I jumped down and walked toward the group. Odin was walking towards me shaking his head.

"There's no race. They called it."

I ran over to the dispersing group, catching comments.

"They lost the trail." "It's all melted." "See you in January."

I just stood there in disbelief as people walked past me. I could feel my heart beating in my throat. My head dropped, staring at the gravel and grass at my feet. Then I turned and looked back at the truck. The dogs were all tethered, standing, beautiful. How was I going to load them up? I walked back to the truck and just stood there. Winnie looked up at me and we shared a gaze. He seemed to know before I did.

"What happened?" Sherri broke the silence.

"They called the race. That's it."

She gave me a hug and left me to the dogs. I sat on the ground as the tears came.

"Not yet, it can't be over yet." But it was. The season that started out with a third place finish at White Oak two months before, with strong finishes in both the Beargrease and UP had come to an end, in that muddy parking lot in Ely. Again I felt like I let the dogs down, put them through the pre-race routine only to put them back in the truck for the drive home. Somehow, when I went around to embrace them all, like Winnie, they knew we were going home. The dogs weren't acting like they were about to race but standing there, resigned.

After circling the truck, I sat on the wet ground, next to Fly, and put both my hands around his chest as he put his head up under my chin. I cried and he rubbed his nose against my face, in the tears. I looked at Fly, then Winnie and Wolf next to him. They deserved another race, another long run.

"We'll run tomorrow puppies. I promise." Letting out a deep breath, I got up.

"But now you deserve a big meal!"

I went to the back of the truck and pulled out the dog food and mixed up the meal they would have gotten at the first checkpoint. They all knew this routine and started to bark and bark. With full stomachs they all were happy to go back in the truck for the ride home.

There was plenty of snow still on the North Shore and we headed out for a fifty miler the next morning. We went fast. Winnie and Wolf led the whole way with Acorn and Fly right behind. I imagined us passing teams on the trail and that we passed the first place team in sight of the finish line. On March 7, the same day the last race of the season was scheduled to end, we crossed our finish line at Trout Lake and I pulled up next to the truck with my team of champions. We loaded up and made the short drive for home with only ten months until the next race, the 2011 White Oak.

Tulip (photo by Sherri Moe)

Chapter 15

Summer at Moetown Kennels usually means puppies. With so many other kennels having puppies, we usually just tried to bring some in from other mushers who had accidental breedings or found they had more than they could handle. The past year that's what we had done and brought Jake, Ben, Cowboy, and Pony into the kennel. This year we'd decided to breed our superstar leader Wolfie to Tina, the mother to the rest of the fastest dogs in the kennel.

"Has she had em yet?" "When are they coming?" "Can we come up to see the puppies?" is what we heard whenever we were in town. Lisa kept coming over from Bemidji hoping she'd be here when they were born. She even had a long list of names that she thought would be good.

"Lisa, we can't name them until we see them. We don't even know how many she's going to have."

"How about Tulip and Tater?"

"Lisa!"

"OK, but you've got to name one Iris."

I just looked at her. "It's no use." I was mostly glad people were so excited.

Finally the day came. It was early July, after a warm sunny day Sherri and I had been out to dinner at Trail Center, trying to sneak some time together. While we were gone, Lisa left to go buy herself some onion rings at My Sisters Place in Grand Marais. When Lisa got back, Tina didn't come out of the shed to greet her as she normally would. Lisa ran into the shed to find Tina giving birth to the first puppy, who we later agreed to call Iris…Lisa was already calling her that anyway. Two more, Tater and Boo, arrived before Sherri and I got home. We drove up to find Lisa lying in the puppy pen. Her jacket was off and under Tina, providing an extra bed for her and the arriving puppies.

"She's already had three!" she said as she stood up and ran back to the car to get her now cold onion rings. Puppies were only so exciting.

Sherri and I sat with Tina while she gave birth to Duke and Tulip. One of us stayed with her for the rest of the night, not knowing for sure if she was done or not. Her last litter, two years before, had been ten puppies. It took her a whole day to have them all. This litter would only be five. For the first two weeks mom and puppies were all healthy.

Sherri and I were having a rough summer. Some of our old demons were coming back to haunt us and we'd been taking them out on each other. I wasn't eating and Sherri and I had both started to smoke again. A few days after the puppies were born Sherri left to go stay at her friend Trish's to "get some space." I was honestly wondering if we were going to make it. I was at work, at an outfitter in town, when I got a call from Sherri. She and Trish were at the house to see the puppies.

"Frank, Tulip is sick."

"Whatta you mean? She was fine this morning."

"She's not eating, just sleeping while the other puppies feed. When I picked her up she didn't even wake up."

"I'll be right there."

It's a half-hour drive to our house from town and the whole way I was thinking about Tulip and remembering Acorn's litter of puppies five years earlier. She had had five but the smallest male stopped eating and died the next day. The vets had told us there was nothing they could do about it. "This often happens. The puppy was born with some kind of defect." I had desperately tried to nurse it with formula and an eyedropper. His little mouth and tongue took some food at first then it just ran out of the corners of his mouth. I stopped, worrying that it might be going into his lungs. For hours I held him, hoping that he'd come back, somehow.

The puppy died in my arms that night, before its eyes had ever opened. We hadn't even named him yet but when we buried him we called him Little Man and put him into the ground wrapped in one of my shirts, next to the dog yard where his brothers and sister would grow up. One of his sister Tina's puppies was now in trouble.

No one came out when I drove up. I walked into the shed to find Sherri and Trish in the puppy pen. Both of them had obviously been crying. Trish left as I stepped into the pen. The four healthy puppies were feeding and Tina was looking up at me as I walked in as if she was hoping that I could do something. Sherri handed me Tulip. She was no bigger than my hands. Her eyes, that had only recently opened, were closed. Tulip was sleeping soundly, felt warm and seemed to be a good weight. But she wasn't eating. Puppies always eat. I sat down in the straw with Tulip in my arms next to Tina. Sherri sat on the other side of me. We hadn't said a word. I looked up into her eyes. She was crying fresh tears. We were both scared, about losing Tulip and about losing each other.

"I love you, Sherri. She'll be OK. I promise you that I'll do everything I can…she'll be fine."

Sherri leaned over and kissed me, and for the next hour we sat together with Tina and her puppies. The whole world in that puppy pen. I laid Tulip next to the other sleeping puppies. The craziness that had crept in that summer started to fade that afternoon.

Sherri stayed at the house and I checked on Tulip and the rest of the puppies throughout the night. At first light I went out to find all of them eating, Tulip too. Tina watched my every move and I sat down next to her, put my face down next to hers.

"You're such a good mama, Tina." I ran my hand over her ears and neck.

Tulip was tucked in between her brothers and sisters, pumping away with her little paws, sucking out her breakfast. I put my hand on top of her tiny white body.

"Thank you, little girl."

Tulip would be fine. Maybe she had a bug, who knew. Puppies are like babies, they get sick but usually get better. Somehow, again, these beautiful dogs were taking care of us. The fear of losing Tulip called me home from work, Sherri home from Trish's, brought us both home to our little cabin in the woods. The dogs were our lives, together, and a two-week-old puppy named Tulip reminded us of that.

❦

"Half way there. Six months to the start of the Beargrease."

After the morning ritual of crossing one more day off the calendar, I sat drinking coffee and pulled out the training journal, leafing through it. The journal had an entry from every run for the last three years, how many miles, which dogs led, if any got sick or injured, the temperature, if it snowed or rained, how many total miles we had run so far that season. The last entry was April 10. It was forty-five degrees and we had trained puppies: Clyde, Blue Jean, Maple, Jake, Ben, Cowboy and Pony.

Remembering the chaos of one of their first runs made me laugh; all the barking, chewing, dragging, and tangles. I got out a pen and turned the page. It was July 30. I began with a list of all our dogs, starting with the main race team from last year and concluding with the yearlings who had their first runs three months before. Then I made a list of the races we planned on running in 2011: the White Oak, Beargrease, UP 200, Wolf Tracks, maybe add the Can Am in Maine or the Copper Dog in Calumet, Michigan. After writing each one down, I thought about the race, which dogs ran it if we ran it last year, which ones would race this year.

Stopping, I looked out into the yard and watched Socks get out of his house, stretch and trot around his pivot. He began with a limp and then smoothed out as he loosened up.

"I should have dropped him at Trail Center," kicking myself again for not taking better care of my dogs. Socks made the top ten-dog team that took third place in the White Oak, now his limp reminded me of my hypocrisy. If it were really about taking care of the dogs I would have left Socks at Trail Center with Sherri. Now he limped, with each step reminding me of my ego and its price.

Each morning from there on I'd get up before sunrise and look at the temperature outside, hoping it was in the forties and we could hook up the dogs. That July morning was in the fifties and humid, still too warm to train. The morning would come though, any day or week now, where we could start. The tired, achy feelings of March faded by May, and I longed to get back on the trail with the dogs.

Later, after feeding and scooping the dogs I pulled out the harnesses and training gangline. They needed to be repaired and organized before the first run of the season. Acorn watched my every move. She announced my hauling the gear out of the shed. The dog yard erupted. It was now in the seventies and even the shortest runs would risk overheating the dogs. We would wait. I hung the repaired gangline next to the four wheeler along with the harnesses. Hooking it up would take only minutes now. The morning would come, soon, when the temperature would be right, and we'd be ready.

I walked over to Acorn who was shedding her summer coat. She was sitting at perfect attention, then jumped up as I approached.

"Not yet Acorn. Soon, very soon."

Bart (photo by Kathleen Kimball-Parker)

Chapter 16

"I can hardly walk in all these clothes." Nothing's colder than sitting on an ATV for three hours on a windy night when it's below zero. It was December and I didn't have any choice. Four weeks until While Oak and rain had turned the trails to ice. Running a sled could kill me on that stuff. I'd tried. The dogs couldn't wear boots on ice.

They didn't get any traction and might injure a shoulder. The ice might cut their pads but that would heal quickly. An injured shoulder could put them out for the season. Down the road the ATV slid with the brakes on. Sixteen dogs ran like I was behind them on ice skates. I might as well have been.

"Crack." We hit another tree, no control.

"Just hold on Frank and hope the gangline doesn't break... again."

Soon we were off our windy road and on the Bogus Hill Trail, an eight-hundred-foot climb in only two miles and the dogs slowed to a manageable speed. I started to breathe again.

"This should be our breakout year, I thought. "After finishing the UP 200 and Beargrease last year, finishing third in the White Oak, this is a great dog team. I just need to get them ready." That meant training every day, regardless of trail or weather conditions.

"Why don't you ever plan a day off?" Sherri'd ask. I knew my competition wasn't taking days off and if they did, I'd get an edge... because I never did, even if I had to train on ice on an ATV in a thirty-below wind chill.

Thirty minutes in and already I couldn't feel my throttle thumb. In the rush to get started I'd forgotten to put a heat pack in my mitten. When we crested the hill I put the ATV in neutral, squeezed the hand brake with my left hand and stepped on the foot brake locking all four wheels, and swung my right hand around in circles as we slid down the other side. The ATV fishtailed sideways around the corners as the dogs sprinted down the hill. I didn't want them going nearly that fast but was at the mercy of ice and gravity.

At the bottom of the hill the trail Ts with a road, a ninety-degree corner either way.

"Gee, Acorn, Gee, Wolfie." The team made the corner at full speed and the ATV cracked the whip into the snow berm on the other side, sending me airborne. Rolling down a hill I came to a stop hitting a tree. Picking my head up, I listened and heard the dogs barking.

"Good, they stopped."

Making my way through the crusty snow I got back to the road and found the ATV on its side with sixteen banging dogs dragging it and a five-foot mound of snow down the road. The snow was breaking up and the ATV moved faster. Acorn looked back then turned and gave all she had to her harness. I had just grabbed the handlebars with one hand and was holding on as my ATV slid down the road on its side at fifteen miles an hour.

"Don't let go. Don't let go."

Bam. We were in another snow bank. Somehow I got my feet under me and pushed up with all I had and righted the ATV. Still in neutral we were going twenty miles an hour and I had one hand on the handlebar and the other on the back rack. Clawing my way into the seat I again hit the brakes. Sliding we slowed to fifteen, then twelve miles an hour as we climbed the next hill. Acorn looked back again. I could swear she was smiling, like she did that stuff on purpose. It was her sixth year leading, and she got bored.

"I hope that was fun." We had two hours left and I was packed with snow. I stood up, shook out as much snow as I could, and took a deep breath. "Just another run."

I prefer the quiet of not having the motor on so I turned it off and let the dogs pull it in neutral while holding on the brakes. I'd have run that way all the time but the brakes wouldn't have lasted very long, so I usually ran with the motor on, not giving it any gas so the dogs could pull against the resistance of the motor and transmission.

Despite the icy road the landscape was winter. Snow still on the ground and trees, a quiet cold that only comes that time of year. It was my favorite time. The dogs were almost ready to race and none of the races had come yet. All those starting lines were yet to happen and we were at least even with all the other teams. Watching the team run I went through the incessant ritual of planning which dogs would run which race, who would lead and how fast we'd run each leg of each race. This team would compete to win. Winnie and Wolf would start the White Oak in lead but Tina's pups were rising stars. Bart, Storm, Esther and Nita would all lead. They were only two and already the fastest dogs in the kennel.

The team ran in a perfect rhythm, a wave flowed from the leaders back, as their feet fell in sync. The wind in the trees, the sound of their breath on a starlit night; dreams happen then. I wondered if they were dreaming too but then knew they weren't. Acorn, Wolf and all the rest were just running, right there and then. My dreams were my own.

Storm and Wolf in lead, White Oak 2011 Start (photo by Jerry Szymaniak)

Chapter 17

We drove into the White Oak parking lot in Deer River on January 7, 2011, with the fastest team we'd ever had. Some trusted veterans: Winnie, Wolf, Ace and Tina but with them many of our promising young dogs: Tina's pups Bart and Storm, Jake, Ben, and two rising stars who weren't yet two, Cowboy and Pony. Some of the older reliable dogs, Acorn, Fly and Ajax, we decided to leave at home, not because they wouldn't have finished this race well, but I had to have them for the Beargrease in less than three weeks. That race was a lot slower and longer. Those three would be my key leaders for the Beargrease and I needed to keep them running slower, so they could pace the team for the almost 400 miles we'd face on that grinding North Shore Trail. My Super Girl leaders Nita and Esther were also at home. I'd need their speed in the middle of the race to keep us going, when the team began to tire, as I knew they would.

Sherri and I dropped the dogs around the truck readying them for the vet check. I looked at these honed athletes. We'd been training every day now for almost five months, and now was our chance to race. There's a tension and excitement at the first race of the season. Most mushers think their team can compete but nobody knows for sure. I did know. Our dogs were ready and fast.

"Sherri, we could win this thing. This might be our year. You know Winnie won this race as a two-year-old leader for Matt. They beat Ryan that year. I think he can do it again." I was already writing the speech in my head, Winnie being back in the winners' circle after five years.

"Just take care of our babies. They'll do the rest."

I knew she was right but I felt I had something to prove. Sure, other mushers had good teams but they weren't running this team. At that moment I didn't believe we could be beat.

"Jake! Why won't you pull."

There we were, on the first leg of the White Oak on a cold sunny day on the way to Northolm from Deer River. We were wallowing through soft powder snow and it felt like we were going to get passed by every team in the race. We needed power and Jake, one of my wheel dogs, was coasting, looking back, not pulling at all. Jake is a large, powerful, fast dog. He was almost three and I had assumed that he would be a star. We got him from Jason Jones as a puppy and his parents were both champions from the Galloway's kennel. So much potential and now was when we needed his power. Jake was more focused on the other teams in front or behind us, the trees, anything but looking forward and pulling.

It was easy to focus on something not going right in a sled dog race, start to get negative. The dogs would pick up on my attitude quickly. I couldn't let that happen.

"Good dogs, nice job." As we swam through the deep powder snow, I told myself that every other team was running the same trail. Energy spent now wouldn't be available later. We were only fifteen miles into a 130-mile race. We needed to take it easy but keep moving and get into Northolm ready to race the last seventy miles to Marcel. Jake still wasn't pulling. I ignored him.

"Trail." I looked back and Amanda Vogel's team was behind me. She started ahead of us but had taken a couple of wrong turns and now was trying to make up time. I slowed my team to let her pass. "Hey, if you keep that team on the trail, you could win this thing." I was teasing her a bit but also recognizing that she was moving fast.

"Frank, don't get negative, it's a long race," I told myself despite feeling discouraged.

We dropped down onto marsh and the powder got deeper. Ahead of me I saw Amanda's team and one other. I knew that two other teams had started ahead of me, Kevin Malikowski and Ryan Anderson. I rightly guessed the team I could see ahead, close to Amanda's, was Kevin's. We were gaining on them quickly. The powder snow was slowing them down too. Out of the corner of my eye I could see that Jake saw them and along with the rest of the team, was starting to chase. I didn't say anything and just let the dogs run.

Outside of the first race checkpoint, Squaw Lake, the trail climbed out of the marsh. Being less than thirty miles into the race, teams only needed to sign in and out there. I pulled in as two teams I saw ahead on the marsh pulled out. Leaving the checkpoint I picked up a mitten on the side of the trail. Soon we were right on their heels, passing Amanda at the next road crossing, "Dang it" I heard her say. Kevin pulled over to let me pass.

"Here you go, Kevin." I tossed him the mitten that I'd picked up on the trail. I smiled at him and kept going, feeling pretty cocky. Jake was looking back at the teams we just passed, not giving much into his harness but the others were pulling hard. With Wolf and Winnie in lead we were on our way to Northolm. The only team now ahead of us was Ryan Anderson, last year's champion. They all began to really drive like they could smell him ahead of us.

The sun sank lower in the sky and the dogs picked up their pace, loping the last thirty miles to Northolm. The last ten miles were on an old railroad grade. The sun set and I turned on my headlamp. In the twilight I thought I could see a headlamp moving ahead in the distance. "Is that Ryan?" I wondered. I kicked next to the sled trying to help all I could. Turning around I could see no headlamps close behind. We were solidly in second place.

"Come on, Wolfie. Good boy, Winnie." I loved hearing Sherri call in the dogs as we approached the checkpoint.

"How're they doin?"

"They look good, even Jake's pullin. How far back are we?"

"Ryan came in ten minutes ago. Don't worry about it, Frank. Let's just take care of our dogs. The truck's ready."

With Lisa and a couple of volunteers' help we ran them over to the truck for a rest. They all were still charging and we could barely hold onto them. After sixty miles they acted like they could've run the rest of the race without rest. But we knew better. Six hours of rest was mandatory at Northolm. After tying them all to the truck we put down straw, took off their boots and gave them their meal. It was already ten below and falling. They'd need all the energy we could get into them. After licking their bowls they all curled up in their straw. Lisa covered them with blankets. Within half an hour of arriving all were sleeping, except Wolfie and Ace, of course. Blankets on their shoulders, they both watched over our every move.

"Such good boys." I sat between them rubbing their heads and got licks on both cheeks.

"Drink this." Sherri shoved a water bottle in my face. "You need to get something to eat and lie down in someplace warm."

"OK, OK. See you guys. Get some sleep." I scratched their heads one more time, got up and walked over to the Community Center where I'd heard they had some food.

"Your sleeping bag's in the building behind us."

"Thanks, honey." Then I turned and walked away. Ahead of me I saw that Odin had just come in. He and his brother-in-law Paul were feeding the team.

"How was the run?"

"Good, Frank. I think we're in fifth place. How about you?"

"We came in second but my guys might be cooked. We'll see if I can get them to Marcel." I smiled and he knew I was bluffing.

"Right. Sure, well, good luck."

Walking into the Community Center I saw Ryan at a table with his family and handlers.

"Don't you ever get a tangle or your dogs stop to take a crap or something?"

Ryan's eyes opened wide and he sat back before he realized I was having some fun with him. He stammered a bit: "Well no, yeah I guess. Just not today."

I smiled. "Nice run," I said, and walked over to get some food.

The trail leaving north from Northolm stays on the railroad grade next to Highway 71 for seventeen miles. It was after midnight and the temperature had continued to drop to twenty below. There was no moon and not a town for miles. All you could see were the countless stars and bright beams of mushers' headlamps. Leaving second, ten minutes behind Ryan, I could easily see his headlamp a mile ahead when he turned around to check my progress. One by one the other twenty teams started behind me, their headlamps looking like a freight train trailing me for miles. Modern headlamps are as bright as car headlights and when they're behind you they seem right on your heels, even if they're over a mile away, which the closest one was to me. I soon realized they were getting even farther behind me. We were gaining ground on the rest of the teams, except Ryan's. I hadn't seen his light in a while. He must have already made the right turn into the woods. Standing on the sled on that wide open trail I was getting cold and thought of coming back on this very trail after Acorn rescued me from my stupor three years before. It was a cold night like this. I missed her. This was the first race I'd done without Acorn since she was one. I started wondering if that was a smart idea.

"It'll warm up some once we get off this trail and get into the woods." Storm was now leading with Winnie and looking like the star he was becoming. Winnie seemed a bit off, was drifting and didn't always have a tight tugline. That never happened and I began to worry. Soon that was interrupted by a trail sign signaling the turn ahead, a ninety-degree turn to the right. The team cut the corner and we tipped over, plowing through the snow.

"Whoa, whoa!" I scrambled to get back on the runners. Soon I was standing upright, brushing off the snow and again watching Winnie. His line was tight. The excitement of a windy trail in the woods must have been what he needed. "He was just getting bored," I thought.

Running that trail was a homecoming. When we lived in Bemidji I'd drive the team up here for long training runs. The part of the trail we were on now was my favorite, winding through alternating marshes and old forests. I figured it was another twenty miles to Effie and we should be coming to a bridge soon. Then Winnie stopped, right on the trail. The rest of the team piled into him before I could slow the sled. Now Winnie could sometimes be temperamental, not wanting to cross a bridge or trying to take the team down a trail that he thought might be a quicker way home, but he rarely just stopped. I quickly untangled the team.

"What's wrong, Winnie? You OK?" I led him out to the front, walked back to the sled and said: "Let's go!"

Winnie and the rest of the team charged down the trail for another couple of miles, got to and crossed the bridge and on the other side he stopped again. Something was clearly wrong. I'd been watching his gait and Winnie seemed to be running normal. I decided to put him back at point and bring Storm's brother Bart up into lead. Soon we were again flying down the trail. When it was cold and calm like that the dogs could run fast for a long time … and they were. We'd lost some time, though, and I was looking over my shoulder. We heard or saw nothing for an hour.

The quiet darkness was interrupted by the first road crossing outside of Effie, then the town, and soon I could make out the bonfire at the checkpoint.

"C'mon, Stormy. Here, Winnie." Sherri's look turned to concern when she saw Bart leading.

"What's wrong with Winnie?"

"I don't know. He didn't want to lead. He's still running fine and Bart's doing great. We'll just keep them this way to the finish."

Effie was the last checkpoint before Marcel, twenty-seven miles away. There was only a ten-minute mandatory layover there, and that was all we intended to take. Quickly Lisa brought over the bowls and we gave every dog a ladle of meat broth. They lapped it up quickly.

"Check the boots, Sherri." She already was and replaced a couple that had come off. I checked over Winnie myself and couldn't find anything wrong. He was pulling hard in point so I wasn't too worried. His boots looked fine so I didn't change them.

Steam was rising everywhere, from the dogs, our breath, our clothes.

"The timer said it's thirty-three below. "

Sherri was showing the cold of standing around in the checkpoint waiting for us to arrive. Her face was pained, and she and Lisa were both jumping around trying to keep blood flowing to their feet and hands.

I called over to Dan Bergerson, the Race Marshall, "How long ago did Ryan leave?"

"Five minutes. His team looked pretty good."

I knew we'd have a tough time catching him now and I was more worried about someone coming behind us. We'd lost time with stopping and moving dogs around on the trail. We could leave ten minutes after we arrived and I didn't want to leave a second late.

"Pick up the bowls, Lisa. We need to go."

Sherri asked me, "Are you ready?" The dogs had already started lunging and barking that they wanted to chase.

"I'd better be. They are."

We brought the team up to the starting line as the third-place team, Amanda Vogel, came into the checkpoint. We were almost ten minutes ahead of her but still over ten minutes behind Ryan.

Sherri was holding the leaders. I quickly set the hook.

"Twenty seconds."

I ran up and gave her a kiss and checked over the team quick for tangles. Winnie jumped so high his head almost caught me in the face.

"Five, four, three, two, one..." We were on our way to Marcel.

From there on the dogs didn't slow once. I watched them all as they loped down the long straight trail leaving Effie. The leaders Bart and Storm ran in perfect unison, front and back feet hitting the snow in synch. Wolf and Winnie were in point running like the champions they were. Brother and sister Ace and Tina were next powering down the trail.

In the fourth row were Cowboy and Pony, only twenty-two months old, in their first race. I knew watching them that night, ears and tongues trailing behind, that they were already stars. I thought about the morning I first saw them, two pudgy fun-filled pups. They still loved to bark and play but Cowboy and Pony were no longer pudgy. They were beautiful racing huskies and belonged on this team, the fastest we'd ever had, with our best dogs.

In wheel ran Jake and Ben. Jake was now running with all he had to catch the team ahead, no longer distracted. Ben, who we'd also gotten as a puppy from Kelly Engle, was now just two. He was all white with one blue eye and one brown and was the quiet dog; the one whose running always seemed effortless, never caused a problem but always, always had a tight tugline.

Quietly we moved through the night, through the town of Big Fork and towards Marcel. We travelled alone not seeing another team, person or animal. Two hours later the horizon ahead began to show the first signs of dawn. A sliver of a moon was setting to our right as we crossed Ranier Lake just outside of Marcel. No team was visible ahead on the lake. Looking back for the first time since Effie I didn't see any teams coming either. The small early morning crowd greeting us at the finish line gave an honest, hearty applause as we crossed. Tina and Winnie barked and lunged as I tried to stop, pulling me beyond the finish line and almost into the road ahead before Sherri, Lisa and a couple of volunteers helped to stop the team.

"Nice run," I heard as I signed the timer's sheet.

"Ready?" Sherri led us across the road and to the truck parked at the Marcel Community Center. It was still thirty below but I didn't notice because I was still reveling in the feeling of running that dog team, better than any I'd yet been behind.

Ryan Anderson had kept his ten-minute lead on us but we'd widened our lead on the rest of the field and the third-place team didn't come in for almost another twenty minutes. Our team had arrived. We'd run with the best and I was already thinking about our first Beargrease Marathon, less than three weeks away.

Storm and Bart (photo by Rebekah Chapman)

Chapter 18

"What's the matter, Winnie?"

After a race I give the dogs the next day off. Two days after the White Oak I was getting the team ready for a short training run. Winnie was barking and running around his circle, as excited as he always was to run. But he was limping, favoring his right foot. I sat down next to him and he immediately ran up to me, putting his paws up on my shoulders.

"Let me see that foot." And I grabbed his right foot with my ungloved hand and palpated all his toes. He didn't pull it away or even flinch. I pulled his foot close enough to where I could see the bottom well. His front toe pads were grey, as opposed to their normal black color. They also felt strange, like the skin was all dead and about to peel off. I put pressure on the end of his two front toes, right at the base of his nails and he flinched then, pulling his foot away from me.

"I wonder if you froze the end of your toes Winnie? You'll get today off."

Harnessing up the rest of the team, I kept looking over at Winnie. Hoping I was wrong, that there was nothing the matter with his foot, that tomorrow the pain and discoloration in his toes would disappear, in my heart I knew it wouldn't. The Beargrease was less than two weeks away and I was going to be without Winnie, my best dog.

❁

Their look is burned in my memory, a combination of fear and trust. The dogs were all sick, some throwing up, others crapping straight blood, their muscles digesting themselves. Their magnificent sleek bodies were shutting down. Almost two in the morning and the temperature had dropped to twenty-five below. What was normally a comfortable temperature to be out on the trail was making a serious situation even worse. Twenty miles ago we'd left Trail Center, the halfway point of the Beargrease Sled Dog Marathon, with twelve dogs, none of which were anywhere near one hundred percent.

After a five-hour rest we'd limped out of Trail Center and I had planned to take it easy on this seventy-mile leg. That slow nine-mile-an-hour pace was now stop and go, barely. Two other teams had easily passed us as I ran alongside my sled giving the dogs all the help I could. Fly and Kimi were throwing up. Bart and Ben were pooping blood. Ace, Storm and Jake had started limping. Tina's wrists got so sore she wouldn't run at all and had to be carried. And now Esther, one of my Super Girl leaders, was passing what looked like straight blood.

I'd been getting more worried with each additional dog showing trouble, now Esther being seriously sick, and the look she was giving me had me scared, real scared. But no matter what, I couldn't let them know. These incredible animals all trusted me, completely, and we were still twenty miles from anywhere. On my knees, next to Esther, I was rubbing her shoulders and holding her face next to mine.

What had happened to my team of super dogs? These same dogs had sprinted to a second place finish at the White Oak only three weeks ago and now I felt helpless, cold and wet.

I looked at the clear eastern starry sky just in time to watch it being lit up by a shooting star, bright and a beacon of hope. To that moment I had been racing and now my task was clear. I had to get these beautiful dogs, my companions, teammates, back to Trail Center.

Looking up, I muttered, "Please give me the courage and strength to get us all safely there." I paused and took a couple of deep breaths.

Walking up and down the team, petting and encouraging each of them, I looked into their eyes. Their looks showed fear but also love and trust. In spite of how sick they all felt, they were still with me. We were on a knife edge, push them even a hair too far and that trust would be broken. The team would stop there on the trail, lie down and we'd have to hope for a rescue. Hours would pass while the sick dogs would get worse and my soaked-with-sweat body would descend into hypothermia. We had to move and soon.

Digging into my sled I pulled out a couple of bags of high-energy snacks for the dogs and encouraged them all to eat a couple. Most did. Nita and Wolf both hungrily grabbed the treat out of my hand. Ajax ate a few too so I moved him and Wolf into lead, putting Nita and Esther in point behind them. They would all need to help me pull the rest of the team in.

Again I dug into my sled bag and pulled out my own emergency ration, a bag of peanut butter cups already taken out of their wrappers. The sugar would hopefully keep me from getting any colder. There was also a small thermos of coffee which I quickly drank. One more jog up and down the gangline; I touched all their heads and tried as best I could to look excited. They were all standing and Nita let out a bark. Wolf leaned into his harness and slowly and steadily we started to move. It was two thirty in the morning.

Two hours, two more snack stops and a dozen peanut butter cups later I saw the headlights of the truck stationed at the Gunflint Trail crossing only five miles from Trail Center. We were going to make it and the dogs knew it too. They picked it up a bit and soon, in the glow of my headlamp, I could see the road crossing ahead. We were about to formally scratch for the first time in our racing career but that was the last thing on my mind. Putting in the snow hook I jogged over to the two people who got out of their truck. It was John and Barb Bottger, friends of ours from Grand Marais.

"Frank, is everything OK?"

"No, we need some help. Can you radio Trail Center and have the vets and Race Marshall there waiting for us? I've got a sick team."

I also gave them Sherri and Lisa's cell numbers. "Ask them to have Sherri meet us at Trail Center."

The last five miles of Beargrease 2011 came a day and a half sooner than we expected. Watching our team, as sick, sore and tired as they were, I could see their hearts at work. They weren't quitting. Limping, coughing, and bleeding they found the strength to bring us home. My tears flowed freely and I stopped one last time on Poplar Lake within sight of Trail Center. Walking to the front of the team I began with Wolf and Ajax holding each dog close and thanked them. I was wondering what decisions or mistakes I had made to cause their pain when Nita starting licking my face. She didn't know of any mistakes. Nita and all of my beautiful dogs just had a job to do and they were almost there. Esther let out a bark, then Nita, Storm, Wolf and Ben.

"OK, puppies, let's go home."

❧

Sherri hadn't shared with me at Trail Center her fears about the condition of our team. She'd watched my headlamp disappear across Poplar Lake with a sick feeling in her stomach. Sherri, Lisa, Steve and David, who had come with Steve to see what handling was like, packed up the truck and drove it down the Gunflint Trail to Devil's Track Landing. They were all getting the checkpoint ready for us to arrive when Lisa's phone rang. The message wasn't clear, something about four of our dogs being sick and that they needed to get back to Trail Center. Sherri later described what she found when she got to Trail Center.

"When he arrived, Frank was exhausted beyond anything I had ever seen in him, even more so than when he arrived at Finland in the Beargrease the previous year. Frank was soaking wet from running for twenty miles to get the team back to the checkpoint. Many dogs had shut down, were throwing up, had explosive diarrhea, but still looked at him with loving eyes saying, what's happening? It was all he could do to get them back through the toughest leg of the race where the hills were steep and endless. Frank was both hypothermic and emotional about whether he was possibly going to lose a dog or two. They were all so sick. I worked with a team of four vets checking over the dogs. Again they didn't want to eat. Bart was taken inside to get IV fluids and had myopathy (muscle breakdown) in his rear end and couldn't stand up. Many others exhibited similar symptoms but at the time did not need critical medical attention. I was given a litany of medications to distribute to each of them.

"At that time Frank officially scratched and was beside himself. We took a break, had breakfast and started to process what had happened. This was unbelievable for all of us. We had never scratched at a race so were dealing with the mental torment of that, but more importantly we were terribly worried about our dogs.

"After packing up at Trail Center, Steve and David took Frank to Grand Marais to shower and sleep. Lisa and I headed back to Devil's Track to get the rest of our gear and to check on Bart.

"We arrived at Devil's Track and let the dogs out to go to the bathroom and check them over. We were immediately in a crisis situation. Bart still wasn't able to stand and had to go back for more fluids and further observation. Then Tina, one of our veteran females, who is a honey, couldn't walk and also had dark brown urine. I carried her into the vets and stayed by both the dogs' sides as the vets put catheters in for IVs and worked on them for other myopathy and kidney issues. After two hours and five liters of fluids we still needed to watch Tina and Bart because they wouldn't stand up. I went out to check on the rest of the team and found that Ace was going down fast too and had brown urine. I carried him into the vet and they put him on an IV. For the next four hours the race vets worked on our dogs, probably saving three of their lives."

Sherri returned to Grand Marais that afternoon and came up to the apartment, that we'd been loaned from Stone Harbor Wilderness Supply for the race and woke me. I jumped from bed, thinking I was still in the race and had overslept. Quickly realizing where I was I sat back down on the bed. Sherri looked shaken.

"You've got to know what I've just been through," she said and told me about the condition of our dogs. We quickly packed up and got down to the truck to take the dogs all home. Sherri had spent the last several hours nursing them and talking to the race veterinarians and marshals about what could have happened to our dogs. Even in the Beargrease, one of the most challenging races in the world, they had rarely seen this many critically ill dogs. Their consensus opinion was that there was something in the food that had made the dogs sick.

We had just gotten a new shipment of beef the week of the race. Unless we were to run an expensive battery of tests, we'd never know for sure but we were taking no chances. We stopped on the way home at a friend's and picked up some new meat. Most of the dogs rebounded surprisingly fast on the new diet. During the Beargrease most of the dogs had stopped eating the meat by Sawbill. Now they all were devouring their new food.

When we got home Fly and Esther were both well enough to be out in their doghouses. Acorn, Moo, Tina, Bart and Ace were all pretty shot and slept in the house that night. By the next day, Wednesday, every dog except Ace, Tina and Bart had recovered enough to be outside. Ace and Tina were both pretty stiff and Bart still had trouble walking. The muscle myopathy resulting from the food-caused illness ended up being a long-term health problem. None of the seven dogs who were sick fully recovered during the race season. Ace, Tina, Moo would race well again later in the season. The rest were obviously slower than they had been. Our dogs were all safe at home but we were never the same team we were in early January when before the Beargrease the *Duluth News Tribune* had named us "The team to watch."

That night we were all in the living room in front of the woodstove, eight dogs, three cats, all my wet smelly Beargrease clothes steaming around us. Everyone was sleeping, except me. A year ago we had still been out on the trail, between Sawbill and Finland, struggling for survival. Yet I would have given anything to be back out there, as cold and tired as I'd been, just to still be in the race. Instead I sat there, feeding the fire, reliving every minute, every decision I made or should have made, for most of the night.

The next morning I got up at dawn to stoke the fire and take care of the dogs. We were all stiff and sore but I knew I had to get back on the runners, now. Sherri watched in disbelief as I put all of my mushing clothes back on and after giving all the dogs their normal morning ration of baited water, hooked up seven dogs and hit the trail.

My body would barely move, only with great effort. I was stiff, sore and weak but I needed to be on the sled, for my sanity. I left the yard with the seven dogs that weren't on the Beargrease team. Wolf's brothers, Gnasher and Rippie were in lead.

Brian Tiura, who we got Wolf from, had moved to Alaska the previous September and sold his dogs. I'd called Brian the day I heard to ask to buy Wolf's brothers. If they were anything like him, we wanted them on our team and definitely didn't want to race against them. Brian had four kids with another on the way and hadn't had much time to train or race the past two seasons.

Gnasher and Rippie were three years old but only had the experience of yearlings so we weren't pushing them to race yet. They'd just started leading and this would be their first lead together. None of the seven had run at all since before the Beargrease. Their excitement to run made me smile for the first time in days. They didn't know anything about the hardship and desperation of the day before. These seven dogs just wanted to run and before I knew it, my feet were off the sled and I was running with them, up Bogus Hill just two miles from our house.

Cresting the hill I felt the sun on my face, warming my skin that had been splashed with snow from branches on the narrow trail. My senses tingled, reminding me that I was still alive and running dogs. We passed Bogus Lake. The surface snow was untouched, sitting on top of at least three feet of ice. It was only mid-winter. All year long I mark off the days, one at time, until winter comes, being able to run the dogs on snow. There were at least two months of snow left, three maybe four races.

I watched the dogs in front of me, so happy to be running after six days off. They weren't throwing in the towel on the season. With all the sick and injured dogs from the Beargrease, many of these dogs would be called upon to race in the UP 200 in only two weeks.

Gnasher and Rippie both looked good, especially Gnasher. "Maybe he'll be the dog his brother Wolfie is after all."

Cowboy and Pony were only yearlings but future stars. They were both on the second place White Oak team and would also make the trip to the UP. That morning, at the same time as the Beargrease was finishing a hundred and fifty miles away in Duluth, I started putting together the team that would run down the streets of Marquette, Michigan, in two weeks. We still had some racing to do.

Sled dogs are remarkable creatures. Just two days after returning home from the Beargrease, the dogs were all bouncing back. The season was not even half over and we had been through so much. After the Beargrease, those dogs needed to convalesce for a week, followed by some short easy runs. Initially it wasn't clear if we were going to race again this year but enough of the dogs progressed quickly. By the week of the UP 200 we had twelve dogs that were ready to make the trip to Michigan.

Moo (photo by Kathleen Kimball-Parker)

Chapter 19

I could barely hear the announcer over the 7000 cheering fans for the nighttime start of the UP 200 in downtown Marquette, Michigan. The fans lined the street as far as I could see. The third team out of the chute, we soon were leading the race. The week before had seen fifty-degree days and some rain, leaving the trail along Lake Superior in rough shape. It was pretty much all just frozen gravel. There were some reroutes around the worst sections that were poorly marked. Often I found myself off the trail. It turned out that the rest of the teams followed our tracks when we made wrong turns, so we stayed in front. The sixty plus miles of gravel ground off almost all the plastic on the bottom of my sled runners. The right runner was down to the aluminum.

The Wetmore checkpoint was unassisted so we were on our own there for about five hours. The dogs were still wound up, and even though it was the middle of the night, I wondered if they would settle down to sleep at all. After feeding them, taking off their shredded dog booties, putting down straw for them to lie on and covering them with blankets, they started to calm.

There's a small building at Wetmore where the veterinarians, timers and radio operators stay. The first-leg results were posted in that Wetmore checkpoint, showing that even though we'd come in first, some teams behind us actually had faster run times. We were in fourth place and only a couple of minutes behind the leaders.

I was planning on staying in Wetmore no more than five hours. As my planned departure time came, no other teams were ready to leave. It was clear that with such a challenging trail, nobody wanted to be the first team out. It was now snowing and the winds were gusting to fifty miles an hour causing total whiteouts. My plan was to rest at Wetmore for five hours. My leaders, Wolf and Ajax, were great in snowstorms and I got impatient, so we hit the trail, again the first team out of the chute.

Snowmobiles had gone ahead two hours before but the blowing snow had completely covered their tracks. The trail was poorly marked and I couldn't see the trail signs until they were just feet in front of my face, far too late to call to the dogs to turn.

Turning the team around for the sixth or seventh time, I got back to the trail to find a team waiting for me to again break trail for him and the other teams. I had had enough. He could lead. I was going to snack my dogs. I stopped and Rene and his team passed on the trail. We followed less than a minute behind, only to find Rene camped out on the side of the trail snacking his dogs. Clearly he didn't want to lead either. We passed him in a tight spot of the trail and caught his sled runner in my sled, bending it a bit and flipping his sled over.

"What the hell, dammit, you busted my sled."

It wasn't really broken, just bent. I choked out a "Sorry" between my laughs. I thought it served Rene right for not taking a turn at leading. He'd won a couple of races already in January out east and didn't need me to always break trail for him.

The trail soon dumped us out onto a gravel logging road. The snow was getting blown off the road as fast as it was falling. The grey gravel road disappeared ahead of me into a tornado of snow. I spent the next six miles running next to and tipping the sled up on its side trying to conserve my sled runner plastic. When we finally got off the road and into the woods with a snow-covered trail again, I found that the sled no longer had any plastic left on the bottom of the runners. We were on the aluminum runners which pretty much stuck to the snow. We slowed way down. A few teams passed us with runner plastic intact. They had either brought extra plastic in their sleds or had thicker plastic than we did. I had the normal quarter-inch thick plastic and no spares in the sled, so I kicked and ran as much as I could, trying to keep my aluminum runners from getting ruined. I was getting another expensive lesson.

The storm had passed, leaving a foot of fresh snow. There would be no more running on gravel. It was a mild ten degrees and the sun was setting as we left Grand Marais for the return trip to Marquette. Fly, Acorn, Tina, and Esther hadn't fully recovered from the Beargrease, so hadn't made the trip to Michigan. Ben, who had a sore shoulder, and Gnasher, who was running in his first race, were going to stay behind with Sherri at the Grand Marais, Michigan, checkpoint. This still left us with ten strong dogs for the last run of the race. We were leaving in seventh place out of eighteen of the best sled dog teams in the country. Of course we'd like to have been winning, or close to it, but coming off our trial at the Beargrease and leaving several of our best dogs at home, we were happy to be in the race at all. Moo and Storm started to bark and lunge. Soon the whole team was jumping and barking to go.

As the full moon rose through the partly cloudy sky, the Upper Peninsula woods opened up. Turning off my headlamp I could see like it was midday. For the next five hours we didn't see another team. It was just me and my ten dogs racing down a moonlit trail, doing what we loved to do best, what we had worked all year for.

We finished in a respectable seventh place and spent the drive home planning for the next two races in Ely, Minnesota, and out in Maine. There was racing still to do and we had plenty of great healthy dogs to race.

Ajax and Wolf (photo by Jim Stoner)

Chapter 20

"You know this is your race to lose."

"Don't say that," I said as I grabbed and shook Odin, another musher at the race.

We were at the vet check for the Wolf Track Sled Dog Classic in Ely, Minnesota. Sure, we had a fast team but eight of the ten dogs had just raced hard a few days before in the UP 200, and two others, Winnie and Acorn, hadn't run much in weeks. Like most mushers, I had my favorites. Both Winnie and Acorn had run almost every race I'd been in for the past four years. Winnie's foot had been frostbitten at the White Oak, when the temperature dipped to over thirty below zero. Winnie was the best dog I'd ever had, and I just couldn't help wanting him to race. His foot appeared healed but he hadn't run in six weeks, except for a short training run two days before the race. Without our best dog we were definitely not as fast a team. Winnie needed to, wanted to race, but I would be taking a chance that he was in good enough shape to run 130 miles.

Acorn was the first dog to have trouble in the Beargrease. We'd had to leave her with the vets at the Sawbill checkpoint only 120 miles into the race. She'd only run once since. But Acorn and I had a bond, a connection that went beyond racing. She's saved my life twice, and I owed it to her to give her a chance to race one more time this year.

The trail from Ely through Tower to Cook had plenty of snow and the temperatures were forecast to be around zero, perfect for a fast sled dog race. With Winnie and Acorn, the team had their heart back and were so excited to go that six handlers and I were fighting to keep them at the starting line. I drew the last starting time at the bib draw, so every other team was ahead of us on the trail. We had some teams to pass.

The next sixty plus miles to Cook were a blur. The dogs were on fire, running as strong as they did in the first race of the season, the White Oak, where we placed second. The dogs always ran faster when it was cold and it felt colder than zero. I was wishing I had brought my fur mittens and swung one hand around in circles while the other held onto the sled.

About ten miles from Cook, I saw a dog team ahead with a headlamp that was waving all over the trail like a searchlight. Driving my team up next to the team, I saw who it was.

"Hey, Tom, are you OK?"

"No I can't see. My glasses are fogged up and I can't fix em. How much further to the checkpoint?"

"It's about ten miles, I think. I'll pull ahead of you here and see if your dogs will follow me in."

"Thanks, Frank. I can't see a thing."

For the next few miles I tried to keep Tom in sight behind us. When I'd look back I'd see his headlamp waving around in all directions as Tom kept trying to see the trail. I found out later that the temperature where we were travelling, through a low spruce bog, had dropped to twenty-five below. That along with a thirty-mile-an-hour headwind, had frozen Tom's corneas and he couldn't see. Tom recovered in a few days but had to scratch at a road crossing before we got to Cook.

Sled dog race checkpoints all have their own character and some, like Cook, make an extra effort. Arriving in Cook just after 9:00 p.m. we ran through a trail lined with luminaries past two large campfires and into the dog-staging area. I saw that only two other teams had arrived. We had already passed every other team but two, and the race was only half over. We were running fast, over eleven miles an hour, and the team looked great.

We spent four and a half hours at Cook, where my handlers Julie, Teri, and Jay helped me wrap wrists, feed, massage and bed down the team. As usual Wolf and Ace sat up the whole time, with their blankets over their shoulders, not wanting to miss anything. They are such incredible dogs. Neither had ever had a slack tugline since their very first run as puppies. There's no quit in them, ever.

Winnie and Acorn both seemed a bit tired. The lack of training over the past six weeks had affected them but as we started getting all the dogs up to go, putting new booties on them all, Winnie and Acorn resumed their roles as team leaders and started howling, the signal to the rest of the team that it was time to race.

With Wolf and Nita in lead and the whole team jumping and lunging, we got back on the trail for the return trip to Ely, with a planned stop at the halfway checkpoint in Tower. We continued the fast pace until the last ten miles when we hit some hills outside of Tower. Acorn started to slow on the uphills; she was getting tired, and Winnie was a little slow on the downhill. His frostbitten foot maybe hadn't completely healed. I slowed the team down to their pace and we came into Tower still in third place.

Every race has a minimum rest that your team needs to take at the various checkpoints. The 2011 Wolf Track required eight hours. We had just over three left to take in Tower, enough to get everyone fed, massaged and bedded down. Winnie and Acorn went to sleep immediately, a sign they were getting tired. Ace and Wolf still sat up looking around.

I'd heard they were serving pancakes up at the Tower Community Center, so I walked up to get some breakfast and check the leader board. I knew we were near the front but didn't know how far back we were. The departure times were posted and it showed that we were in the lead, by twenty minutes. I was surprised to see that we had the first departure time, over twenty minutes before the next two teams. We'd thought we were close to the lead but didn't think we were in the lead.

Terri sat down next to me while I was devouring a stack of pancakes. "I think our time is wrong. It has us leaving 25 minutes early."

"Naw, we're just having a good run." I wanted to believe we were in the lead and had already thought about the first-place prize money. Sherri wasn't working because of her second bout with pneumonia of the winter. We had never raced for the money before and rarely even knew how much the prize money was prior to a race. My mind had crossed a line that winter. Maybe it was Sherri's illness and our being totally broke. Maybe it was my ego still smarting from our trial at the Beargrease. Maybe I was losing the drive to run dogs just for the pure love of it and the dogs.

Terri and I wrote down our departure and arrival times then calculated our rest. A rough estimate showed she was right. Our departure time was early. I didn't want to believe it and tried to make excuses.

"I think we took more rest than thirty-eight minutes at the first checkpoint. That number must be wrong. We've been cruising. How can we not be in the lead?"

Terri walked away unconvinced. I sat there, no longer interested in my pancakes, looking at the leader board then over to the timer's table. The race judge and the timer were talking. It was clear to them that we were not sure they had posted the correct time for us. I again looked down at the numbers I had written on a napkin. I added again, including the seconds, and looked up at the departure time. It was wrong and I knew it but I didn't think that our official rest times were correct either. The race judge came over to talk to me about it. He told me that our departure time *was* wrong. I agreed and he handed me a revised departure time. Instead of leaving more than twenty minutes ahead of two other teams, now I was leaving twenty minutes behind them. That time didn't match my calculations either.

I walked over to the timer's table and talked to him and then the judge again. They were now convinced that they were correct. About to boil over, I returned to my pancakes. In a couple minutes we went from leading to being too far behind to catch the teams ahead of us.

Head in my hands, I went through my choices. I could make a scene, file a protest or have some other confrontational response. The serenity prayer ran through my mind again and again.

Then it came to me that there was nothing I could do about the departure time. Even if it was wrong, I knew in my heart that we wouldn't likely win anyway, not on that day.

"And why am I all of a sudden so obsessed with winning?" I asked myself. "Because we're broke." For the first time in my mushing career I had thought about the prize money, how we needed it to pay our bills. Staring at my pancakes, my mind went to Sherri. It sucked not having her there. From the beginning, racing was our thing together but Sherri was home sick with pneumonia and hadn't been able to work in a month. I remembered talking to her the night before I left for Ely.

"We need to win this one, Sherri, the prize money will cover us for the month."

"How can you be thinking about it that way? What's happened to you? You've always done this for the dogs."

"Yeah, but we're broke."

She was right, something had changed in me. I'd felt the pressure of not having any money, but it was more than that. The Beargrease was haunting me. There was the humiliation of having to scratch but worse than that was feeling responsible for how sick the dogs got. Somehow I needed to redeem myself, prove that I could run dogs, that I knew how to take care of them. Prove to who? I didn't know, maybe just myself.

I got up and tossed the rest of my pancakes in the trash. When I got to the truck I saw our dogs resting on straw in the morning twilight. I knew that Wolf and Ace would be sitting up already waiting to go, and they were. Their blankets had fallen around them. Wolf's tail was wagging as I walked up, and Ace got up and stretched.

It was 7:30, a half hour before our scheduled departure. Julie and Teri had the food ready. I mixed it up and gave the dogs a bowl of meat broth. They all stood to eat, except for Acorn and Winnie. I would have to decide whether we would all go on together or if I'd leave one or both of them behind. It would have been an easy decision if I could have made it logically but I couldn't. I'd never been able to. Often it's in the best interest of the dogs and the rest of the team to leave dogs behind at the checkpoint. For me, though, the dogs and I were in this together. Sherri wasn't there and I was feeling alone. How could I take off without Acorn and Winnie too?

The team would be slower with Acorn and Winnie than without them but selfishly I wanted them along. We were now almost a half hour behind the first and second place teams and I knew we weren't going to catch them. There was also a group of teams ten to twenty minutes behind us that I wanted to stay ahead of.

"The heck with it. We'll all finish this thing we started together and will take whatever place we get."

Arriving at the starting chute a few minutes early, I had some time to thank our handlers and our beautiful dogs: Wolf, Nita, Storm, Moo, Cowboy, Ace, Tina, Jake and Acorn and Winnie. Holding Winnie, then Acorn, brought tears to my eyes. We had been in this same place so many times, the last run of a race. Acorn licked my face and, trying to be the tough musher, I covered my eyes with my glove, thinking I was hiding my tears from our handlers, the race judges and fans. Catching the eyes of Teri and Julie, I saw they were crying too. We were seeing a team of dogs giving so much and then still be willing to go again, for one more run.

The run from Tower to Ely travels along the south edge of the Boundary Waters Canoe Area on a trail lined with towering red and white pines and views of the granite cliff-lined border lakes. The whole scene was bathed in the sunrise. Winnie's foot was bothering him on the steep downhills and Acorn was slow going uphill, so we travelled only as fast as they could comfortably go. While our speed didn't allow us to challenge the leaders, it kept us in third place. Every dog came to the finish line in Ely looking strong, including Acorn and Winnie. In the finishing chute I walked up and down the team hugging and thanking them all. Acorn and Winnie both gave me big licks. It was their last race of the year, and both being seven, I didn't think that they had many race years left. The thoughts from only four hours before about prize money were gone, lost in the feeling of companionship that I had for those two dogs.

Esther (photo by Mark Tessier)

Chapter 21

We returned home from the 2011 Wolf Tracks to find Sherri still recovering from pneumonia. I had signed up for the Can-Am Crown Sled Dog Race for the next weekend. It started in Fort Kent, Maine, and I had arranged to carpool with Ward Wallin, which meant I was going to pack up and leave in two days. Looking at Sherri, still sick in bed, I knew I couldn't go.

"We're not going to Maine."

She looked at me with a look that showed both relief and guilt. I'd be home to take care of her, the house and dogs, but Sherri knew that racing was what I worked for all year.

That night while feeding the dogs I couldn't handle the thought of the season ending early again this year.

"How can we not race? A farmer doesn't just leave his crop in the field in the fall because someone in the family is sick."

It was still February, and the snow conditions were perfect for racing. After feeding I sat in the snow next to Esther. She was licking my face, just happy to have had dinner and that I was sitting there next to her. She looked perfect. Her muscles shown through her sleek brown coat. Esther and her siblings Nita, Moo, Storm, Bart, and Socks were only two but already the fastest dogs in the kennel.

"I guess we'll have to wait until next year to race again, little girl."

By Thursday of that week I was crazy with the thought of races still going on and not being able to go. As much as I was trying to be a good husband around the house, I couldn't hide my true feelings. I was pissed about not being able to race and my not talking much to Sherri made that clear.

"It's not my fault I'm sick!"

"I know, Sherri."

I left to go talk to my friend Dennis who was leaving the next day for another race in Michigan, the Copper Dog 150. It's a stage race which generally means shorter, faster runs than the distance races that we usually ran and trained for. There was also a lot more rest with only one stage of the race being run each day. The dogs, mushers and handlers got to sleep at night before running again the next day. I'd always called these races the "Hot Tub Circuit."

"We've got room in our truck, Frank. Why don't you just come with us? You can still register and we'll only be gone three days."

Without giving it any thought, I asked, "What time are you leaving in the morning?"

I knew that even though Lisa was coming for the weekend and could take care of the rest of the dogs, this would be hard on Sherri. Had I gone to Maine I'd have been gone for over a week. Now I'd only be gone for three days and would get to race one more time this year. If I didn't go I'd be resentful.

"Just go," Sherri finally said. "I'll go stay at Robin's."

The next morning I loaded up our truck to meet Dennis in town. The season had taken its toll on the team and not many of our dogs were ready to race again that soon. I've since learned that dogs need two weeks between races to fully recover. Looking around the dog yard I picked out the ten dogs that looked like they were up to one more race that year. The only veterans would be Wolf, Ace and Tina. Two-year-olds Nita, Esther, Storm, Moo and Ben would also come along with our rising star yearlings Cowboy and Pony.

The first stage of the Copper Dog starts under the lights in downtown Calumet, Michigan, and finishes after midnight in the town of Eagle Harbor. At the end of the first leg we weren't challenging for the lead but finished the leg in a tight group just a few minutes back. In spite of her being angry that I went to the race and being sick, Sherri stayed up late the first night of the race to see the results come in.

"I was so nervous and excited I couldn't sleep," she told me.

There we were, again at a race without Sherri, and it felt like we were just going through the motions. The dogs were running fine but definitely without the edge they had to begin the season. This was not the team we brought to the White Oak. Not only weren't our big stars Winnie and Bart there, but the season had worn on us all.

"Good puppies." I scratched all their heads as I went around to pick up their bowls at the Eagle Harbor checkpoint. Their straw beds were down, booties off and they were all covered in blankets. All but Wolfie and Ace were almost immediately asleep and even they were already curled up.

"You guys never sleep the first night of a race." I was kneeling between them and felt like lying down right there. I was tired too.

"Just go to sleep in my truck. We'll watch the dogs for you."

Clay Rumph and his son Beckley had come along to help Dennis. Dennis already had his longtime handlers along, his son Charlie and friend Chris Lang. Clay and Becks had offered to help me and since I was there alone, I was glad. It was two in the morning, and while Sherri was at Robin's back in Minnesota watching the computer for results to come in, I fell asleep in Clay's truck. Not taking the time to take off my boots or parka, I just collapsed on his seat.

The next morning started before sunrise. I woke the dogs to give them another light meal before the day's run. Moo, Esther and

Ben didn't even sit up to eat. The rest of the team also still seemed tired. They'd slept for four hours but clearly could have used more. Once we started hooking them up, the barking of the cheerleaders, Nita, Esther, Moo, and Storm, was enough to get the rest of the team lunging into their harnesses at the starting line.

The second leg of the Copper Dog quickly climbed a thousand feet up away from Lake Superior. As dawn arrived I could see my team ahead of me was tired. They were still running, giving all they had into their harnesses but they were all just trotting. Most of them never trotted. Their gait was always a lope, which is naturally faster than a trot. At the White Oak earlier in the year, the team loped the whole 130 miles and took second place. That race seemed like forever ago. So much had happened since, so many miles and illness had taken their toll. Nita and Esther were leading. We'd started calling them "our super girls" because they were so fast and always gave all they had in lead. Nita was running strong but Esther's line was occasionally slack. That had never happened. Just a few miles into the second run I was already kicking and running up the hills. Looking back I saw a team was catching us. As they passed I saw it was Kevin Malikowski.

"Frank? I didn't think we'd catch YOU."

"Hey, Kevin. You're looking good."

I tried to sound like I was happy for him. Kevin is a good musher with fast well-trained dogs but he'd never passed us in a race. This race was different, though.

"It's OK, puppies. We'll get there when we get there."

A couple more teams passed us as Esther's line kept going slack in lead. I switched her with Wolf. I had planned on saving him to lead the last day. He'd have to start a day early. The team's speed picked up and Esther's tugline was tight again now that she was in point, the second row.

I was starting to question why I had taken these dogs, who were clearly tired, to one more race. Most of them had been really sick a month before at the Beargrease and seemed to not have fully recovered. At the very least everyone was tired from just finishing a race only five days before. Sherri couldn't come because SHE was still sick.

"Why couldn't you just stay home, Frank? Weren't four races this year enough? Do you have something to prove?" These thoughts were running through my head as I saw Nita's ears perk up. She really loved to see what was around the next corner or over the next rise in the trail. We crested the top of the ridgeline halfway between Eagle and Copper Harbor. The panorama of the Upper Peninsula opened up before me. The hills descended for miles until they blended into the great Lake Superior far below. I smiled, as the picture reminded me of the gifts of sled dog racing. The dogs picked up their pace too as the trail began a twenty-mile downhill run.

"See the lake, puppies? We live on the other side. We'll be home soon."

They loped again, all the way to Copper Harbor. We were now way behind the race leaders. The dogs didn't know what place we were in as I praised them at the finish line. After I gave them their well-deserved meal I went around to massage them. Esther wasn't putting weight on her left front foot. Her shoulder was sore, probably never totally healed after the Beargrease. I held her close.

"You're done now, Esther. Thank you, little girl."

2011 Copper Dog (photo by ADAM JOHNSON – brockit inc.)

Chapter 22

The next day was March 6, the last day of the Copper Dog, our final race of the 2011 season. My nine dogs were pulling me along a high ridge on the Keweenaw Peninsula on the west side of Michigan's Upper Peninsula. To my right was Lake Superior, the massive freshwater sea. My home was on the other side, 100 miles of water away. To my left were the hills of the Copper Country. Waves of mining booms and busts had left a legacy of leaking abandoned copper mines, towns scrambling for a future, scattered across this unique Great Lakes' landscape. In many ways it was a scene so similar to the one I'd return to across the lake in Minnesota. There was one big exception. My home had never seen the type of mining that had left the toxic legacy that flowed through the Keweenaw.

My mind flashed back to August, 2010. Conservation Minnesota, which I am on the board of, had just awarded Minnesota Conservation Citizen of the year to one of my best friends, Dann

Siems of Bemidji. Dann and I had taught together at Bemidji State University and spent many days on the trail in those wild outdoor places that we both called home. Dann was dying of brain cancer. He had weeks, maybe a few months to live. Dann stood before the crowd gathered to watch him receive the award. The normal routine would be for him to say a few thank yous, shake hands and sit down. But Dann was never one to miss a chance to lecture on what else needed to be done. There he stood before us, bald and puffy from months of failed chemotherapy, and began a story. He told us of a group camping trip that he went on as a young student. One night on that camping trip one of the leaders organized a play about the trees and animals that lived in them. The main character was dying at the end and asked all the others in the play, "Who will protect the land, the trees, the water and the animals when I'm gone." In unison the other characters replied, "We will."

Dann paused. The quiet became obvious as he looked around the room of Minnesota's conservation leaders. Then he said, "Who will protect the places we love when I'm gone?"

No one spoke. Again the quiet was obvious, growing awkward. Someone clapped and we all nervously joined in. Dann shook our hands, took the award and walked back to stand next to his wife Lenore, who had long since been able to hold back the tears. A few of Dann's closest friends asked to speak and all told stories of how Dann had inspired their work but I couldn't pay attention to their words. Dann's were still ringing in my head.

"Who will protect the places we love when I'm gone?"

Hadn't I done my share? I'd run for and won a seat in the Minnesota House of Representatives. Didn't I get the first law in the country passed to protect a native species, wild rice, from genetic contamination? What about the other work I did there to protect the environment? Wasn't it someone else's turn? I knew the answer and, worse yet, Dann knew the answer too. I walked over to him. We both smiled a knowing smile.

"Dann, I'm not done yet. I promise, I'm not done yet. "

As I embraced him, he just said, "I know."

I only saw Dann one more time, in a hospital bed in his living room surrounded by loved ones. He died a couple of months later, on the fourth of February, 2011. The celebration of Dann's life was on the very same day, March 6, that I was scheduled to be finishing the last sled dog race of the season. I was torn about whether to go to the race or the service. In the end I knew Dann would expect me to race, and I did.

I thought of my promise to Dann as I looked over Michigan's Copper Country with its boom and bust legacy; thought of the pollution that ran through those streams and it became clear. No, I wasn't through yet. In fact I was just taking a break. My dogs ran forever and never quit unless I forced them to; the dogs and I would do it together. They were going to deliver me, and the message that we need to protect Minnesota's water from the type of mining that polluted the Keweenaw, all the way from Grand Marais to the Capitol in Saint Paul.

That idea came to me at the hour of Dann's service back in Bemidji. The second thoughts about not going to the service left me. I was where I was supposed to be. On that ridge at the top of the Keweenaw, Dann was with us. I smiled.... and said, "Thank you".

"Let's go, Wolfie, Nita. We gotta get home. We've got work to do." Watching these two leaders, I thought of our adventure to come, not yet knowing how its success or failure would ultimately depend upon them both.

Gus (photo by Kathleen Kimball-Parker)

Chapter 23

Sitting at my kitchen table I was looking out at the first snowflakes of another winter storm to hit the North Shore. It was April 3 and there were three feet of snow still on the ground. It felt like a heavy wet Thanksgiving snow and I soon had made up the list of dogs that would pull the sled. The depression that comes with the end of winter was forgotten and replaced with visions of riding the sled down a fresh snow-covered trail. Running the dogs would give my mind a break from the constant torture I put myself through this time of year. What had begun as longing to be back out on the sled with the dogs, quickly had jumped to questioning myself on all levels.

I looked down at the day's list of dogs to train. The snow was piling up.

"Time for one more run yet this season."

I put on my gear and headed out, not wanting to let go of the salve of winter.

❧

It rained hard the next day and there I was again at the kitchen table. I looked over at Gus, my housedog. He never got worked up about anything, was just happy sleeping in my easy chair or riding next to me in the truck. "Why can't I be more like you, Gus?"

Staring at the pile of bills that had built up over the winter, I thought: "What the heck am I doing with my life? Ok, I don't give a damn what people think about me becoming a wood tick up here in the hills, or do I? At least I need to be able to pay my own way, not put Sherri through this poverty."

I had recently been asked by a few to consider running for another political position. Of course it was flattering. My ego toyed with the idea for almost a day. But after sitting with it, wearing the role of candidate and politician like a hat, it no longer fit. That night I sat next to Sherri napping in her chair surrounded by dogs and cats. I looked out at the sled dog yard where all the dogs were looking to the house for some sign that I was going to come out and take them for a run. I couldn't even bear the thought of turning my back on all this, my current life and those who were so directly affected by my decisions.

My mind then jumped to "well, then what?" For a living I guide people who want to experience the outdoors and train other guides to do the same. This is something I've done off and on all my working life. "But shouldn't I be striving to do more?" It's a question that never even entered my mind when I was harnessing up the dogs. It's funny how we can look at someone else's job and see where the great service possibilities are. My own vocation, helping others learn how to do outdoor activities, to experience the wilderness, often felt futile.

"What about your plan to run the dogs to Saint Paul?" I asked myself. The idea had faded after I returned home from the Copper Dog. My mind jumped on it. I pulled out a pad of paper and pen and began to make a list of what I needed to do to make it happen. First I had to see if it was possible, which meant surveying the route. How would a sled dog team travel from Grand Marais to Saint Paul, Minnesota? I would need to get all the snowmobile trail maps for the State of Minnesota, plan the route from start to finish, every turn, road crossing, where we'd stop every night, how long it would take. I realized I'd need a lot of help. It would be more of an expedition than a trip. Really it would be an expedition in reverse, going from our rural cabin in the North Woods all the way to the Minnesota State Capitol in very urban downtown Saint Paul.

After a quick online search I had trail maps that covered most of the route, but there were gaps leaving Grand Marais, through Duluth and the last few miles before the Capitol. Looking at a bike trail map of the Saint Paul area I saw that a paved State Trail, the Gateway, started eighteen miles northeast of Saint Paul and ended just two miles from the Capitol. I pulled out my calendar. I needed to go see the trails and route, as much of it as possible before I got there with the dogs. Before I told anyone else about the plan, I needed to be sure it was possible and wrote in scouting trips to Duluth and Saint Paul on my calendar. After doing my dog chores in the deep slushy snow that morning, I headed into town. Gus rode in with me, and we parked next to Harbor Park, right in the center of Grand Marais.

"We need to start right here, Gus. We'll have a rally, harness up the dogs and head down the street." My dog was the first one I told the plan to. We got out and walked around town.

"Gus, how are we going to get out of town and get on the snowmobile trail? I guess we'll just have to run on the street. Acorn and Fly will have to lead us through town."

⁂

"Mud and slush, that's all that's left of winter. The last day of April, nine months until the start of Beargrease 2012."

On paper I had begun to plan our run to Saint Paul but my heart longed to be racing. I had just come in from moving the dogs around to get them onto as dry a ground as possible. Everyone was healthy and well muscled, ready to train now for the next season, which was still four months away. It had started to rain and was forty degrees. With their heads hanging they gave the look that they hated the weather as much as I did. If it were sunny I would be able to pull out all the gear, clean and pack it up for next year. All the bags of used dog booties needed to be rinsed, sorted and laid out to dry. Far from work, it was all part of the ritual, anything to be focusing on mushing.

It was the day of the Beargrease annual board meeting, and I almost drove down to Duluth, six hours round trip just to talk dogs for a couple of hours. Instead I decided to stay home and do my best to deal with a muddy dog yard.

We usually have or buy puppies every year and were planning to breed our new superstar female leader Nita to Winnie, but none of the females had gone into heat yet, probably because of the late spring. If it got much later we risked Nita missing too much fall training to be ready to race in January. So I waited to have puppies, to sort gear, to train dogs, and sat dreaming of next year.

Again I found myself reaching for last season's training log. Each entry represents a day of training, the dogs that ran and how they did. The miles all add up to a total for the year and I second-guessed the training plan for the umpteenth time. The reality probably was that the training plan was sound, and even if it wasn't, the dogs were good enough to overcome my mistakes...which I'm sure I'd made more of than I knew.

Setting it down, I looked back out to the dog yard, watching them sit, stand, walk, dig, sit, as restless and bored as I was. Four months to go.

Once the road and trails dried out I would be able to do some short runs with the ATV, training the pups Wolf and Tina had the previous June. They all had as much energy as Wolf. Iris was mostly white with black on her face and flakes in her coat. She was the wildest dog we've ever had. It was impossible to get out of her circle without a muddy paw on your face or even in your mouth. Yuck. Boo was all white, the smallest but clearly the boss. After running her only once I was convinced she'd be a leader. Their sister Tulip was also white and had the best build of the three but wasn't too sure of herself yet. The two boys, Tater and Duke, were good sized and seemed to be a cross between their dad and grandfather Winnie. Their gait reminded me of Winnie's. Duke's face was half black and looked like his dad, every bit as wild too. Tater was the biggest but acted more like his mother, crazy in harness but on his pivot he loved to put his face right up next to mine. I'd whisper in his ear what a good boy he was and scratch behind his ears. Optimism always was high but those pups looked good. I couldn't wait to hook them up again but it was raining on a muddy slush-covered trail, so we all sat and waited.

❀

"Remember what you said after the race?" Sherri was beside herself. "You were never running the Beargrease again. You said it's too hard on the dogs, costs too much. How can you forget what happened? We thought that Bart and Tina might not make it. You were sleeping when I was at Devil's Track with the dogs. Five were on IVs. Tina needed four liters. Bart needed five. Ace got three or four, too."

"I know, I know, don't forget that I was with them all on the trail when they got sick." Not the smartest answer to give to your wife who was the one that picked up all the pieces at Trail Center, four thirty in the morning and twenty-five below.

Sure, Sherri was right. For a couple of months I'd said that I'd never put us through that race again. Looking back, it seemed we could be reasonably sure that the dogs got sick from something in the food. Once we'd changed their diet, they all eventually recovered. It was pretty clear really, but my self-doubts remained.

"What if I make a worse mistake next year? What if it wasn't the food at all but something else that you'll just do again?" I knew those questions would run through my head until we finally neared the finish line of the Beargrease once more.

"Sherri, both Dennis and Odin scratched three times before they finished. We'd never scratched a race before. Not once."

I stopped and we looked into each other's eyes. "If we don't do the Beargrease what are we going to do for the whole month before the UP? You knew I was going to run the Beargrease again, no matter what I said then. How do we not run it?"

Sherri's exhale was long and audible. "I know Frank. I've known it all along."

Dog Truck (photo by Sherri Moe)

Chapter 24

Driving home from the Twin Cities I stopped in Beaver Bay where the Beargrease checkpoint was almost right on the highway. I turned up the hill and drove into the field that served as the dog yard for the checkpoint. I grabbed a smoke out of the glove box (I've since quit, again) and walked over to where our team had rested five months ago. I sat on my heels, lit my smoke and scanned the ground. Through the grass I could see some straw that had been put down months before for our dogs to lie on. I closed my eyes and felt the wind off of Lake Superior. The smells and sounds of this spot during the race came flooding back: diesel trucks, propane cookers, dogs barking, teams coming and going, all in the darkness of a cold Lake Superior night. Headlamps had told where mushers and handlers were caring for their teams. All was clouded with the steam of hundreds of dogs breathing and their food being cooked.

Here we were only eighty miles into the race. Most of the race was ahead, all still a possibility. Any mistakes we had made, or would make, had yet to take their toll on our team. There they were all strong, healthy, happy and had hungrily eaten their food. Sherri, Lisa, and Julie were busy massaging the dogs, looking over all their feet and covering their bodies with blankets, hoping they would rest. Our team was in the race and looked to have as good a chance to win as any other.

I sat and savored the memory. Five months had passed, and it would take seven more of planning, training and waiting before we would all be here again, with that same possibility ahead of us. I thought about each dog that was there with me on that night, how much they had given and would give in the twenty-four hours to come. I was crying, again feeling like I'd let them down. After all the miles they had run, all the trust they had put in me, I had made the mistake that had cost us—them—the race. Some had gotten so sick that they didn't race again all season. But there, at Beaver Bay, we'd had a full team, and they were racing the Beargrease.

Now, Cocoa, my old leader, was out walking, smelling the ground, all the ghosts of the checkpoint. I stood and watched her, thought of all the miles that she and I had travelled together, and finished my smoke. Walking back to the truck, I called Cocoa. Turning around, I could see my team all lying there, covered in blankets and peacefully resting on the straw. Wolf turned to me, with a look that he was ready to race.

"We will, Wolfie. We'll be back and next time I'll try and be as good as you are." Cocoa and I got in the truck and continued east on Hwy 61 towards home.

〰

Spring came very late in 2011 on the North Shore. The weather stayed unseasonably cold, which was good for some late season training but seemed to keep the females from going into heat. Like every other year, we were either going to have a litter of puppies or bring some in from another kennel. Gus and I were checking all the females every day to see if any were in heat.

Gus didn't know he was neutered and tried his chances with all the females. After his cue, I then looked for drops of blood. We weren't having any luck and it was already June, getting too late to have pups. If one of our main females, Acorn, Tina or Nita, were to breed then she'd be lost for the upcoming season.

Sherri heard that Kelly Jo Engle in Houghton, Michigan, had an accidental breeding between Rodney (Fly's brother) and Tina Fey (Cowboy and Pony's sister) and asked if we wanted the pups. After two months of staring at the butts of female dogs, I jumped at the chance and again made the drive to Michigan. It's only about a hundred miles across the lake but driving around takes eight hours. I came back with six beautiful pups. By the time I'd gotten home I'd already named them: Bacon, Pork Chop, Popcorn, Pepper, Ginger, and Ruby. We had thirty-six sled dogs to train and I was only seasonally employed as a canoe, sea-kayak, and climbing guide. It was perfect.

※

Most people who celebrate the summer solstice are happy that it signifies the formal beginning of summer, the longest day of the year, another two months or more of warm, mostly sunny days. For me the solstice means the countdown to winter, halfway from the last snow to the next. If it was anything like the last year, we were only two months from ATV training. When I walked around the dog yard, I didn't see any injuries. Every dog was healthy, happy, and eager to run. Again Acorn led them in a howl. They were ready, and it was only June.

Our last litter of puppies was one year old yesterday and looked like adult dogs but would still need at least another year to mature. They got to run a few times at the end of the spring and would train with the main team until November or so this year. We'd ease up on their training then to not put too much pressure on them at such a young age. Lisa came over from Bemidji to celebrate their birthday, she even brought a cake...that none of them got to taste. I ate most of it.

※

July 18 hit ninety degrees. On the North Shore that could be the high for the year. The biting flies had hatched too. They swarmed the dogs, mostly going after their ears. We normally coat all the dogs' ears with a salve that protects them from bites. The flies had gotten so bad that salve no longer was working so I resorted to spraying them with a fly repellent made for horses. I hated to use that kind of stuff but there was nothing else that worked when the flies were that relentless. Left untreated the dogs would get open sores from all the bites.

Looking at the calendar each day was a ritual, counting down one more day. "Hey Sherri. Do you know that we are now over half way between the last training run of the spring and the first training run of the fall? Seven months from now we'll be on the Beargrease Trail."

"What? Can't I just enjoy my garden for a few more weeks?"

We're not always on the same page.

For many years we were the kids our parents liked to brag about. We owned a business, had a nice log home on a pond and eight acres of land. I taught at the university and served in the Minnesota Legislature. Now they asked us: "How much longer can you live like that?"

"Do you mean how much longer can I crap outside?"

My mom's the only one of our parents who has visited us here on the North Shore, and it took her two years to make the six-hour drive. She didn't want to stay more than two hours because she was afraid to use the outhouse. Something about spiders. Once she'd been here, seen how beautiful it was and that we didn't lock her in the outhouse, she came once or twice a year. We weren't sure, but we thought it was more to see the dogs than us. They were her only grandchildren.

Sometimes I still worried about doing something with my life, having a job again that might impress people when they asked, one that my parents would feel proud telling their friends about. But when I was honest about it, I really didn't care. All those jobs would just get in the way, take me away from the dogs. I quit another one in June. The owner was temperamental and self absorbed, probably too much like me, but that's not really why I quit. Maybe it tipped the balance but, really, I needed the time to work on the dog-sled trail leaving my house. Having to use the road last year cost me several days of training. It was too hard packed and dangerous to run a sled on. Those were days that I did not want to give up next year, so I had to get that trail done. Heck with the job.

Tank (photo by Kathleen Kimball-Parker)

Chapter 25

In March Lisa had stopped at the Voyageurs Outward Bound School in Ely to check on Peanut, Buck and, most of all, Tank. He had been her favorite. She walked around the dog yard and immediately recognized their loud, almost roaring barks. After the slobbering reunion with her boys, Lisa went looking for Peanut.

She couldn't find her. Lisa went into the office to ask and heard that Peanut had died of cancer that winter. On her way home, she called and told Sherri, but they held off on telling me until the season was over. Peanut had been one of my first race leaders and I had had a rough time with letting her go. They knew that I'd blame myself for her dying.

I hadn't gone to see Peanut, Buck, and Tank since I dropped them off. I didn't know if I could handle it. After hearing about Peanut I knew that I would have to go visit Buck and Tank. On my way home from teaching a canoeing class in Nett Lake, I took the long scenic route through Ely. What I'd find when I got there had long been on my mind, and a sick feeling in my stomach grew the closer I got to the school on the east side of town. The mile-long driveway to the Outward Bound school seemed to go on forever, much longer than I remembered.

Suddenly to my right was the gate. I quickly stopped. There was the dog yard where I had left Peanut, Buck and Tank almost three years ago. Looking at the gate, the memory of seeing them through it, with confused looks on their faces as I drove away, came rushing back. I quickly got out of the car, jumped over the gate with its No Trespassing sign and began scanning the dog yard for Buck and Tank. There were rows and rows of at least sixty dogs. Most were running in circles, the excitement of somebody new walking amongst them.

A guy started my way.

"Can I help you?"

"Yeah, I'm looking for Buck and Tank. I raised them."

"Buck was just adopted, a guy who just got out of the military. I think he's in Ohio or some place."

As he talked I saw that Tank was just a few yards to my right, sitting in the sun, dusty, with one ear dropped and a look like he'd been waiting for me. There was one of my boys, from our first litter, looking just as big and handsome as he did when I left him there. Maybe it was just me but he looked sad, alone. His brother Buck was gone. He cocked his head as I walked up to him. I fell to my knees.

"How's my big boy Tank?"

He let me hold his head next to mine and started giving me his big slobbery kisses. I stood up and, like he always used to, he put his paws up on my shoulders and kept licking my face.

"Oh, Tank, I missed you. I'm so sorry"

The guy there hadn't stopped talking. "Yeah, his hair is too short. Buck's was even shorter. I don't know what they were thinking taking these dogs. It must have been to get Peanut. She was a hell of a leader."

Looking over at me he continued: "Do you even know what we do here? We go on mushing trips. These dogs camp out..."

He saw my tears. "Hey man, do you need some time?"

"I'm taking Tank." I unhooked his collar.

"Well I don't know, can you go check at the office?"

"No, I'm goin now. He's coming with me."

"Can't you call the office tomorrow and if it's OK come back and get him?"

Tank heeled right next to me as I walked back to the truck barely holding his collar.

"How'd you do that? That dog would be dragging me through the yard, running circles around me if I tried to hold him like that."

The guy followed me out of the yard. Seeing Tank and me together, the guy changed his tone.

"Hey, do you want some food for him, so he'll get used to yours?"

I thanked him for the partial bag of food and opened the door of the truck. Tank jumped right in, like he'd done it every day of his life, sat in the back, waiting for me to take him home.

I held back most of the tears until we pulled away and then the sobbing was uncontrollable. I pulled over and held my head in my hands.

Facing back, I scratched behind his ears: "Tank, I promise I'll never leave you anywhere again."

My tears went on. They flowed for all the dogs that we no longer had, that had given everything for us; dogs that we'd buried, some that were now stars for other mushers, for Buck who was somewhere in Ohio, for Peanut who I never got to see again before she died, and for Tank who was coming home.

Ravens are a fixture in the dog yard. They walk, usually in pairs, among the dogs looking for scraps of food. The older dogs ignore them, and the younger dogs watch closely. When a raven gets close enough, the young dogs give chase but they don't plan to eat it. It's more like when one of the housedogs gets close enough to them, they just want to play with it.

The ravens are a higher form of life and the dogs know it. There's a respect there that the dogs don't have for another bird, a frog, vole or red squirrel. I've often found these other unsuspecting animals dead in the dog yard. Ravens feed in pairs and at least one always is facing the potential threat. I doubt the dogs could ever catch one but even if they could, I don't think they would try and hurt it.

Ravens started showing up in September, just sitting in nearby trees and watching. After a few days they would land close to the dogs and wait for reactions. Slowly the dogs got used to them and the ravens learned which dogs would ignore them and which would give chase. Now they walked among the dogs registering little reaction, just an interested stare from some, that was it. So many animals up here in the north spent their fall squirreling away their supplies for the winter. The ravens prepared by learning and cultivating what was available.

I was sitting in the Grand Marais Senior Center talking to a friend about quitting my job, venting a bit. He sat, looking amused then said: "Well, it's done."

"What?" In my head I wanted to keep stirring it up but stopped talking for a second. I caught something out of the corner of my eye in the window next to me. The thump nearly made us jump out of our chairs. Looking out the window, I saw a young raven lying in the garden next to the building below the window. Its beak was open and it was breathing rapidly. For a minute I sat down and tried to continue the conversation until my friend stopped and stared at me.

"Frank. Frank?"

"I wonder if the raven is OK."

I looked out the window again and the raven was still upright but its head was turning back and forth quickly.

"I gotta go." I was almost running as I left and circled the building to the base of the window. The raven was now on its side. The feeling that it was no longer alive dropped me to my knees. Clouds were moving in and the last rays of the sun caught the sheen of its black feathers. As that light faded, I exhaled, closed my eyes, opened them, and carefully picked the raven up. It was surprisingly light for its large size and its head lay limp, eyes now closed. I could feel its warmth through the feathers. Still kneeling, I dropped my face next to the raven as if to shelter it from the gusting wind and coming rain.

Several people walked behind me on the sidewalk and the road was busy with the summer tourist traffic. The raven needed to be somewhere else, free of this place. I stood up, cradling it in both of my hands and walked toward the lake, two blocks to the Coast Guard station, and then out on the rocks at the edge of the harbor.

The spray of the crashing waves landed around us. I could see the sun setting below the clouds to the east, even as the rain fell. I carried the raven down the rocks and as the next wave came in I tossed it into the lake, imagining that it would fly.

For several minutes the raven floated nearby, not washing up on the rocks but not getting washed out into the lake either. I sat and watched, as it rained, windy, and the sun set. Slowly, the raven drifted out into Lake Superior and in the twilight could no longer be seen.

The wet rocks were barely visible as I climbed back up to the Coast Guard parking lot, often stopping to turn and look into the darkness of the lake.

Ben (photo by Kathleen Kimball-Parker)

Chapter 26

Cool nights come early to the North Shore, usually in August, and with them the hopes of a new season. This year they'd come in July and for the last three mornings we'd been training. After a couple of uneventful runs I decided to move up to running fourteen-dog teams. That night I hastily put together the longer gangline and barely noticed a place where one of the dogs had chewed most of the way through the main center line. There was nylon coated steel cable inside, so I didn't think anything of it.

In the morning I began harnessing up the dogs, and Lisa, who was visiting again, came running out to help. She was watching the dogs on the line as I brought the last three big dogs, Winnie, Ace, and Tank up. Just as we were about to take off, Tater and Duke got tangled up. I jumped off the ATV and ran to them. I got to Tater, lifted him over the line to remove the tangle and heard a snap. The gangline broke right there, and off went the front eight dogs at a sprint, leaving me behind with a team of six dogs attached to the ATV, Duke and Tater in the front.

I liked to ease yearlings into leading, give them a chance to gain some confidence before they led for the first time. I hopped on the ATV. "Lets go!" and after the front eight we went with Duke in lead. Tater was still a bit tangled but was able to run alongside. Tank and Ace were in wheel and ran like champions. Ben and Jake were the next two. They had started to fight and somehow kept the fight up while we were travelling down the road at twenty miles an hour.

The next two minutes felt like hours. All the possibilities of dragging and injured dogs were running through my head when we rounded a corner, and there they were. Acorn had stopped the team and she was sitting, waiting for me. The rest weren't sitting. Tina and Tulip were in heat. Winnie couldn't make up his mind which he was going to jump, his daughter Tina or granddaughter Tulip. I turned off the ATV, hit the emergency brake and got to him just in time to prevent incest. My grabbing Winnie gave Fly an opening, and soon I was wrestling them both.

Ben and Jake were still fighting.

Lisa rode up on her mountain bike. "Do you need any help?"

"Please, grab the leaders!" She did.

"Straighten them out!"

"Oh yeah. OK."

I grabbed the frayed end of the front section of gangline and tied it to the back section.

"Ben, Jake, NO!" I grabbed and shook them apart. Looking up the team I saw that both Tater and Winnie were now tangled in the gangline and all the dogs in front of them were lunging, making it impossible for me to untangle them.

"Lisa! Come here!" Lisa let go the leaders and ran back to me.

"Grab the gangline here and pull." I motioned to a place right in front of Tater and Winnie hoping that she could take enough pressure off the line for me to untangle them.

Lisa grabbed the line and pulled away from me, tightening the line. "NO! The other way."

"Oh." She pulled, relieving enough of the pressure for me to untangle Tater, then Winnie. Every other dog was lunging and barking, dragging the ATV with locked brakes down the road. Ben and Jake started fighting again. I gave them another good shaking, hopped on the ATV and took off the brake.

Lisa went airborne. She'd been standing with her feet in the gangline and was now rolling head over heels down the road next to fourteen screaming dogs.

Brakes on again, then I turned off the ATV and then ran up to check on Lisa.

"Guess I'm outta practice," she said as she pulled herself out of the ditch next to the road.

Winnie and Tater were again tangled. As I went to untangle them one more time, I was having visions of the gangline separating again. I hopped on the ATV as it dragged on past me, took off the brake and started the engine. And just like that, they were all running in perfect formation, all fourteen dogs, as if nothing had happened. I throttled them back to our training pace, ten miles an hour.

"How was the training run today?" Sherri asked.

"Duke is going to be a great leader."

"What? Why was he leading?"

∬

In spite of the near disasters, nothing was better for me than training the dogs. I could be on the verge of suicide, wake up on a cool morning, run the dogs and then wonder what I was so upset about. All the dogs' illnesses, injuries, and aches from last season were gone. My back and shoulder, on the other hand, were already bothering me. Handfuls of ibuprofen, Tylenol and aspirin seemed to come earlier and earlier every year. At least my knees were feeling better. I could hardly walk, back in March, even with the drugs.

Winnie, Bart, Tina, Esther, Fly, and Ace had all finished last year with injuries. That was a lot of dog power. They now all looked one hundred percent. The next day, sitting on the ATV, watching them running perfectly took me to the upcoming racing season. I caught my ego visualizing winning each race, then I stopped and remembered: "Do right by the dogs. That's it. If I do that, the races will take care of themselves."

My ego and ambition used to take me away from the dogs. For years I spent most of my time in Saint Paul. Pulling out of the driveway on Sunday nights to make my weekly drive to the Capitol was brutal. Their looks showed they knew I wouldn't be there to train them for days.

We moved to Grand Marais so I could be with the dogs all the time and my ego came home. For the last couple of years I had put my ambition on the dogs, focusing on winning races. Sure we'd had some success but at what cost? I was crazy for weeks before and after the Beargrease. Dogs, like human athletes, are going to get injured, but my reaction to those injuries was totally out of whack. I blamed myself for everything, like I was all powerful.

My obsession led me to training the dogs at 5:00 a.m., starting in July, over five months before the first race. I sat on the ATV running down our road at dawn wondering if we were going have time to get ready for the first race. Seriously. All the dogs' injuries were healed up and they looked great but that fear would stay with me through the race season.

I reminded myself, "I'm just going to try and do what's in front of me: feed and clean up after the dogs, fix the gangline and a couple of harnesses, order the next round of vaccinations, treat their ears for flies, and find time to sit in the puppy pen. Maybe it'll be cool enough to train again tomorrow."

Our Cabin (photo by Lisa Boulay)

Chapter 27

Sherri and I moved to the North Shore of Lake Superior, near Grand Marais, because it was the best place in the lower forty-eight to run sled dogs. Winters were long there in the hills. Snow was normally deep enough to sled on by Thanksgiving, and rarely was it gone before late April. Storms coming from the south picked up moisture off of the lake and then dumped snow as the clouds hit the hills, sometimes feet at a time. The power of Lake Superior could make the country inaccessible to those without snowmobiles or dog sleds. Those who lived there developed a respect, even a reverence for the great lake Gitchi Gumi. It had a weather all its own, its moods shaped those in its shadow. Our lives there depended upon its gifts of tourism, food, and recreation.

Over the hills from Superior lies the Boundary Waters Canoe Area Wilderness, the most heavily visited wilderness area in the United States. Hundreds of thousands seekers of solitude travel its million acres of lakes every year. Many of those drive up Highway 61 along the North Shore of Lake Superior and base their trips out of Grand Marais. In the months where the lakes are unfrozen, every other car or truck in town is either carrying on top or pulling a trailer full of canoes. They can slow down travel in town but it's easily worth it, given the sustainable dollars they bring to town.

I'd been visiting and bringing people to the North Shore and the Boundary Waters Canoe Area Wilderness since I was a kid. Research done on the formative experiences of those who advocate for the environment and wilderness has shown that those people all had formative wilderness experiences when they were young. All my early trips to Lake Superior and the Boundary Waters have memories attached to them, memories that I now know were why I believed in protecting wild places.

One night, when I was a teenager, it finally sank in that there was a power in the universe greater than myself. I was lying in my sleeping bag, on the south shore of Lake Alice in the Boundary Waters Canoe Area. Our high school church canoe trip had been hammered by a typical Northern Minnesota afternoon storm and we barely made it to shore before our canoes were swamped. While eating dinner under a tarp we watched the rain stop and eventually the clouds part. After finishing setting up camp and hanging all our stuff up to dry we decided to throw our sleeping bags down on the beach. Out of the north a strong wind was now keeping the mosquitoes in the woods, and we lay on top of our sleeping bags staring up at the northern sky. We were expecting to look at the stars but instead watched the sky catch fire. First the lights were just vertical flickers of white but then there was also yellow and green. The streaks turned to waves that covered us in a virtual birdcage centered at a point overhead, extending to the horizon in every direction.

Now, I was not a religious kid and only went on Boundary Waters trips because my friends went, and I liked to canoe and fish. Also my home life was pretty tough, and what trouble I didn't have at home I found for myself out on the streets. A hard week in the woods calmed me down a bit, and that night, after what had been my toughest ever on the trail, I looked up and felt like I was being held in God's world. I was safe. It was a sense that, from that point on in my life, I sought out but only found there, in those wild places. For years since I'd brought others to the Boundary Waters, including troubled teenagers like myself, hoping they would find some clarity of their own.

Starting in 2009 several companies began the permitting process to mine copper, zinc, and other metals in the Superior National Forest, in virtually all the country between Lake Superior and The Boundary Waters Canoe Area Wilderness. The more I learned about it the more it seemed it was as if a massive bull dozer sat at the edge of our home, waiting to plow it into the lake. The Canadian company Polymet, whose primary investor is multinational mining giant Glencore, was the furthest along in the permitting process. Glencore's legacy was one of human rights violations, massive environmental contamination, child labor atrocities, and then taking the money and running. To punctuate that history, Glencore hired Tony Hayward, the BP CEO who presided over the Gulf Oil Spill, as their environment and safety expert.

Sulfide mining, the process used to extract the non-iron metals from the ore, had a long history of creating environmental disasters. No matter what was said about new mining technologies, how corporations had learned their lessons, how "they" would return the site to its natural state, their history was clear. The United States Environmental Protection Agency has stated that forty percent of all the water pollution in the US came from hard-rock sulfide mining. Abandoned mines, that are now Superfund Sites without the money to clean them up, dotted the American West.

Polymet/Glencore was most likely to drag out in court any efforts by the state or federal government to make them stop polluting the surrounding lakes, rivers, and streams. When the mine was no longer profitable it would be abandoned, leaving the state and the Minnesota taxpayer with the impossible task of cleaning up the mess. The mess would be massive and toxic. Sulfide pollution would have run off in both directions, polluting the Boundary Waters Canoe Area Wilderness to the north and Lake Superior to the south and east.

Polymet's proposal had been twice labeled a failure by the US Environmental Protection Agency. The existing settling pools, where the mine proposed to store the sulfur tailings, were already leaking and were clearly going to pollute the Saint Louis River and Lake Superior with massive amounts of sulfuric acid.

There was support for the mines in the towns on the Minnesota Iron Range. Many of those towns had never recovered from the industrial decline of the 70s and 80s. Unemployment was chronically high and there was almost a mythology of the "good old days" when Grampa worked in the mines. The prospect of this new, potentially more polluting type of mine, had opened up the old wounds, pitting the Iron Range pro-mining advocates against those in the recreation and tourism economy whose livelihood was dependent upon clean water.

Duluth Twin Metals, the second mining project in line, succeeded in stirring up even more controversy about their proposed mine by naming it Nokomis, which is the Anishinabe word for grandmother. The mines would be surrounded on three sides by Native American reservations who were all already strongly united in their opposition and are now publicly outraged by this latest insult. The Nokomis mine would be the largest in North America, and one of the largest in the World, a hard-rock sulfide mine that would drain right into the Boundary Waters Canoe Area Wilderness.

It was reported in the media that the Duluth Complex was the third-largest untapped deposit of copper and other precious metals in the world and that there was little sulfur in the deposit so the likelihood of sulfide mining pollution was low. But that information came from The University of Minnesota, Duluth Precambrian Research Center. It sounded official and trustworthy until the curtain was pulled back. Their so-called research center was funded by a collection of mining groups, including Twin Metals and its parent corporation Antofagasta.

Jim Miller, PhD, who wrote an assessment that there was nothing to worry about with the Nokomis Project, had worked as a geologist for a mining company prior to coming to UMD. His research was funded by the very companies that stood to benefit from his conclusions. More and more of those mining dollars would no doubt flow to the UMD Precambrian Research Center if Twin Metals succeeded in getting its permit to mine near the Boundary Waters Canoe Area Wilderness.

For twenty-five years Lake Superior was the dumping ground for thousands of tons of mining waste every day. Beginning in the early fifties Reserve Mining Company daily dumped tons of waste rock directly into the lake, turning it gray and muddy for miles around. Duluth's drinking water, fifty miles away, was contaminated with an asbestos-like fiber, that also was in the mining waste, which could cause cancer. Federal Judge Miles Lord ultimately forced Reserve Mining to stop the dumping, establishing the precedent that people and our government could force industry to clean up its pollution.

After thirty years the lake is finally recovering. The fibers are no longer in our drinking water and the fishing has come back, but now we find ourselves looking at an even greater threat to Lake Superior's water. The difference is that we have a chance to stop it from happening, before it begins.

Minnesotans have a history of protecting our natural heritage. Along with the decision to stop dumping mining waste into Lake Superior, citizen efforts in the 1970s led to the designation of the Boundary Waters Canoe Area Wilderness and Voyageurs National Park.

More recently Minnesota became the first state to protect a native species from genetic contamination. In 2007, I authored a bill in the Minnesota Legislature, supported by a coalition of Native Americans, sportsmen and women, and environmentalists, that successfully fought off Monsanto and other multinational agribusinesses who wanted to cultivate GMO wild rice in our state. A law was passed that made it illegal in Minnesota to release any genetically modified strains of wild rice. With the proposed sulfide mining we face the same kind of David-versus-Goliath battle, but our history tells us that we can win.

⚘

During the summer of 2011 I made several trips to the Twin Cities, and each time I would scout out a different portion of the route the dogs would have to travel to Saint Paul, to deliver the petitions opposing sulfide mining to Governor Dayton. By August I was convinced it was possible to drive a dog team all the way there from Grand Marais. That was assuming there would be sufficient snow, which turned out to be an optimistic assumption. I was sure enough, though, to start sharing my ideas with the people I'd need to help me make the trip.

Sherri: "Frank, if anyone can do it, you can."

It's nice to have such a blindly supportive wife.

Molly, my friend and Government Affairs Director for Conservation Minnesota: "You're gonna do what?"

OK, less optimistic. I had some more work to do there.

Adam Harju, friend and the person I had hoped would coordinate logistics for the trip, after I explained the idea to him a second time: "I'm in. Tell me what you need me to do."

Jerry Vanek, DVM: "Well, I've got a race to vet in Alaska, maybe two, the White Oak here in Minnesota, going to Norway, not sure when I'm coming back…When are you going?"

That was as much of a yes as I was going to get from Jerry.

"Molly, when do you think the best time to make the trip would be?"

"Probably the end of March, maybe early April."

"OK but how about when we might have snow, February or early March?"

We decided the best time would be the first week in March. There was still a chance that there'd be snow and that the Minnesota Legislature would still be in session. Hopefully they and the Governor would be there when we arrived. The plan was also to have rallies along the way, to try and build attention and momentum around the trip. Everyone I asked to help said yes.

"Adam, can you help me set up a meeting in Grand Marais of people who would plan a send-off rally?"

"No problem. I'll make a list of people and find a place to have the meeting. How about at Stephan's place? He's still got a couple weeks before he gets evicted."

Ian Kimmer, the Northern Minnesota Organizer for Friends of the Boundary Waters loved the idea and knew a lot of people in the Duluth area that he thought would be willing to help.

"Ian, can you help me set up a meeting in Duluth to plan a rally there for the trip to Saint Paul?"

"Yeah, no problem. Hey, how about if I join you and ski the whole way … at least to Duluth?"

"Thanks, Ian. How fast can you ski?"

I had thought about somehow including Ely in the trip and plan. Ian came up with the idea of having a sled dog team leave Ely and meet with my team in Finland where they'd hand off their petitions to me to add to the pile I was taking to Saint Paul. Paul and Sue Schurke of Wintergreen wanted to help but they were going to be tied up with sled dog tours. Dave and Amy Freeman, who are well known for their Wilderness Classroom program and guide for Wintergreen, heard about our plan and jumped at it. They wanted to hold a rally in Ely, collect petition signatures there and run a sled dog team from Ely through Isabella and on to Finland.

"We'll be running Schurke's Canadian Inuits, Frank. They're a lot slower than your racing dogs. It may take us a while to get there."

"How much slower?"

The plan was shaping up. Groups formed around rally events in Ely, Grand Marais, Finland, Duluth, and Saint Paul. The plan was to collect as many petition signatures as we could opposing sulfide mining. On March 1 sled dog teams would leave rallies in Ely and Grand Marais. The Ely team, driven by Dave and Amy, would travel to Isabella, collect petition signatures there, depart the next morning and finish at an outdoor bonfire event in Finland. My team would leave a rally in downtown Grand Marais, travel to Sawbill Canoe Outfitters and leave the next morning for Finland where I'd meet up with Dave and Amy's team. Water Legacy, a grassroots organization founded to oppose sulfide mining, would organize the Finland event with a bonfire on the night of the 2nd, a pancake breakfast the morning of the 3rd and an educational rally at the Finland Community Center. From Finland I'd travel to Two

Harbors, then on to a big rally at Lester Park in Duluth on the afternoon of Sunday, March 4.

The Duluth organizing effort would be critical. That was where we hoped to first get the attention of the statewide media. The event needed to include all the major groups and people organizing against sulfide mining in the Duluth area: Water Legacy, Protect Our Manoomin, Friends of the Boundary Waters, The Sierra Club, Save Our Sky Blue Waters, Friends of Cloquet State Forest, and the Center for Biological Diversity. The leaders of those groups had all been working against sulfide mining for several years and here came this guy they didn't know who was asking for their help to plan a rally, so he could run his sled dogs into and out of Duluth on his way to Saint Paul. They must have been desperate because they all said yes.

⚥

By the time the first real snow fell on December 15, I'd been training the dogs on the ATV for over four months. My ass was sore, I was tired of the engine noise and just sitting in the cold. There were four inches of snow, not enough to run a big team on a sled, but I convinced myself that I could control a nine-dog team on the new thin snow cover. With Nita and Esther, the fastest craziest leaders in the kennel in lead, I pulled the snow hook. Hitting the first tree leaving the yard, I realized there wasn't enough snow to slow or control the sled. Two trees later I was dragging on my face.

"Don't let go, Frank. Don't let go."

A timely long, steep uphill slowed us enough for me to get on my feet, start running and jump back on the runners. There was no time to rest either as we ping-ponged down the trail at between fifteen and twenty miles an hour. This was the opposite experience of sitting on a big heavy ATV. I wasn't cold or bored but instead was hanging on for dear life. Twenty-four miles later I rolled the sled rounding the corner of our driveway, dragging in just the way we left. The dogs stopped next to the house, as they always did and all started rolling in the snow. I quickly looked at my watch.

"An hour and forty-five minutes. That's fast. Too fast." Back to the ATV tomorrow.

Full of pride I looked down at myself. My parka had ripped down the side and on the sleeve. Several of the dogs were trying to catch the feathers that were falling out and now blowing around the driveway. After securing the leaders I went to the house to try and save as much of my parka as possible.

Sherri looked at me. "What happened to you? You're face is bleeding."

I wiped my face. Looking down at my hand seeing not too much blood, I took off my jacket.

"When's Lisa coming? I need her to sew up my parka again. We hit a tree. You should have seen how fast they were going. We need more snow... My head hurts."

Until Sherri pointed it out, I didn't know I'd hit my head on one of the trees we'd bounced off of. Putting on another jacket I went back out to put the team away and fed all the dogs. Before putting the dogs back on their pivots I had to take off their booties and harnesses. This was often the best part of the run. There was something about having just shared the sled time together where the dogs gave everything they had. They trusted me to guide them through the run and back home, and I was relieved that we made it back without anything serious happening and were one step closer to being ready for the first race of the season.

After taking each dog's booties off, I removed their harness and gave them a quick going over, looking for any cuts, abrasions, soreness, anything that would need some extra attention. Each dog got praise for its work. Almost all of the dogs ran back to their pivots on their own, and I just followed to hook them back up to their chains.

The leaders were usually unhooked last. Nita and Esther were chattering at me as I walked up to them. I kneeled down between them and quickly my face was getting licked in stereo. We'd only gone twenty-four miles and for these two it was just a warm up. I scratched behind both of their heads.

"Good girls, Nita, Esther. You're both champions, aren't you?"

It was mid-December. Training was in full swing. The first race was less than a month away and the whole season was still a possibility. I was feeling optimistic. These two girls and the rest of our team were as fast as anyone else's. We were registered for three races already, the Voyageurs (formerly the White Oak), the Beargrease Marathon and the UP 200. Two weeks after the UP we were going to leave from Grand Marais for Saint Paul. It would be a full season.

"But we're going to need some more snow, girls. It's back to the ATV tomorrow."

When there was not enough snow to run a sled in December I started to worry. "Will there be enough for the races?" We only had four inches on the North Shore and there was less everywhere else. There'd need to be another foot before any races could go off. There was nothing I could do about that part of the equation so I focused on training the dogs, and pathologically checked the weather forecast.

✳

"They've cancelled the Voyageurs' race already. It's still two weeks away but there's no snow over there at all."

Sherri just looked at me. She knew that whatever she said wouldn't make any difference. I just needed to go out and train the dogs. It was New Year's Eve, 2011. We'd had another six inches on the North Shore so I was back on the sled. Nita and Esther were up again as leaders along with a team of big boys: Ace, Tank, Winnie, Jake, Bart, Storm, Cowboy, and Pony. We were going to be going fast but we had new snow. "It'll be fine."

A mile and a half after leaving the yard our trail merged with Trout Lake Road, which was often plowed, sometimes down to the gravel. This was one of those times. To try and save the runners I was running alongside the sled but was tiring fast. After another mile there was a sharp right that took us up the steep, frozen gravel-covered Bogus Hill Road.

"Gee, Esther."

She made the turn no problem and we started the long climb up to the top with me running as much as I could next to the sled.

At the top the trail veered off of the road to the right, then came to a Y. Going right would take us back to the house, about three miles away. I wanted us to go left, over the top of the hill and down the other side where we'd cross the Brule River and do a loop over on the Hovland side.

"Haw, Nita. Haw! Haw, Ester, Nita, haw!"

Instead they took a right. I tried to get the snow hook in but with still only about eight inches total snow on the ground it wouldn't hold and all that dog power took us right, back towards the house. I wasn't going to give up that easily and reached out with the snow hook and hooked a tree.

"Whoa, girls. Whoa!"

Hooking a tree made them all stop abruptly. With Nita and Esther as cheerleaders the whole team was barking and lunging. The six-inch diameter tree I'd hooked was bending over and looked like it was about to break. I quickly ran up and grabbed Nita and Esther. Running back the way we came, I turned the team around. The team just kept running and the snow hook popped off the tree. I jumped on the sled as it came by me. We were travelling full speed down the trail. The Y was approaching quickly and this time I needed the team to take a right so that we could go over the top of the hill and down what we called the Chutes trail which would take us two miles down towards the Brule River. I was standing on the brake as hard as I could as the Y approached.

"Gee! Gee, Nita. Gee!…Gee! Gee!!"

We missed the turn and were gaining speed. I threw the sled down on its side to try and slow the team enough for me to try and catch another tree with the snow hook. At that point the trail was again a road with snow berms on the side. Dragging on top of the tipped over sled, I reached out with the snow hook in my right hand frantically trying to catch a tree, but all were just out of reach. I considered lunging for one but would have to let go of the sled. If I missed, the sled and dogs would be gone, off on their own. I just held on.

The trail merged again with Bogus Hill Road and what was a steep gravel-covered uphill was now an out-of-control downhill bobsled run. With Nita and Esther in lead the team sprinted down the mile-long road towing me behind on the sled tipped on its side. I kept trying to pull myself up onto the sled but it was moving too fast. Each time I'd fall back to where I was, only hanging on with my hands, dragging on my stomach behind. We were on ice-covered gravel, travelling at least twenty-five miles an hour.

"Just don't let go. Don't let go."

And I held on. About half way down the hill my arms started to tremble. I was getting tired. I could also now feel the gravel on my knees. My bibs, actually Sherri's bibs because I'd already destroyed my own, were wearing through. I tried to pick my knees up and drag on my toes. That was too hard, and back down on my stomach and knees I went. I lifted my head enough to see the approaching stop sign. Bogus Hill teed with Trout Lake Road, and we were about to take a ninety-degree turn either left or right. The right hand turn was sharper and since the sled runners were on my right, if we went right I would swing out and crash into the frozen snow bank. We needed to go left so the sled runners would hit first and I'd have a better chance to stay holding on. It was coming fast. This would be it. Either they'd make the left turn, and maybe I'd stay holding on, or they'd turn right and I'd crash hard into the snow bank, with no chance of holding on.

"Haw! Haw, Esther! HAW!"

Waiting till the last second they made the left turn and the sled hit the bank on the right. The sled bounced, I fishtailed behind at twenty-five miles an hour. My left hand slipped off. Only my right hand was holding on…then my fingers, sliding to the very last digit.

I looked at my hand, focused all my attention on it, gripped as tightly as my remaining strength would let me and reached with my left hand. I missed and my hand hit the ground and quickly was dragging behind me again. With my body still fishtailing, I waited and timed the next reach.

"One, two, NOW!" I lunged and caught the handlebar. Both my hands again were on the sled. I took a breath.

Trout Lake Road continued downhill for another quarter mile before it crossed the Kadunce River after which there was then an uphill section. I hoped maybe then they'd slow down enough for me to get back on the sled.

"Hold on, Frank. Hold on. Just a few more seconds."

Over the bridge the team ran and then we began to climb and with all my remaining strength I pulled my knees up under me and flipped the sled back on its runners. One hard pull up on the handlebar and my knees were on the runners. After a deep breath I stood up and immediately put both feet on the brake. We slowed for the first time in two miles, since we were on the top of Bogus Hill only five minutes before.

I looked down at my parka and bib overalls. The dragging had opened up the zipper and exposed the whole front of my (Sherri's) bibs. My bloodied knees were showing through the legs and the pockets and the zipper had ripped off the front. My clothes were packed with snow and gravel but I hadn't let go. If I had, the dogs would be running free, who knew where. They could find their way to a highway, get tangled in the line and drag and maybe get choked. I was tired, sore, and my clothes were shredded, but I breathed a sigh of relief. Disaster was averted. I had planned to run the dogs fifty miles that day but we headed for home. We'd barely make twenty … and I was spent.

When we pulled into the driveway, Sherri came out. "What happened?"

"I've decided that Esther and Nita shouldn't lead together anymore."

It might seem like every time I hooked up my dogs, I got into trouble. That was really not the case. Writing about the runs that go smoothly isn't as much fun. Each season I went on between one hundred fifty and two hundred runs. There were always going to be a few crashes or mishaps of some kind. I often said, "If you hook up a bunch of dogs to a sled you never know what's going to happen."

Snow was limited and came late in winter 2011/12. That meant that most of the runs I went on were on hard icy trails where trying to steer and use the brake for the sled was far more challenging. Now some mushers would just say, "It's too dangerous. I'm going to wait for more snow." Or, "Just run smaller teams." Either of those options would mean less training and fewer miles. I always assumed my competition was training and therefore that I needed to also.

The night after getting dragged down Bogus Hill—New Year's Eve, 2011—it snowed about eight inches, the most we'd had yet that year. The bad news was that only the North Shore got much snow. Duluth only got a dusting. The Beargrease was at risk of being cancelled. For our Sled-Dogs-to-Saint-Paul, what we were calling the planned trip to the Capitol, planning groups were meeting. Rallies were getting planned with music, Native American drumming, speakers, media. Everyone kept asking me: "What are you gonna do if it doesn't snow?"

"Oh, it'll snow. We've got a lot of time left. But don't worry, we're going no matter what. I'll run all the way on concrete if I have to."

Privately I was thinking, "It had better snow."

Adam and I were having coffee with Dave and Amy Freeman, talking about their planned trip from Ely. They guide for Paul Schurke, who has travelled across Greenland and all sorts of remote places, often times over miles of rock and hard ice.

"Dave, how do you guys do that without trashing your sled runners?"

"Paul has had extra thick and wide plastic made for our sleds. I'll ask, but I'm sure he'll let you have a set."

Between the heavy-duty plastic and extra five hundred dog booties we'd ordered, we could literally run all the way without snow…if we absolutely had to…I thought, maybe. At least I could tell people that we had it covered and I hoped they'd believe me.

There was another growing issue. I was sick. What had started as a sinus infection was getting worse. My normal routine of a handful of ibuprofen and more coffee was only just keeping me moving. I was always tired, coughing, and moving slowly. I kept trying to ignore it, hoping that it would go away, that everything would be fine.

"Frank, I made an appointment for you to see the doctor tomorrow at 12:30. You've got to go."

"That's right in the middle of the day. How am I supposed to get a run in?" The look on Sherri's face let me know she was very concerned. "OK, I'll run at night tomorrow then." She didn't say anything and walked away.

"Frank, you have pneumonia again. You really need some rest... but I guess that's out of the question."

Dr. Terrill was a former musher and knew that getting me to take a day off from training in January was impossible. So he prescribed a potent antibiotic and a steroid to help it work on my lungs.

"Good luck," was all he said when I left.

The prednisone made me feel better for a few days but the pneumonia stayed with me. I made sure to act as though I was fine whenever I was around Sherri. She didn't say anything about it but suspected that I wasn't getting any better. It was all I could do to get out of bed and then just power through the day with my pain relievers and coffee, crashing into bed every night, coughing myself to sleep.

Between the first of January and the first of March, when we were planning to leave for Saint Paul, we had signed up for three races. The Voyageurs was already cancelled and even the Beargrease was at risk. It had only been cancelled one time in its twenty-five-year history. The Beargrease Board was considering their options: reschedule for March, have the race start in Two Harbors, or cancel. When asked, I gave them a status report on the snow conditions on the north end of the Beargrease Trail but other than that there was nothing I could do but train the team on what soon again became hard, fast, icy trails.

The only time that I didn't feel sick was when I was holding onto the sled for dear life. The excitement of it, the adrenaline rush, kept me from thinking about my pneumonia. It never dawned on me that being sick was having anything to do with my performance on the sled. "At least I'll have a lot of material to write about," I thought after hitting another tree and wondering if I should buy a helmet.

The Mail Run (photo by Mark Tessier)

Chapter 28

"Sherri, the Beargrease has been cancelled."

"What? Why? Can't they reschedule or start up in Two Harbors? I'm sorry, honey."

It had been almost two years since we first ran the Beargrease Marathon and barely finished. The next year was almost a disaster after our dogs got so sick. I'd thought about that race every day since and hoped this year would be our chance to make it right. It wasn't to be. My mind first jumped to anger. I had been focused on that race for a full three years, and now I'd have to wait one more to exercise those demons. There was no relief in knowing that I would get a reprieve from the long training runs.

"Why can't they just reschedule for March or move the start further north. It's not all about Duluth!"

It was the morning of January 16. I put on all my mushing clothes and went outside to water the dogs. I felt so defeated, completely powerless and exhausted. I stumbled out to the dog yard. They all were just as excited to see me, to eat, and to run as they were every morning. They had no idea that there wouldn't be a Beargrease. I stuffed my list of the dogs that were going to train that day back into my pocket. It was time to have some fun and take out our puppies.

Once sled training started in the winter, the puppies—yearlings really—didn't get as many runs in. While most of the rest of the dogs had been training hard and had various nagging injuries or soreness to show for it, the puppies were wound up and ready to go. After harnessing up our most reliable leaders, Acorn and Fly, I hooked up Bacon, Pork Chop, Pepper, Popcorn, Ruby, and Ginger. Several chewed necklines later we left the yard, dogs jumping all over each other as we haltingly made our way down the trail. It was a perfect fifteen-degree day. Soon I was laughing at the show in front of me.

After I got home from the puppy run I went into town and called Odin. He and Betsy Jorgenson were mushers who lived near us. Odin grew up mushing near Grand Marais, and his dad Arleigh was one of the original Beargrease mushers.

"I can't believe they called it off. The trails on this end are fine. What if we try to pull off a race up here on the Beargrease weekend?"

Odin responded, "We gotta try and do something. It sucks that we're stuck with a decision made down in Duluth. Jack Stone called me and asked if we were going to try to do something. We've only got two weeks."

I said I'd call Jack and see if he was interested in helping. Jack Stone was the owner of Stone Harbor Wilderness Supply in Grand Marais. I had worked for him for a year setting up his outing and gear-rental programs. We'd butted heads often, but he was a real doer.

"Hey Jack, it's Frank. I just got off the phone with Odin. We want to try and pull off a shorter race on the Beargrease weekend. He said you might be willing to help."

"When I heard it was cancelled I thought the same thing. You and Odin will have to figure out if we can pull it off. Let me know. I'll do anything I can to make it happen."

From that point on nobody that we asked for help said no. The Grand Marais area has a long, storied mushing tradition. Many of the greatest mushers ever have lived or still live there. Before the

John Beargrease Sled Dog Marathon there was the Gunflint Mail Run, which in the seventies left from downtown Grand Marais and traveled up and down the Gunflint Trail. In the early eighties that race was absorbed into the Beargrease, with an organization based in Duluth. Grand Marais and Gunflint Trail area volunteers were still called upon to mark, groom, and provide safety for the north end of the trail. This didn't always sit well with the seasoned volunteers, many of whom predated the Beargrease. Now that the Beargrease was cancelled, those same volunteers were more than willing to put on a local race.

It was decided that the resurrected Gunflint Mail Run would leave Devil's Track Landing on Monday afternoon, January 30, do a loop near Gunflint Lake, and layover that night for six hours at Trail Center. Trail Center was the historic heart of the Beargrease, being the unofficial halfway point where mushers, handlers, and fans always mingled, reveling in the mood and excitement of the race. The teams would then leave Trail Center and retrace the route back to Devil's Track, finishing on Tuesday morning, after a total distance of one hundred twenty miles.

On a cloudy Monday afternoon in January, nineteen sled dog teams and a couple of hundred volunteers and spectators gathered on the lake at Devil's Track Landing to celebrate winter and the North Shore mushing tradition. There was minimal prize money and only the local media, but that was just fine. We had a race, our first of the year, and it had only been two weeks since the night we'd heard the Beargrease was cancelled.

Jack was the self-appointed master of ceremonies and stood in front of the teams at the start, hands in the air and leading the countdown.

"Five, four, three, two, one, GOOOOOO!!" and the first two teams, Odin's and Thea Schneider's left the starting chute. Apparently Jack didn't know how fast the teams would be going and didn't get out of the way in time and got tripped up as the teams went racing by. After rolling to a stop he got up stunned, then smiled and everyone laughed. It was that kind of day, where everything about winter, and where we lived, was good. We came together to be a part of something that was more about tradition than competition, an impromptu reclaiming of celebrations passed.

The race, such as it was, quickly shaped up to be between the two local mushers responsible for putting it on, me and Odin. My twelve dogs blazed the sixty miles into Trail Center in just over five hours. Odin was only a few minutes behind.

"I'm going to just try and hold on to second." Odin said to me.

I knew better. Odin's strategy is usually to start out slower, come from behind. Mine is the opposite. I like to start fast and try and hold that pace. We were essentially tied.

"Time to get up, Frank."

Sherri had stuck her head inside the car where I'd laid down to get some rest. I lay in my sleeping bag, coughing. It took a minute for me to remember where I was. I struggled outside and felt a mist in the air. The temperature had risen to almost freezing and a light rain/snow mix was falling. "Sherri, the dogs are gonna get warm, I wonder if we should even boot em."

"It's a long run, sixty miles, to go without booties. If their feet get sore it'll be tough to get em back in time for the UP."

She was right. It was the first race of the year and all twelve of these dogs would likely be lining up in Marquette for the UP 200 in only two weeks. Booties protected the dogs' feet but did slow them down some, especially when it was warm. Sure I didn't want Odin to catch me but I really didn't have the energy to argue and decided to just agree, be cautious, something I rarely was.

"OK, we'll boot em all."

I took a handful of ibuprofen, chugged a large coffee, and got ready for the run back to Devil's Track.

Just after two in the morning we brought our team down to the starting line. The bonfire was still going on Poplar Lake. After hooking down, I signed the time sheet and walked up to the front of the team. There was Sherri. She gave me her familiar loving smile. I kissed her and then turned to our dogs, our beautiful, amazing dogs, here for another year of racing, ready to give it everything they had one more time. I worked my way down the row, the leaders Bart and Storm, and Nita, Wolf, Gnasher, Winnie, Tank, Ace, Pony, Cowboy, Ben, and Tina. I praised them all, and as I stood back on the sled I was overwhelmed with the gratitude of being the one who was there that night on the back of that sled.

Odin caught us half way back to Devil's Track. The night continued to warm up and the trail softened. For miles I'd seen the light of his headlamp behind me. My dogs were getting warm so I stopped them to give them a chance to cool down. Odin passed with his team and I saw that none of his dog were wearing boots.

"Hey, Odin. You can lead now."

"So I'm going to break trail, huh?"

We were playing games with each other. His team was travelling faster than mine and I knew it. It wasn't clear to Odin, though, if I was sandbagging or not, so maybe I could catch him later. I hoped my dogs would save energy by chasing his, then be able to catch him at the end, but I doubted it. I wanted to keep him guessing, though. Maybe having the boots on was making my dogs too warm to run very fast but I was going to stick with the plan and keep them on. If we were going to be competitive at the UP, the dogs would all have to be one hundred percent. I watched Odin slowly pull away. At first I started kicking, thinking that I needed to try and keep up.

"Let's go, Stormy. Let's go, Bart."

The dogs surged and we stayed close behind. Once I stopped kicking and calling up the dogs, they slowed a bit and the gap between our teams grew. I looked down at my dogs and watched them run. They were giving it all they had, and I knew then we weren't going to catch Odin. He slowly pulled away from us and I relaxed into the run. It was warm and foggy, just before first light. All I could see was the tunnel of light from my headlamp that my dogs were running through. The story of the race played in my head. We'd pulled this thing off in only two weeks. It had brought local volunteers and businesses together and played off of the mushing heritage of the area. The story would conclude with Odin, the next generation of one of the North Shore's original mushing families, winning.

I smiled to myself. We had always finished well ahead of Odin. Our relationship and conversations had always had that tone, too; me telling him what I thought, more than the other way around; Odin making jokes about hoping one of his females accidentally was bred to Wolf or Winnie. Things had changed. He was leading now and we couldn't catch up. It actually felt like I wasn't supposed to win, as hard as I might have been trying, as if there was a bigger plan for this race, for my dog team, for me. It was as if we were part of a story that had already been written.

We came out onto Devil's Track Lake and I saw that Odin wasn't too far ahead of us. I called up the dogs one more time.

"Come on, Stormy. Let's go, Bart."

They picked it up a little. In the distance I saw Odin turn around then begin kicking. He must have called up his dogs too. Then the fog settled in thick again and he disappeared. I knew he wasn't going to slow down enough for me to catch him. He had the fastest team on that day, the last in January, 2012. Thirteen members of his family, some that had travelled a long way to be there, all celebrated as Odin emerged first from the fog on Devil's Track Lake. The Jorgenson's family tradition of mushing was going to live on in Grand Maris.

A few minutes later we came out of the fog and arrived at the Landing. Sherri and Lisa were waiting, along with another hundred handlers, volunteers and spectators. I heard Sherri above them all.

"Come here, Stormy, Bart. Come on, punkins."

I was always happy to see Sherri at the end of a run and looked forward to it. Often it was what got me through a run that was tough. But that morning the end of the run came too soon. It felt like the dogs and I were going somewhere that we hadn't gotten to yet, that I'd been woken from a foggy dream and found myself at the Devil's Track Landing. In spite of my pneumonia and exhaustion, I wanted to get back out on the trail, to keep racing.

⁂

I spent the day after the mail run in bed. "I'm just tired from not getting any sleep." Sherri knew better but didn't say anything.

The next day I decided to give the dogs another day off so that Adam and I could drive down to Duluth to see if and how I'd be able to run a sled dog team through the city. The map showed a snowmobile route all the way through town, but there were sections that ran along and across highways. We needed to go down and see for ourselves what we would be dealing with. It was theoretically possible that we could run the dogs the whole way. With enough planning and volunteers we could cross any obstacle, but our time and resources would be limited. Our full-time handling crew would be only three, Adam, Mark, and Jerry.

"A lot of roads to cross, Adam, and we'll be doing it in the middle of the afternoon."

We parked the car on the side of US Highway 53 and got out to look at the snowmobile trail crossing. Our conversation turned to yelling over the sound of the traffic.

"We'll just have to run them across. Stop in the median like the snowmobiles do."

I yelled back: "The median's not wide enough to stop a ten-dog team." I looked behind me at the snowless trail, the highway, the median and tried to picture my dog team there. The thought terrified me. I got back in the car, shaking my head.

"It has to snow or there will be no way to stop, anywhere."

For the rest of the afternoon we drove around Duluth, scouting the trail and taking notes. We talked less and less as the immensity of our task, to get a sled dog team safely through the Duluth metro area, sank in. Our final stop was Lester Park, where I would drive the team into a rally and where we hoped to make our first major media splash.

Adam looked around. "There's no snow here either."

"We've got plenty of time."

I doubted my own optimism. There were still six weeks before we planned to leave Grand Marais, but this winter was proving to be a dry one. It was the middle of January and the only place in Minnesota that had any snow was the hills up the North Shore, where we lived. Down in Duluth it looked like it was still November, leafless trees, frozen, but no snow anywhere.

"There's the trail."

My eyes found the steep downhill trail that led to the park where the rally would be. Adam and I climbed the trail, which was covered with rocks, some as large as basketballs. I thought of driving a ten-dog team down the steep rock-covered trail, combined with crossing highways, there not being any snow, and a doubt first crept into the back of my mind. After a quick shake of my head: "It's gonna be tough but we can do it. I know we can."

Adam didn't say anything. I hoped he believed me. Any doubts I had I was trying to keep to myself. My outward confidence was critical to keep everyone else going. There was a lot to plan, the rallies along the way, the arrival at the Capitol, all of it.

"Frank, there's no snow." "That's a heck of a long way." "Are you sure you can make it?"

I always responded with a confident: "We'll get there. I guarantee it." I was putting it all on the line, my word, my dogs, myself. I was sick and just hoping by some miracle that I'd be well enough, that there'd be snow, that somehow the dogs and I would arrive at the Capitol in Saint Paul on March 8, at 11:05 a.m., only five weeks away.

Ace, Pony, and Bart (photo by Mark Tessier)

Chapter 29

Even with the immensity of the trip to Saint Paul hanging over us, we still planned to run one more race in February, the UP 200. Our annual trip to Marquette had become a kind of homecoming for Sherri and me. Our host family, Phil and Patty, had become close friends, and we had many supporters who stopped by to see us during the race. I was looking forward to focusing on a race, after all the worry and planning for the Saint Paul trip.

If there was going to be snow anywhere in the United States, it was the Upper Peninsula of Michigan, but the dry winter of 2012 was even affecting the UP. The normal downtown Marquette start was moved twenty miles away to Chatham, where there was plenty of snow up in the hills away from Lake Superior.

Sherri had to drive most of the way to Michigan because I was too sick. I woke up the morning of the race at our host family's house with a fit of coughing. After powering through the morning's dog feeding, we drove in for the race vet checks which were part of the show and open to the public. I did my best to be pleasant and talk to the race fans, but I was on fumes.

Our friend and handler Donna met us at the vet check. She could tell immediately Sherri and I weren't our normal happy talkative selves. She quickly busied herself greeting the dogs and helping out the vets and vet techs with checking over the dogs. They were all in great shape, and all of their feet were in perfect condition.

"Your team looks good, Frank." That was as much of a compliment as I ever remember getting from the vet crew.

"Thanks, Kathy." And a smile was all I could say in return.

At the UP 200 there were eight veterinarians, a dozen vet techs and not a single human medical professional. They were there solely for the sake of the dogs, to protect, advocate for, and take care of them. The joke is if there were an accident, the vets would all rush to care for the dogs. The mushers would be on their own.

As soon as the vets gave our last dog the OK, I collapsed into the passenger seat of the truck. Sherri got in after saying a few thank yous and good byes.

"Look at you. How are you going to stay up all night tonight running the dogs? The checkpoint in Wetmore is unassisted. I won't be there to help. I'm calling your doctor."

I dozed while Sherri made a few phone calls.

"OK, your prescriptions are going to be waiting for us at the Target pharmacy. Let's go."

Soon I was sitting in Target with my head in my hands, waiting for the pharmacist to fill another dose of antibiotics and prednisone.

"Your insurance card doesn't work," I heard the pharmacist say to Sherri.

"How much is it?" she asked.

"Twenty-eight dollars."

Sherri paid, opened the bottles and handed me some pills. "Take these." Then she gave me her water bottle.

Back in the truck we were on the way to the musher luncheon. I drifted in and out of sleep. Sherri didn't say anything while driving us there. After a quick appearance and dropping off our checkpoint drop box—my supplies for the unassisted checkpoint—Sherri drove me back to our host family's house so I could lie down. We had four hours before we needed to be at the race start. I would sleep for as much of that time as possible. There was really no question as to whether I was going to race or not. With only two races this year, scratching wasn't an option.

It seemed my head had just hit the pillow when Sherri shook me awake. I sat on the edge of the bed and then, on autopilot, put my mushing clothes on, as I'd done a thousand times before. We thanked Phil and Patty.

"Are you sure you're OK?" The concern in Patty's eyes was obvious.

"I'll be fine. It's just another run."

↕

Twenty-four teams, with twelve dogs each, were at the Chatham start on that February night. Maybe it was the prednisone or maybe the excitement of the race, but I wasn't thinking about being sick. We were in race mode, and our team was as good as any there. We had all veterans. Wolf and Ajax would start in lead followed by Bart, Storm, Nita, Gnasher, Tina, Winnie, Ace, Tank, Cowboy, and Pony. The worries about lack of snow, was there even going to be trail, a race, were all behind us. We were now racing, what we'd been training for at least five months.

We were the seventh team out and by fifteen miles into the race had passed all the teams that started ahead of us. For the first time we were leading the UP 200. Wolf and Ajax had led this leg the year before and they seemed to remember the way. I often didn't see the trail markers until after the dogs made the turn. It had started to snow, so any excitement I may have had by being in front was doused by the worry of staying on the correct trail.

"Dammit, where's the crossing?"

The snow was falling harder. The trail came out of the woods and paralleled Highway 28. I was having trouble seeing where the trail went. We arrived first at the Wetmore checkpoint and as we approached what I thought was the highway crossing, there were no crossing guards. It was after midnight and even though it was a busy highway, I didn't see any approaching cars, so continued across. As we reached the other side, volunteers with flashlights ran out to the trail to guide us into the checkpoint. I quickly forgot the danger of an unmanned highway crossing and tried to brake my charging team. We had only travelled thirty miles since the start and they weren't even close to tired.

"Whoa. Whoa!" They dragged the sled past the race officials before a group of volunteers arrived to help me stop the dogs.

"Sign here, Frank, Nice run. Remember, you have to stay and rest your dogs here at least three hours."

"Rest em? Are you kidding?"

The team dragged me and four volunteers into the campground, that served as the Wetmore checkpoint, and through the campsite that was my designated rest spot.

"Whoa. Whoa. OK we gotta back em up." The dogs were barking and lunging like we were at the start of a race leg, not the end. I quickly jumped off and unhooked all of their tuglines, limiting their power.

"OK, let's back em up!" and we pulled the team back into the campsite. I pulled ropes out of the sled and tied the team to nearby trees and began my checkpoint routine of taking off booties, putting down straw and feeding, except none of the dogs were ready to rest. After only thirty miles they would eat, but that was it. Instead of lying down they barked, played, and chewed.

"This is going to be a long three hours."

The snow fell harder and all of my gear quickly was covered. I spent the next three hours trying to keep the dogs from chewing themselves free of the gangline. By the time the three hours had passed, four inches of snow had fallen, and it wasn't letting up. I looked around the checkpoint and saw that nobody was getting ready to leave. Even though all of our teams were well rested, nobody wanted to leave first and break trail in the deep snow. All the front group of teams slowly put on our dogs' booties, putzed with gear and kept an eye on each other. Finally after four hours David Gill, a Michigan musher, pulled the hook and headed for the starting line. I followed along with several others right behind me: Nathan Schroeder, Troy Groenvold, Ryan Anderson, Andrew Letzring and Martin Koenig. The race again was on, and the snow continued to fall, only harder.

I left with my two best snow leaders, Wolf and Ajax, in front. The wind was straight off Lake Superior and the lake-effect snow made it impossible to see the leaders. The snow was so hard that my headlamp turned the whole world white and I had to take it off and hold it down to my side, shining it at the side of the trail to be sure we were still on it. Often only the two wheel dogs were visible. It was times like that that I really marveled at the dogs. Where we see the world mostly with our eyes, they have a multi-dimensional view, feeling the trail ahead with their feet, smelling the team ahead, even hearing the subtle differences between the trail and the surrounding woods. We stayed on the trail and didn't even slow down that much. Soon I could no longer see David's trail ahead of me. I wondered if he had gotten off the trail, or maybe I had.

Out of the corner of my eye I caught sight of another trail marker. We were on the trail. I hoped David still was but was helpless to do anything about it if he wasn't. Times like that mushers are on their own and completely dependent upon their dogs. Mine were running strong, seemingly oblivious to the whiteout. Time seemed to go on and on. I wasn't sure if I'd been on the trail for one or five hours. Seeing only white and getting tired, I began to get dizzy. The vertigo came and went. I held onto the sled as tight as I could, afraid I was going to fall off the side.

Out of a stupor I became aware of a slight lightening of the sky above. It created the sense that we were running through a canyon with the trees next to the trail being the canyon walls.

"The sun must be coming up."

I pulled up my sleeve with my mouth and shined my headlamp on my watch.

"Seven o'clock. We've been on the trail for six hours. We must be getting close to the checkpoint."

Grand Marais, Michigan, was the halfway point, and I became aware that the trail was on the long descent out of the hills towards the shore of Lake Superior. There still was no sign of David's team. The headlamp was of no use, so I turned it off. Through the snow I watched the shadows of my dog team in the snowstorm at dawn, and ever so slowly the snow-covered world lightened up around me. It was still difficult to look ahead because of the heavy snow blowing into my eyes, but with one mitt over my face I was finally able to see. The trail came out onto the gravel road outside of Grand Marais, and I recognized the trail. We were only a couple of miles from the checkpoint. The dogs knew it too and picked up the pace the rest of the way to town, knowing that Sherri, food, and their beds were waiting.

"Did David make it in?"

"Yeah, he just got here, maybe five minutes ago."

Sherri looked at me, covered head to toe in snow. "Are you OK? I was so worried. It was snowing so hard we had to pull the truck over on the way. We just got here."

David Gill had only been five minutes ahead of me and it was snowing so hard that I never saw his trail, but my dogs must have known he was just ahead. I wondered what his dogs were following. It was time for a rest. The dogs and I were now very hungry and tired.

In spite of being awake all night, it was always hard for me to sleep during the day at a checkpoint. The Grand Marais checkpoint was a celebration of the UP 200. Hundreds of race fans and volunteers were everywhere, and they all wanted to talk about the race. I was tired but it was daylight, and after Sherri and I took care of the dogs, I went into the checkpoint to get some food and to find a place to lie down. Walking felt like I weighed five hundred pounds, every step a chore. The pneumonia wasn't getting better, but at least it didn't seem to be getting any worse either.

"It must be the prednisone," I thought. "Thank God for modern pharmacy."

Lying down on the floor of a small library room I tried to sleep, but my mind stayed out on the trail and with the dogs. Five hours after we arrived, and no sleep later, I was back out with Sherri getting the dogs ready for the trip back to Wetmore.

"I'll be fine, Sherri. I can sleep at Wetmore. It'll be dark there."

"OK." She looked skeptical. "Take care of our babies. Don't forget to eat." And we were off for the second half of the race.

We left in third place. David Gill, from Michigan, and Ryan Anderson, the last two years' champion, left ahead of us. With two of our fastest leaders, Bart and Storm, in front, we raced out of town. We knew our team was as good as anyone's there, and we were in the race to win.

The race had been lengthened from previous years by adding a five-mile loop to the Grand Marais-to-Wetmore leg. The new section of trail was up on a high scenic plateau which we had travelled the night before in the snowstorm. This time we reached it at sunset and I was captivated by the glorious colors of the clouds, forests, and meadows at the end of the day. My team was running hard, in perfect form and I fell into a trance, watching them. Fatigue took hold, and soon I was in that zone between being awake and asleep.

In the twilight I saw a dog team approaching from the other direction. At first I thought it was a dream; then I snapped out of my stupor and saw that it was Troy Groenvold.

"Hey, Troy. Are you turning back? You're going the wrong way!"

He had a look of shock on his face. "What? What?" and he went past us.

I turned and looked at his team disappear down the trail.

"I wonder what's up with Troy. Maybe something's wrong with his team?" His look of confusion confirmed that he doubted that he was going the right way. Later I found out that he had just turned around after taking a wrong turn and wasn't sure if he was back on the trail or not.

After another five minutes I saw a second team coming. The tall musher I soon recognized.

"Hey, Andrew. Aren't you going the wrong way?"

"No Frank, you are."

"I AM?"

"Look at the trail markers! They're supposed to be on the left!"

I was fully awake now as I watched Andrew and his team also disappear behind me. It sank in that he was right. In my stupor I had missed a turn but had no idea where. The rules are clear. If a team leaves the trail it has to go back to the exact spot where they left it and begin again at that spot. So I had two choices, either turn around and try and find the spot or follow Troy and Andrews' trails until I recognized where I had already been then turn around. I quickly decided the latter, hoping I would be able to stay on the trail.

After only a few minutes my choice was confirmed as I passed a remote race officials' table. They were positioned at places on the race trail to radio teams' progress and to be sure that every team ran the entire trail.

"Hey, I made a mistake and have to go back," I yelled as I passed four people with clipboards and confused looks on their faces.

After another few miles the trail teed with the main trail again and I saw one set of tracks that missed the turn. They were obviously mine. I could legally turn around there. We turned around and wanted to make up for lost time so I called up the dogs.

"Let's go, Stormy. Let's go, Bart."

They picked up the pace and in only a few minutes we were back at the official race table. I put the snow hook in to stop and to tell them what happened. The team popped the hook and I quickly stamped it back in. A woman stood on it with one foot and another on the sled runner to help me keep the team stopped while we quickly talked.

"OK. No problem, Frank."

"Thanks." And I grabbed the snow hook.

"Let's go!" We took off a little too fast for the woman on my sled and she fell off sideways into the snow.

"Sorry!" I waved and looked back to see that woman was now running after my sled. I looked down and between my right hand and the handlebar was her mitten. I grabbed it and threw it in the air. I looked back to see her pick it up and wave. I waved again, too.

The missed turn cost us at least a half hour, probably more. It was now dark. No moon and a star-filled sky. All twelve dogs were loping. We now had four teams to catch. All of my senses were totally awake and focused on the run, the dogs and the race. I still felt like hell but didn't care. For the next two hours we didn't see another team but I started hearing barking in the distance. I kept expecting to see a team tied off on the side of the trail, stopped. Dogs don't usually bark when they're running.

"Maybe we're close to a house with dogs tied out," I thought, but the barking stayed in the distance.

We rounded a corner and down a straightaway I saw a dog team. The dogs were running AND barking at the same time. I'd never heard that before. Eventually we caught the team and it was Andrew's. I drew up close behind.

"What's up with your dogs? Do they always bark like that?

"Hey, Frank. Yeah, they never shut up. It's driving me crazy."

We passed on his left and the barking got louder. Andrew's dogs didn't like being passed and they tailed us all the way into Wetmore, barking. We had spent a lot of energy catching up to and passing Andrew and didn't have enough left to separate from his team. Most of my dogs ignored his, except Nita. She kept barking back. Usually I revel in the quiet of the trail during races, especially at night. That night I laughed all the way back to Wetmore. It was better than beating myself up for the mistake that could cost us the race.

The trail into Marquette was still not safe to travel, so the race had us again return to Grand Marais to finish. In spite of our lost time we would leave Wetmore for the final leg in third place. Sherri was optimistic, but I was worried that I had tired the dogs with the added miles and pressing them to try and make up for the lost time. Gnasher and Tank both had slack tuglines on the way into Wetmore and to be cautious we had the vets mark them out. They'd ride in the truck back to Grand Marais.

While I readied the remaining ten dogs to leave, I saw that they weren't acting tired at all. I was, and popped another prednisone, a handful of ibuprofen and chugged a big mug of coffee. This was the race we had focused our training and planning on. I was prepared to leave everything on the trail.

Nita started the barking and by the time we had them all bootied the whole team was up, howling and banging into their harnesses to go. Nita and Bart would lead the final leg.

"Look at Bart and Nita!" Sherri yelled over the barking. "They're frothing at the mouth."

Our dogs had watched Ryan, then David, leave ahead of us and were crazy to chase. They obviously knew it was a race, and wanted to win. Two other teams, Martin Koening's and Nathan Schroeder's, would start just minutes after ours but my mind and eyes were only looking forward.

Is was below zero when we left just after three in the morning. There was no wind and for hours all I heard were quiet footfalls of my dogs' bootied feet and the occasional slight jingle of the snaps on their collars. Four hours into the run my dogs hadn't yet even broken into a trot. They were loping, running hard all the way.

There was a long straight uphill on the trail to the plateau two thirds of the way back to Grand Marias. In the distance I could see the faint light of a headlamp. The dogs knew before I did that the next team was close ahead and continued their lope up to the top of the plateau.

"This might be our year, puppies. We could win this one."

Once we crested the top the snow softened. The team ahead was no longer visible and the dogs slowed to a trot. We were still at least twenty miles from the finish. The dogs were tired and just like that my dream of catching the teams ahead vanished. Immediately my mind flashed back to earlier that night, the mistake that cost us so much time and energy. My own exhaustion caused me to relax back on the runners, hang my head just a bit. Quickly I shook my head, to say "No" to the self-doubt. The dogs keyed off of me, and I couldn't show my disappointment. I called up the dogs, knowing now the two teams close behind would have a chance to catch us.

"Let's go, Nita. Come on, Bart."

In the soft snow Bart's line went slack. Last night's sprint into Wetmore was showing up. I was now running and kicking behind the sled, on all but the steepest downhills.

"Maybe a short break and a quick snack will help."

On the other side of the plateau, I hooked down and grabbed the bag of snacks and tossed them all a small chunk of frozen water and dog food. Everyone ate it immediately, most catching it out of the air. In less than sixty seconds we were back on the trail.

In a race you can feel a dog team on your heels, and I knew the next team, probably Martin from Montana, was right behind me. On the next short straightaway I quickly turned my head between kicks and there he was, gaining fast.

"Trail."

I had to slow my team to let him pass.

It's really not a bad thing to get passed by a team that's moving faster because your team will usually pick up its pace a bit to give chase. To give us a boost I quickly hooked down and switched leaders, putting Wolf in lead with Nita. Soon we caught up to Martin and stayed within a hundred yards of him. We didn't have enough left, though, to catch and pass him.

"We can still finish fourth, puppies. That's the best we've ever done here. Let's go!"

On the outskirts of Grand Marais the trail dumped out onto a long gravel road. It was a gradual uphill before the final drop into the town on the edge of Lake Superior. We were still tailing Martin. At the top of the hill, I looked back. Another team exited the trail onto the road. Nathan was less than a minute behind us with two miles to go. They were moving fast.

"Let's go, Nita! Come on, Wolfie!"

I ran and kicked with all I had. Nathan's voice calling up his dogs was now a constant sound behind me. At a sprint we hit a steep downhill chute that dropped the trail onto the neighborhood streets of Grand Marais. I stumbled at the bottom, regained my footing, and looked behind to see Nathan's leaders at my heels, trying to pass.

Now in "No Mans Land" I didn't have to give up the trail and we sprinted neck and neck through town.

"Gee, Nita, Gee!"

She tried to cut the last corner onto the straightaway that was the last two blocks to the finish line. Nathan's leaders got there inches before and now had us by a nose.

"Let's go!" I tried to be heard over the deafening screams of the crowd lining the street. It was an all-out sprint to the finish. The dogs running too fast for us to run, both Nathan and I kicked and yelled with everything we had left. His lead grew from a nose to a dog's length.

"Come on, Nita! Wolfie!" came Sherri's screaming voice over the crowd.

We again grew even with a hundred feet to go.

"Come on now. Let's go!" Nathan's booming voice was next to me.

Out of the corner of my eye I saw his red snow suit, slowly, inch by inch, ease ahead of me. The finish line banner came up over our heads and we passed under.

Nathan had caught us for fourth place. Martin was at the finish line only seconds ahead of us in third. We all collapsed on our handlebars. The crowd swarmed our dog teams. My dogs, who had only seconds before been running with all they had, were now cowering at the onslaught of human attention. I looked up to see Sherri in front, holding the leaders. Exhausted, I still wanted to praise the dogs, be with just them and Sherri, away from the excitement and the scene of the race.

"Sherri! Let's take em to the truck."

She nodded.

"Let's go."

With Sherri running in front, I rode the sled for another hundred yards through the checkpoint, behind our incredible dogs, back to the truck. They had given it all and were due a big meal and a long rest. We couldn't have been more proud of them. In spite of being asked to make up for my mistake of missing the trail the night before, they finished with the race leaders. I continued to be the weak link of the team. Not being able to stay healthy or stay on the race trail cost us a chance to win the race.

After hooking the dogs up around the truck and praising them all, I got their food ready while Sherri and Donna went around taking off their booties and harnesses.

"Need anything, Frank?" It was one of the race vets.

"I don't think so, Phil. Thanks. They all seem fine."

"They look great," he said, as he walked around the truck looking at all the dogs.

The rush from the race finish was wearing off, and in its place was pneumonia. After going around and giving all the dogs seconds, I almost fell to the ground between Wolf and Nita. Nita gave me a few rapid licks and Wolf leaned against me. They turned and barked. Another team was being led to the truck next to us. It was Troy, whose wrong turn also cost him valuable race time. He had an excuse though, it was his rookie UP 200 run. This was our third time at the race and I shook my head, feeling like I let the team down one more time. Nita licked my face again. She looked like I could harness her up and she'd turn around and take the team back to Wetmore.

"Next year, Nita. We'll have another chance. I won't screw up here again. I promise."

When Sherri and Donna were done massaging them all, we loaded the dogs into the truck. In spite of being so sick and tired, having been edged out at the end of the race, I couldn't have been more proud of our dogs. The race veterinarians agreed with us and awarded our team the Tom Cooley award for the best cared for and trained dog team. I cried receiving it, knowing that the care we gave the dogs during the year and the race was far more important than whether or not I made wrong turns on the trail.

Our next trip began in only nine days, and it would be all the way from Grand Marais, Minnesota, to the Capitol in Saint Paul. It would require not only the very best dog care but perfect navigation. Beyond exhausted, sitting in the passenger seat on the way home from Michigan, I prayed to have the strength to make the trip. The dogs would be up to it but would I?

I woke up in the truck to the barking of the dogs that had been left at home.

"We're home, finally." Sherri paused, hands on the steering wheel before getting out of the truck. It was after midnight and we had work to do before we could get to bed ourselves. Lisa stumbled out of the house, putting on her jacket, her headlamp on sideways, shining off into the woods. She had stayed at the house taking care of the rest of the kennel. The three of us unloaded the dogs and the wet gear. I hung it all up in the cabin and got a fire going while Sherri put together a quick dinner that I don't remember eating.

The next morning Sherri and Lisa took care of the dogs. My constant coughing and fever kept me in bed where, when awake, I worried about the dogs and how we were going to get to Saint Paul. On the way home I had talked to both Mark and Adam who reported that there was no snow at all on the trails south of Two Harbors. We planned to leave in eight days from downtown Grand Marais. Down there by the lake it looked like October just after the last leaves had fallen. Looking out my own window I saw only ice-crusted snow. I climbed out of bed long enough to sit at my computer and look at the National Weather Service forecast. There was a thirty percent chance of snow that weekend. It was Wednesday. I looked up two more weather forecasts. The Weather Channel predicted a fifty percent chance. I liked that one better, turned off the computer and went back to bed.

The next morning Sherri had to go to work. "Stay in bed today. I'll take care of dogs when I get home."

As soon as she drove off I was up staggering around the kitchen. After a couple cups of coffee, a piece of toast, and handful of ibuprofen, I put on my mushing clothes and went out to water the dogs. Afterwards, I walked over to the dog truck. My sled was still tied to the top and I stood staring at it for a few minutes. I didn't remember tying it up there after the race.

"Maybe Sherri put it up there."

After a deep breath I climbed up on top of the truck, undid the sled and lowered it to the ground. Jessie was barking, as he always did when I was up on the truck. The rest of the team joined in. We all knew that I was going to take some of them out for a run, regardless of how I felt or what Sherri said. Nine of our racing dogs hadn't made the trip to the UP. Most of those were going to be taking me to Saint Paul in eight days but hadn't run in ten. Struggling, one dog at a time, I hooked up nine dogs.

"Let's go!" as I pulled the hook. It was more a statement of fact than a command as they were out of the yard before I was done saying it. With Acorn and Fly in the lead we pinballed down the icy trail for a twenty-mile training run. My feet rarely even left the runners. I just held on, sometimes finding myself slumped over the handlebar.

An hour and a half later we returned to the yard as fast as when we left. On autopilot, I unhooked the team, put away the gear and fed everyone. By noon I was back in bed, knowing I'd done all I could that day...except lie in bed and pray for snow.

Rippie (photo by Kathleen Kimball-Parker)

Chapter 30

"Frank, you look horrible."

I was at the last planning meeting for the sendoff in Grand Marais. It was Friday, February 24, six days before our planned departure. After one day of rest I was now on a schedule of planning, packing, media calls, meetings, and taking care of the dogs. There was no time to even acknowledge my pneumonia, let along try to do anything about it…except more coffee, cold medicine, and my old friend ibuprofen. These, with enough food and water to keep them down, were keeping me going.

"Where are you going to stay?" was the next question from the group.

"We'll camp! We don't have any money for hotels, plus it'll be a much better story if a guy drives a dog team to the Capitol camping along the way. Who'll be interested in covering some guy staying in the Holiday Inn, coming out every morning showered and shaved. I need to try and be authentic."

"You'll be authentically dead by the time you get there." This was Sherri, now worried about her husband. To me, the success of the mission and my credibility were more important than my deteriorating health.

"How can you take care of the dogs if you can barely stand on the sled?"

She struck a nerve. She knew I cared more about the dogs than myself.

The meeting broke up with the plans for a sendoff celebration in Harbor Park, downtown Grand Marais, at noon on Thursday, the 1ˢᵗ of March. I would arrive on the sled at rallies in Finland, Duluth, and Saint Paul. We all walked to our cars with a heavy snow falling on what had been barren streets. The weather forecast for the weekend was heavy snow all over the state, all the way down to the Twin Cities, where there had been virtually no snow all winter. But there was no optimism in our car on the way home. Sherri worried in silence. I immediately fell asleep.

Sherri tried to keep her fears to herself, knowing that there was no way to keep me from going. Too much was at stake. All the momentum was in the mining companies' favor. Even environmental activists were saying not "if" sulfide mining was coming but "when." In the face of a multi-billion-dollar juggernaut I had only this one small card to play.

That weekend saw two feet of heavy wet snowfall from the North Shore down through Duluth all the way to the North Metro. By the time the system got to Saint Paul it was too warm for snow. The snowstorm had turned to rain. Our hopes of completing the dog sled trip to the Capitol were further dampened by pictures in the news of the rain-soaked, snowless streets of Saint Paul. I tried to inspire myself at night, before falling asleep in front of the woodstove, by reading others' adventure tales.

George Attla wrote about the first Iditarod in his book *Everything I Know about Training and Racing Sled Dogs*. Those guys left on a 1000-mile trip to Nome not even knowing the route. Attla wrote that the hardest day was the first, just getting out of Anchorage. A picture in the book shows him riding the sled on a paved road approaching a highway overpass, being pulled by sixteen dogs. He broke his brake off early in the first day and still made it to Knick, where he camped. Every morning, he and the other mushers who finished the race, got up, took care of their dogs and started again. Most days there was no trail but they just kept heading north. Eventually, twenty-two of the thirty-five teams that began, made it to Nome. The last one arrived thirty-two days after the start in Anchorage.

Our trip was hardly an Iditarod but we had a challenge that they didn't have. Hundreds of people would be waiting for us to arrive at a rally on the Capitol steps on Thursday, March 8 at precisely 11:05 a.m. After finishing Attla's account of that first Iditarod, it was clear to me how we would get there. Each day of the trek would be a journey all its own. We'd get to Saint Paul by planning for and completing each individual day.

❦

I woke up in a fit of coughing the day before we were to leave, Wednesday, February 29. Eventually I sat up on the side of the bed trying to catch my breath. Dizziness forced me to lie back down.

"Sherri, can you bring me a glass of water, some cold medicine and ibuprofen?"

She brought them in to me without saying a word. Sherri had given up trying to get me to reconsider and was now like me just hoping I'd get through the trip. I lay in bed for another half hour waiting for the medicine to kick in. Eventually I stumbled out of bed and made my way to the kitchen table where a cup of coffee was waiting for me. The woodstove was already roaring, warming our little cabin. I looked over at it, then to Sherri.

"Thanks" was all I said as I stared into my coffee.

"You have to go to the doctor again today. I'll make you an appointment."

I nodded, wondering how I was going to fit the trip to town into my plan for the day. My clothes, gear and dog food for nine days still all needed to be packed into the truck. Sherri left for work, and after a piece of toast and a second cup of coffee I worked myself into my winter clothes and out into the yard to do my morning chores. The dogs broke into their normal morning chaos in anticipation of getting fed. Routinely I went through pulling out the buckets of beef, chicken and dog-food soup that were the dogs' morning meal. Feeding time had a chaotic tempo all its own. It was overtaken by a silence that got nearer and nearer as each bowl got filled. I sat on the bumper of the truck looking out over the yard at the dogs all licking their bowls and searching the snow for any drops they may have missed. My labored breathing gradually slowed.

"OK, the next thing." The yard needed to be scooped. The first stop was always Acorn's pivot. I grabbed the shovel and a bucket and walked up to her and dropped to my knees.

"Oh, Acorn, what have I gotten us into this time?"

She gave me her normal response. A few rapid licks to the face followed by an "Arr row row" and a wagging tail. Acorn was eight, on the downside of her racing career but still the most reliable leader we had. I was counting on her to lead us through all the difficult parts of the trip, all the cities and towns that the trail would go through and in between the hundreds of snowmobiles we were sure to encounter on the North Shore Trail that upcoming weekend. After scooping her area, I stopped again and looked at Acorn. For the first time I noticed that she looked older. She was still in great shape but there were now white hairs around her mouth, and her eyes had a look to them, not quite as bright, a little weepy. I again dropped to my knees and put my hands around her face.

"One more time, Acorn. I'm gonna need you."

For a long moment we sat and stared at each other.

As I walked around the yard I made the final decisions on who would be going. Some of our best race dogs would be staying home. Winnie, Bart, Storm, Cowboy, Pony, Gnasher, Ace and Tank had all pushed themselves so hard the week before at the UP and would stay home. Fly would begin leading with Acorn. Behind them would be Wolf, Nita, Esther, Rippie, Ajax, Moo, Ben and Jake. In the short training runs since the UP these ten had all looked fresh and without any nagging injuries. Most of the team were also able to lead and with eight hard days ahead we were going to have to switch leaders, maybe often. Wolf, Nita and Ajax had run the UP but never in their lives had shown being tired. There was no quit in them and by the time this thing was over I knew I'd need them.

✦

"There's nothing I can do for your problem, Frank, stupidity."

Dr. Sampson then handed me two sheets of paper.

"Here are admitting orders to the hospital. If you leave tomorrow, you're going to need them."

He said nothing else, got up, and walked out of the examination room. I looked down and briefly read over the papers in my hands. There was no new prescription for an antibiotic or prednisone, which I was hoping for to give me a boost for the next few days.

"What did the doctor say?"

"He said I'd be fine. I just needed some rest. Don't worry. I'll get plenty once this thing is over."

"WHAT?" Sherri didn't believe me.

✾

I fell asleep after midnight in my chair in front of the wood stove with my equipment list in front of me. Everything was packed. All the plans made. Everything set in motion. The dogs' howling from the yard woke me. I put a few more logs on the fire, set the alarm for 5:00 and lay down in bed, clothes still on.

"Frank, Frank." Sherri was shaking me. "The alarm. Wake up."

It was still too dark to see anything, so I fumbled for a headlamp that I kept next to the bed. Finally getting it on, I flashed it on the clock. It read 5:23. The alarm had been going off since 5:00. After a fit of coughing, I looked around for my clothes. I was about to ask Sherri where they were, then realized I was already dressed. I went through the motions of my morning routine, stirring the coals, a few more logs on the fire, kettle on the stove to make coffee, feed the cat, head to the outhouse. The morning cold shocked me fully awake.

"Today's the day. We leave in less then six hours." It was the first time I'd thought about it since I woke up. After coffee Sherri helped me with the morning chores.

"Are you going to be OK while I'm gone?"

Sherri was dressed in her black coveralls, snow boots, my old Carhartt jacket, stocking cap and work gloves. Sherri swore growing up on a farm that she wouldn't marry a farmer. There she was, dressed as a farmer in the winter, prepared to take care of twenty-five dogs for most of the week that I'd be gone. She looked tired. For the first time in days I really looked at her and saw that she too wasn't feeling well. Sherri was overworked already and coming down with the flu, something that she'd been trying to keep from me. She was planning to stay home to take care of the dogs, drive down for the day to meet us in Duluth, then come down the night before we arrived in Saint Paul. I was grateful that Lisa had arrived the night before and would be there to help Sherri all week.

"Will she be able to come down to Duluth? Or Saint Paul." A sadness crept in as I wondered if I'd see Sherri before the whole trip was over. Quickly I put those worries out of my mind. I already had all I could handle.

Lisa came out to help us finish, and together we all loaded up the ten dogs that would be making the trip.

"Let's bring Cocoa down to the rally," Sherri said.

She already had my fifteen-year-old leader Cocoa on a leash, wearing a blue dog jacket with a "No Sulfide Mining" button on it. I stopped, bent down and held Cocoa's head in my hands and looked into her eyes. She hadn't pulled a sled in two years but still barked and howled whenever we left the yard, reminding me that she was ready, could lead the team if I'd let her.

It was eight years to the day since Cocoa had led the team out of Deer River to kick off my first political campaign. She, Rocky, Lola, Jessie, Peanut, and Bobcat pulled me for five days across North Central Minnesota. Cocoa was the only leader in the group and the trip would have been impossible without her. Maybe she didn't understand exactly what we were doing but I've never seen a dog so proud as when she pulled us up to the political rally on the shore of Lake Bemidji, in the shadow of Paul Bunyan. Cocoa was on the next day's cover of the Bemidji Pioneer. A framed copy of that picture in our house shows a barking, thin-muscled lead dog. Now Cocoa was heavier, her back sagged a little and her fur had lost some of its black sheen. But Sherri was right. Cocoa needed to come. Without her I wouldn't have known a trip like this was possible and may have never even started mushing.

Cocoa could no longer get up into the truck so I cradled her in my arms and lifted her in to sit between Sherri and me for the ride into town. Lisa followed in her car as we drove out the driveway with the rest of the dogs barking and howling their displeasure of being left behind. Looking to my right, the last dog I saw was Winnie. He wasn't barking or howling but just sat with his ears dropped flat against his head and watched as we drove on by.

We came into Grand Marais from the east, and as we drove in on Highway 61 I saw the snow-bare shoulder that I would be running my dog team on in just three hours.

"We're going to have to cross the highway right here," I said as we passed the Gunflint Trail intersection. Somehow we'd have to sneak the team across the busy highway before we could pick up the snowmobile trail on the other side.

"And that one's gonna be easy compared to all the highways we'll have to cross down south."

After a long pause Sherri said, "Acorn can do it. She'll take care of you."

I smiled a knowing smile and was glad that Acorn was coming along. She wasn't as fast as our young leaders but when conditions got hard, she was at her best. I didn't lead with her much anymore in training because she was usually bored if it was just training. Acorn would slack off, have a loose tugline and often wouldn't turn where I wanted her to on purpose. She just wanted to go somewhere else, and since she was leading, often got her way. Sometimes I let her decide. She'd earned it.

Harbor Park (photo by Mark Tessier)

Chapter 31

The sendoff event in Harbor Park had become an afterthought to me. It was all I could do to prepare to get the team to Saint Paul, I'd almost lost sight of why we were making the trip.

"Hey, there's Dennis' truck."

We pulled over in the parking lot on the edge of town. I'd gone with Dennis LaBoda to the Copper Dog sled dog race in Michigan the year before, where the idea first came to me to run my dogs to Saint Paul to draw attention to sulfide mining. It was the same crew that I'd traveled with the year before and they were meeting in that parking lot to head again to Michigan for the 2012 race. We both had ten-dog teams in the truck. I had a strong desire to get back in the truck and follow him to Michigan. Sherri and I stopped and got out.

"Hey Dennis, Charlie, Clay, Becks."

We shook hands. Sherri gave a few hugs.

"Good luck, man."

"Thanks, Clay."

Dennis was smiling a knowing smile. Now in his fifties, he'd been mushing all his life and knew the immensity of what we were up against, getting a dog team safely all the way to Saint Paul.

"We'll be back on Tuesday if you need any help. Call Curt if you get into trouble before then. He's got a dog truck sitting at home."

"Thanks, Dennis. You guys go win this one."

As we were all getting back in our trucks, Odin drove up with his snowmobile on a trailer. "I just was checking the trail. It's good once we get outta town. Not much snow until then."

"Thanks, Odin. Good thing I got that thick plastic for the sled. We'll need to change dog booties once we cross County Road 6. Sherri and Lisa will meet us there."

We got back in our trucks, and he followed us into town on the same roads we'd be taking on our way back out. Driving down Wisconsin Street, we turned the corner at Harbor Park. Behind was Lake Superior. The low gray clouds and their reflection in the water blended together on the horizon.

The stage was already set up. Marco Good was putting out clipboards with petitions to the Governor on them, asking him to oppose sulfide mining. After taking off my seatbelt I paused to take in the scene. It was eerily calm, quiet.

"I wonder if anyone will come," I thought out loud.

Sherri grabbed my hand. "They will. Let's get the dogs out."

We started hooking the dogs to the short leashes that snapped to the sides of the truck. Lisa got out of her car, pulling on her jacket and hat, and made her rounds greeting all the dogs. I heard her on the opposite side of the truck. "Acorn. Fly. Wolfie…"

Mark Luttinen pulled up in his Suburban and went straight to the dogs without first greeting any of us. He was the primary handler for the trip. He loved the dogs as much as we did.

I climbed up on top of the truck to get the sled down just as Adam walked up.

"Hey, Adam, can you take the sled?"

I lowered it down to him, then heard some talking across the street. It was Jerry, Dr. Jerry Vanek, who'd volunteered to be the vet for the trip. All the core members of our crew were now there. For a moment I stood on top of the truck. Several more people had arrived. The Stonebridge Singers, a group of young Native American drummers from Grand Portage Reservation, were unloading their drum and setting their chairs in a circle around it. The crowd had grown to fifty, with more coming down the streets. Several of the new arrivals were wearing large paper-mache animal masks. I laughed out loud at the guy with a moose head mask. There were animals of all kinds, including a fish head.

I got down off the truck and got the sled, equipment and harnesses ready. Mark and Sherri were already putting the dog booties on the dogs. The drumming started and what had seemed like a random gathering came to life. "Boom, boom, boom, boom."

Then the singing, an Ojibway song to Lake Superior, GichiGami, "The Great One."

The song seemed to call in more people and soon there were a hundred, at noon on a Thursday, in the small town of Grand Marais, whose very existence depended upon the great lake that surrounded us. What I had envisioned being a rally against sulfide mining had become something far greater; a celebration of our home, Lake Superior and the lakes, rivers, and forests that surrounded its shore.

A few people wandered over to see us, say hello, and pet the dogs, but the attention was around the drum where the crowd stood in a circle with many dancing, bending their knees to the rhythm.

An elder Native American woman leaned over to Sherri.

"Never in my life have I seen drumming in downtown Grand Marais."

Boom boom…Boomboom…

The threat of the water pollution from the proposed massive sulfide mines was in the back of all of our minds, but there was no sense of anger or pessimism. The air was full of possibility, what we could do together.

The drumming stopped and Marco greeted the crowd to cheers. He and Yvonne Mills sang songs of the lake. John Morrin, the Vice-Chair of the Grand Portage Band of Ojibway spoke of honor and reverence for GichiGami. Bill Hansen of Sawbill Canoe Outfitters reminded us of how our livelihoods depended upon the clean water that surrounded us.

Then it was my turn. I looked one more time at the gear laid out on the ground, the dogs now all bootied and harnessed. Their barking was competing with the sound of the drum. I quickly petted a couple more, then walked to the stage. My attention had been completely focused on getting organized and ready for the dog trip to Saint Paul. As I stepped up onto the stage, I heard someone yell, "The eagles!" Many in the crowd were pointing overhead. I looked up to see two eagles circling. I didn't really understand what it might mean but felt there was a blessing there somehow, the drum calling in the eagles to see us off. For a moment all the crowd stared at the eagles circling above our gathering.

"Thank you" came out of my mouth without me even thinking about it. The microphone was on and most eyes dropped from the sky to the stage. To me there was nothing else to say. Adding to the other speeches felt unnecessary, and my mind was on the dogs and getting them safely out of town. After an awkward pause I started again.

"Thank you, for coming out today." The dogs were now barking loudly in the background and people's attention was starting to go where mine already was, to the trip ahead. After a few more uninspired comments I concluded with:

"We've got a long trail ahead of us today, need to get to Sawbill tonight, so I'm gonna get going. Hopefully I'll see some of you down the trail."

Glancing up again I saw that the eagles were still circling, a little farther off and to the south, the direction we'd be going. The urgent barking of the dogs reclaimed my attention, and I stepped down off the stage, shook a few hands and walked over to the truck. The drumming started again.

Boom boom. Boom boom. Boom boom.

Almost screaming to be heard over the dogs and drum, I said, "Let's hook em up! Lisa, Come out front to hold the leaders!"

Sherri was already running Acorn to the front. I grabbed Fly to go next to her on the left. In seconds Mark, Adam, Jerry, Sherri, and I had all ten hooked up. Their frantic barks rose above the drumbeat. I looked down the road and saw that Odin was on his snowmobile looking back, waiting for the signal to start.

Sherri came over to me, gave me a kiss and yelled in my ear, "I'll just see you at the top of the hill!"

She jogged back and got into the dog truck to follow us out of town. On wet pavement there would be no way for me to control the speed of a fresh ten-dog team so the sled was tethered to the truck. After double-checking the slipknot that attached the sled to the truck, I nodded to Odin and he started the snowmobile. I raised one hand over my head and after again making eye contact with both Odin and Sherri, dropped my hand.

Instantly the dogs stopped barking and again sound was dominated by the drum as the ten dogs were now free to charge down Wisconsin Street. Lisa, Mark and Jerry were running alongside the dogs, trying to hold on. Running at fifteen miles an hour, they all looked like they were about to fall on their faces.

"Let go of the line! LET GO!"

They must have seen the wisdom in doing what I said. Instantly I passed by all three as they stumbled and tried to regain their balance. Following Odin's snowmobile we made a quick left, then right, a left and another right. Flying around the corners on the wet pavement it was all I could do to hold on. All that practice on icy trails was paying off. I turned around and gave Sherri a signal I hoped she would recognize as a plea to slow down. She did and the rope held fast on the sled, slowing us down to ten miles an hour. I took what felt like my first breath since I got on the sled.

Across from a Super America gas station the dogs ran up onto the sidewalk. There were two road signs between the sidewalk and the road and immediately I thought of the rope tied to the truck. Before I could even conceive of what might happen if the truck and sled went on opposite sides of the first sign, Sherri hopped the curb with the dog truck and followed right behind. I looked back and Sherri was expressionless, like it was normal; she did that all the time.

We made the sharp right onto Highway 61 in front of Super America and followed Odin's snowmobile down the shoulder of the road. I was trying to run alongside the sled as much as possible because the wet gravel would soon wear down my sled runners. Taking my weight off them hopefully would preserve the plastic on the bottom long enough to get out of town, off the roads and onto the snowmobile trail. At ten miles an hour I could only run so long in all my winter gear. I was sweating hard.

I was struggling, trying to wave at all the people in their cars honking as they went by, when flashing lights in front of us grabbed my attention. A Cook County Sherriff's car was parked up ahead.

"Dang it. We're gonna be stopped before we even get outta town."

The Sherriff's car was parked right at the intersection of Highway 61 and the Gunflint Trail. I started wondering if the dogs and I could somehow get around it and onto the snowmobile trail on the opposite corner of the intersection. Then I saw that the car was not blocking our path but actually was parked across Highway 61, stopping traffic. The Deputy was standing in the intersection, looking back at us.

"It's Julie!!" Julie Collman is a good friend and had handled for us at the Beargrease and the Wolf Tracks race in Ely. I had no idea she'd even be there.

Odin cut across the highway right in front of her, and Acorn and Fly followed right behind. "You're the best, Julie!" I tried to high five her as we passed. She just smiled and waved.

The dogs followed Odin up the Gunflint Trail and over the side of the road onto the snowmobile trail that followed it for a half mile before it made a turn into the woods.

"Whoa!" I threw my snow hook onto the post of a trail sign to stop the team. I needed to catch my breath and for a moment hung over the handlebar of the sled. I felt dizzy and coughed for a minute. The sweat dripped off my face. It was a cloudy and damp thirty-degree day. I hoped that up in the hills, further from the lake, the temperature would be cooler. Odin sped on ahead to meet Sherri and Lisa where the trail again crossed the Gunflint Trail two miles and over a thousand feet of elevation ahead. I took off my parka and hat. We had three hundred and fifty miles to go. I would have to help the dogs up the hills if they were to have the energy to make it to Saint Paul. It didn't occur to me that they might have an easier time of it than I would.

At the top of the hills outside of Grand Marais, I met Sherri, Lisa, Odin, and Adam. The dog booties had all been shredded running through town and needed to be changed. With so much help it only took a few minutes. I was still in "go" mode and was anxious to get back on the trail. Lisa was standing on the sled brake for me, and Sherri and I were standing up by the leaders. Sherri leaned over and I barely heard her whispering, "Acorn, you take care of him for me."

Acorn licked her face in response and immediately barked to go. After I kissed Sherri goodbye, we pulled away. I wasn't going to see her for a week and immediately missed her.

With Acorn and Fly in lead, the team fell into a rhythmic easy pace. It came over me, the feeling that we were finally on the trail, on our way to Saint Paul.

I laughed thinking about how we'd showed up that day without any money for food, gas, anything. Jan Attridge had decorated some donation buckets and we'd passed them around. I had meant to ask people from the microphone to put money in them, that we needed it for gas and dog food but forgot. Mark, the main handler for the trip, told me that people were coming up to him, asking if we needed any help, and, in between putting booties on the dogs, he kept pointing to the buckets. Without me even asking, we would have enough, barely, to get to Finland. We'd have to send the buckets around again there.

Since is it was a Thursday, it was a quiet day on the trail as we headed south and west past Lutsen Mountain and down into the Temperance River Valley. Most of the team had finished the Beargrease Sled Dog Marathon and had been on that trail several times. They obviously knew where they were going and I tried to relax into the ride.

The recent snow was hanging on all the trees, often making it difficult to see any of the green underneath. It was the most snow we'd had all year and came just in time. Then it dawned on me the very forest I was travelling through was at risk from the proposed mines that we were fighting against. This was Minnesota State Land whose minerals the State of Minnesota could auction off to the highest bidder with no regard for the towering pines and maples that covered the surface, nor the animals roaming among them, living in their branches, hibernating in their roots. What about when this snow melted to water, ran down the hills into the streams, rivers and on to the big lake? Wasn't there any value there? Once contaminated with sulfuric acid, mercury and who knows what else, would it support the fish we liked to catch and eat? If we could even eat them?

"But who cares? How many people really know this place, will fight to protect it?"

I wondered who else had been on that trail all winter. How many people's lives would actually change in some way that they'd know the

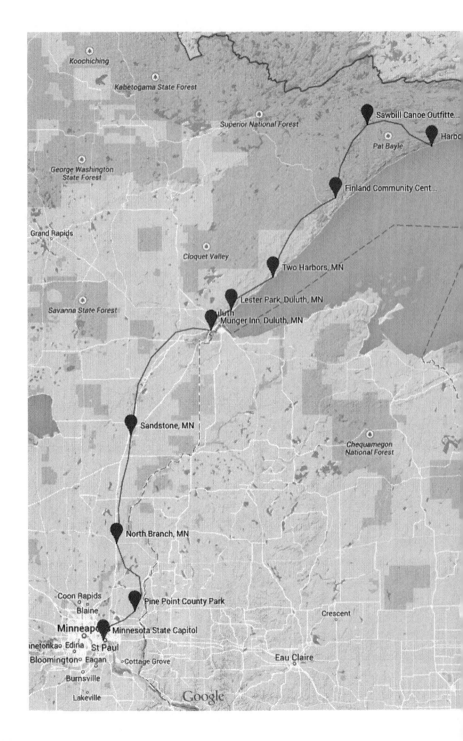

difference, would feel it, if that whole valley turned into one big acid-leaching mine pit. People's lives today were mostly indoors, staring at their screens, big and small. "Gotta get that new iPhone every year."

The thought started bringing me down and I quickly became aware that the dogs weren't focused, wandering side to side on the trail. They were so connected to me, and my emotions were affecting them, directly.

"It's OK, puppies. Let's go."

Acorn gave a sideways glance over her shoulder and then lunged into her harness. The team resumed our ten-mile-an-hour pace. Watching the leaders, Acorn and Fly, I thought of all the adventures that we'd shared, the thousands of miles on the trail, mishaps, and races. Acorn had been with me almost from the beginning and I'd had to learn to not lean on her so much, let other dogs lead more. But today we were on an errand more important than any other we'd been on, and Acorn seemed to know it. I'd trust her with my life, I had.

There I was, again with ten of my dogs on the trail, exhausted, pneumonia and all. There was no place on earth I'd rather be. It was almost perfect. I only wished that others could see this, feel what it was like to be behind those dogs, on that trail, see the valley descend into dusk, the shadows mixing with the fog off the lake, life's great mysteries almost revealed. Then they'd know, understand why this country must remain wild, forever.

Just before dusk, at the bottom of the valley we hit the Sawbill Trail where Jerry and Mark were waiting. A quick bowl of soup for the dogs and then down the road we went to Bill Hansen's place. There would be no camping that night but a home-cooked meal and a bunkhouse. The stress of planning and pneumonia had caught up with me. With only the first of eight days behind us, I wondered how I'd make it.

Clothes on and lying in the bunk that night, the last thing I remember was saying;

"Hey, Mark and Jerry, can you take care of the dogs?"

Acorn and Fly (photo by Mark Luttinen)

Chapter 32

Friday, March 2

I woke up with the first light shining in on my face. It took a minute to remember where I was. Soon it all flooded back in, what we were doing. I sat up and immediately started coughing. Head in my hands the coughs kept coming, and for a few seconds I struggled to breathe. The fit passed, and I was breathing as if I'd just come up from holding my breath underwater. My breath slowed and I reached for the cold medicine and ibuprofen next to the bed and, with my water bottle, downed a handful. Then I grabbed my coat, hat, and boots. The dogs needed to be fed. I knew that and would then figure out what was next.

The meat buckets were thawed and sitting by the door.

"Thanks, Mark," I said to myself.

The noise of the metal bowls hitting the ground must have woken up Mark. Seconds afterwards he fell out the door, trying to put on his boots, coat, and hat at the same time. With one boot still not all the way on, he began pulling the dogs out of their boxes and hooking them up around the truck. I filled the bowls with meat broth just as Jerry showed up to help me pass them out. As the dogs finished eating, Mark massaged them all, and Jerry checked them over. We said little. All of us were coffee drinkers and hadn't had any yet.

"I'm going to go check in with Bill."

When I got to the lodge he was already making blueberry pancakes. The coffee pot was full and ready.

"You guys need breakfast?"

It was more a statement than a question. Returning to the truck I found Mark doing a second, more thorough round of dog massages. I don't know who enjoyed it more, Mark or the dogs. Each dog greeted him with a kiss, and he didn't mind getting it right on the face. Jerry was making the rounds with the poop shovel.

"I even got a kiss from Ben!"

"I don't know, Mark…I wouldn't brag to too many people about that. Bill's got blueberry pancakes and coffee ready."

The dogs were almost instantly back in the truck. After seconds on pancakes and several cups of coffee, the stories around the table really got rolling. Then I looked at my watch.

"We gotta get rollin! Jerry, can you go pick up Adam in Tofte?"

The three of us all thanked Bill for his generous hospitality.

"No, thank you guys for what you're doing. I wish I was going with you."

Adam had had to work the night before, grooming the ski trails after the fresh snow we had just had, but now was going to be with us for the rest of the trip. Jerry went on ahead to pick up Adam. Mark and I packed up the truck.

"You should take a minute to send out an email, let everyone know how you're doing."

Mark's suggestion irritated me. We had to get down the trail, and I kept packing. A minute later I looked over at him. "You're right." And I went back inside and typed up a quick note:

Hello from Sawbill,
I didn't get to give you all thanks as I took off yesterday. It was so inspiring to be a part of that event. What a kick off! I'll try and check in with you along the way and hope to see many of you in Duluth.
So far the trail is beautiful, warm, lots of snow.
Frank

I closed up Mark's computer and carried it outside. We got in the truck and drove back down the Sawbill Trail to the trailhead. We pulled up to the Sawbill Campground and Trail Head where we'd been so many times before. It served as a checkpoint both up-bound and down-bound for the Beargrease. I walked around the truck, looked into the woods and could see the campsite where the dogs and I had camped the winter before, where I had to leave Acorn behind, the first of all the dogs to get sick on that long terrifying day.

Today the whole team was healthy. Acorn, Fly, Wolf, Tina, Nita, Esther, Moo, Ben, and Jake were all back from that team, along with Wolf's little brother Rippie. It was Friday and several snowmobile trailers were already there with the constant drone of snowmobile engines in the air. Normally I'm glad to see people out enjoying the trail, but the rush to embrace the late winter snow had me worried.

"Are they going to be OK with all the traffic on the trail?"

Mark's question was my own.

"They're used to snowmobiles. Acorn and Fly will keep us on the side of the trail. It'll be fine."

We caught each other's eyes long enough to know that neither one of us was really sure it would be fine.

The dogs were all bootied, the sled down and gangline ready, when Jerry and Adam pulled up in Jerry's rusty Toyota pickup.

"Hey, Adam."

My greeting was drowned out by the sounds from a dozen snowmobiles that passed by. We all stopped to watch them pass, including the dogs. There wasn't a wave or even a nod from the group. The engines faded down the trail and the dogs began barking, wanting to chase after the snowmobiles.

I looked at my watch. It was almost 9:00. A dampness hung in the air as it does when the temperature approaches freezing.

"Did anyone catch the weather?" I looked at Adam.

"Yeah. It's supposed to be in the thirties today and cloudy."

The clouds were looking pretty thin.

"If the sun comes out we may have to stop for a while in the heat of the day. Mark, make sure you meet me at the road crossings around noon and after, and bring the dishes and plenty of water. These guys are going to need a rest."

I grabbed Acorn and led her to the line, signaling to the rest of the team we were about to go. The rest of the team jumped up, and soon I was on the trail, waving my goodbye.

"Whoa, Acorn. Whoa, Fly."

The dogs showed how fresh and rested they were by starting off at a fast lope. It was warm and damp and I had to keep them from getting too warm. That would slow them down later today and for the seven days and three hundred miles ahead. Ahead was the long gradual straight six-mile climb up Heartbreak Hill. In the Beargrease Marathon this was nearing the end of the race and I'd always had to run, kick and encourage my team to the top.

I heard them first, the high whine of snowmobiles, then looked up. The train of lights went almost to the horizon and they were moving fast, straight towards us. Here would be the test. It's one thing to be on the snowmobile trail during a race, with signs, other mushers, people at road crossings warning snowmobilers, but we were out there on our own.

"GEE, OVER, Acorn. OVER!"

Fly was pulling into the middle of the trail, and the team followed.

"FLY, ACORN, OVER! OVER!"

Fly continued to fight Acorn and our line put us right on a collision course with the first snowmobile in the group which now was approaching at highway speed. I opened my mouth to scream the command again but before I could get it out of my mouth the group of snowmobiles reached the leaders and, within a few feet, which seemed like inches to me, Fly veered to the right. Without slowing we hugged the right edge of the trail as more than twenty snowmobiles passed on our left, their riders all waving. The final two snowmobiles hung back and stopped.

"Where ya headin?"

"Saint Paul!"

I just caught his startled look as I passed and waved. Terror turned to laughter in seconds.

"Fly! You did that on purpose! Trying to scare the crap outta me."

For an instant he turned his head to the right. I could swear he was smiling.

Fly, a small male with the coloring of a fly, was a little standoffish to everyone but me. He loved it when I'd hold his head close to mine. When I'd do that he stuck his nose up under my chin and wagged his tail. We got Fly and his sister Woolly as pups from a champion mid-distance kennel.

Back in our skijoring days I bought a big strong dog, Bobcat, from this same kennel. He was a Husky Catahoula Hound cross. Catahoula Hounds are bred and raised to hunt wild boar and to round up cattle that don't want to be rounded up. They are tough dogs and Bobcat grew into a powerful dog with bulging muscles and wide intimidating jowls. He teamed up with Lola to make my first winning skijoring team. Lola was the only dog we had that wasn't too intimidated to run next to Bobcat. She was a real happy-go-lucky dog but very ADD. Lola had gone to live with Lisa. Lisa said it was a perfect fit.

Bobcat was a dominating puller but became more and more aggressive the older he got. By the time he was three we had to put up a warning sign in the yard to keep any visitors away from him but he still respected me as his owner. We would wrestle and he'd lick my face whenever he got the chance.

It was December 3rd, 2005, Sherri's birthday. We were planning a surprise birthday party for her, and our friends John and Karen

Filardo came over early to help me get the party ready and to run the dogs. It was dusk and we were hooking the team up for a twenty mile run. Bobcat was particularly wild that day. He was next to Lola on the gangline and kept growling and trying to bite her. Twice I grabbed him to pull him off of her. We were just about to take off when Bobcat bit Lola in the neck and was shaking her around like a stuffed animal. Lola was trying to defend herself but was helpless against such a massive, powerful dog.

I jumped over the gangline to grab Bobcat, when he reared up and bit me in the face, catching my nose and upper lip. Falling back I held my face and then pulled my hand away. It was covered in blood. Bobcat went back after Lola and I knew he'd quickly kill her if I didn't stop him. Already covered in my own blood, I grabbed his collar, with my arms straight. It took all the strength I had to keep him away from my face. The seventy-pound dog was lunging and biting with everything he had. I was only thinking about protecting the other dogs. My adrenaline surged and I was able to focus my strength and attention enough to unhook Bobcat from the team. He was wild, jumping, scratching and kept trying to bite my face, a couple of times missing by so little that I felt his whiskers and spit. Our struggle continued as I dragged him back to his pivot. Just as I was hooking him up to his leash, Bobcat lurched away from me and I felt his teeth sinking into my left cheek. The skin tore as I fell backwards. Bobcat was now wildly jumping and barking but safely on his leash.

Holding my face, I walked back to the team. They were no longer barking to go but just standing in their harnesses watching me walk towards them. My face was wet with blood and tears. I'd lost him. I knew this meant that Bobcat had to be put down. He was dangerous and nobody could handle him, not even me.

"Oh my God, Frank, are you OK?" Karen and John were shaken and looking at my bloodied face.

"I'll be OK. I think I'm going to need stitches. Can you help me put the dogs back?"

"Yeah sure and then we're going to the hospital."

After we put the other dogs back on their pivots, I squatted down out of Bobcat's reach and watched him pace back and forth. I'd failed him. Somehow, I knew I'd failed him.

"I'm so sorry, Bobcat. It's not your fault. You're such a beautiful boy."

We buried Bobcat's ashes in the corner of the dog yard and put his collar on the fence post above. He was the biggest, strongest dog we had, and to this day I've never had a dog that's pulled harder. Not for a second have I regretted the two years he spent with us. I just wish I'd have been a better dog trainer, done better by him.

The people we'd got him from had no way of knowing that he'd get aggressive and felt terrible about what happened. They immediately offered us two more dogs out of their most recent litter and that's how we got Woolly and Fly. Both were leading before they were two, and in 2008 Fly was one of our three main leaders. He was the calm one at the starting line when the other dogs were jumping and barking to go. Fly had a nice steady pace, too. When he was in lead, I'd have to slow the rest of the team down to his pace. When the rest of the team tried to go too fast and I got sucked into letting them, Fly would just stay travelling the pace we were going. He could run faster, if I asked him to, but Fly seemed to have a sense of how fast we should be travelling. When I watched him, adjusted to his speed, we'd do well. When I pushed too hard, in spite of Fly's pace, we all paid the price by slowing down before the end of the run.

Fly had had an off year in 2009. He had gotten worms during the winter and I didn't catch it right away. In 2010 he was back to full strength, having finished with the third-place White Oak team and was one of the eight Beargrease finishers. Fly and Woolly led all the way from Two Harbors to Sawbill. Three of Fly and Tina's pups were on the UP 200 team, Nita, Esther, and Storm. Three others, Bart, Moo, and Socks, became key members of our team. Fly wasn't the flashy superstar of our kennel but no dog had been more important to how far we'd come.

I'll sometimes notice the scar on my face when I look in the mirror and think of Bobcat. I can only smile when I remember his strong graceful body running down the trail, and I thank him. I thank him for Woolly and Fly. I thank Bobcat for Fly's puppies and for the great runs we all had together. My thoughts were interrupted by the sound of snowmobiles. We crested Heartbreak Hill. A large group of snowmobilers had pulled over. Having just climbed to the highest point on the North Shore Trail, the dogs were willing to stop. I braked when we came up next to the group.

"Hello."

"Hey, look. It's a dog sled team."

"Whattayadoin?"

"I'm heading to Saint Paul. Nice day to be on the trail, huh?"

The dogs lunged, the snow hook popped out and we were off down the other side of the hill. I caught a few of the confused expressions my comments left behind. That got me thinking, "Who are the main users of this trail?"

The snowmobilers were out enjoying the same place I was, in a slightly different way. I'd long since stopped judging snowmobilers for their choice of how to enjoy the trail. At least they were out there and not in front of their TVs somewhere. Plus they could put their snowmobiles in the garage for the rest of the year when they weren't riding them. Our dogs needed constant care. Of course that time in the offseason that I spent with the dogs was a great time for me, to get away from the rest of the world's cares, to spend with and get to know each one of them individually. The ugly secret of mushing is that it's not a very environmentally friendly sport. Our carbon footprint is bigger than someone who snowmobiles. The dogs require food, shelter, vet care, all sorts of resource-intensive things. But it's our life. When we're caring for the dogs, we're not doing other things that use resources, shopping, motor boating, whatever. Plus Sherri and I garden for a lot of our food, so I think it's a wash, really. I've come to believe we have to earn our way on this planet, do our fair share to warrant the impact we make on it by being alive, by service to the earth, other people, the environment.

The dogs were also earning their way by heading to Saint Paul. Obviously the people we passed on snowmobiles were interested in the dogs too. I'd just have to figure out how to talk to the people out on the trail about why we were out here, protecting this trail, this place, for all of us. Soon I was rehearsing my thirty-second pitch against sulfide mining to every snowmobiler who would stop to listen. The temperature rose into the thirties and the sun was out. The dogs got warm so stopping them more often became easier... and necessary.

"We're bringing thousands of petitions to the Governor in Saint Paul to tell him to protect all this country from sulfide mining. Every place these foreign mining companies have done this type of mining, they've left massive water pollution and holes in the ground as far as the eye can see. Look around you. This place could be next. If you care about it, let the Governor know."

I handed a father and son on their snowmobiles a flyer.

"See you guys. Thanks." And I waved as I let off the brake and lurched past.

I looked over my shoulder to see the dad putting the flyer in his snowmobile suit.

At the next road crossing, Country Road 2, there was a group of snowmobilers parked off to the side, obviously taking a break. I was hooking a sign to stop for a while and give my pitch, when Mark jogged up.

"Where ya been?"

"Talking to people about why we're out here on the trail."

And I turned to the group who was clearly interested in seeing a dog team on the trail.

"Hey, guys. How's the trail?"

"A little bumpy but heck, we got snow. Can we pet your dogs?"

"Sure. Mark, you got the leaders?"

He already was kneeling next to Fly and Acorn and started answering questions about the dogs to a few guys who first walked over to the team. Ben, who had always been leery of people, gave his best attempt at appearing ferocious, "Rough." He was a looker, the one people were most drawn to with his all white coat and one blue eye and one brown eye.

"It's OK, Benny."

With the sled hooked safely to a sign, I kneeled next to him and held him while I launched into my pitch.

"These dogs are delivering petitions to the Governor in Saint Paul…"

"Cool." "How are you going to get there?" "What's sulfide mining?"

While I was answering the questions, Mark went to his truck and got a petition for them to sign. We had fallen into our routine running, caring for the dogs and talking to the people we were sharing the trail with. What had been our safety concern, snowmobilers, became our audience. When Mark was finished checking all the dog booties, replacing a couple that had fallen off, I said, "Well thanks, guys, I gotta hit the trail. Maybe I'll see some of you in Duluth or Saint Paul."

Mark stood out in the road looking for cars and I pulled the snow hook off the stop sign. We crossed the road and were again on the trail. For another two hours I stopped and talked to all who would listen, but Acorn was beginning to get impatient with all the stopping and starting. She was giving me less and less time before she'd bark and lunge. With the other nine dogs following suit I had to say goodbye before finishing the story of our trip.

It was after two in the afternoon when we got to County Road 1 and time to give the dogs some water and a snack. They'd been on the trail for over four hours on a warm, sunny day. Mark already had their snack ready, and while I tied the sled to his truck hitch and the front to a stop sign, he filled their bowls. The crowd around us grew as we brought the bowls to each dog. Our audience stayed for a half hour, long after we had picked up all the bowls and scooped. A group of mostly teenagers from Iowa, who had started out being too cool to get off their snowmobiles, ended up kneeling and petting all the dogs. One guy took off his helmet just in time to get several quick licks from Nita.

"You guys wanna help us cross the road?"

Mark guided them all to a place on the gangline.

"Wait! I want to get my camera."

One of the adults with them ran back to his snowmobile and then stood in front of us taking some pictures.

"This isn't somethin ya see back home."

After a pickup with a trailer full of snowmobiles rolled on by, Mark led us across the highway.

"Thanks, guys."

It was good to be talking to people about our trip but I was anxious to get back on the trail, have some time alone with the dogs. Instead of a few minutes of quiet, we immediately passed another group of snowmobiles. From that point on there was never a time, for the next three days, when I couldn't see or hear snowmobiles. I began to pick and choose who I gave my talk to. We DID have a schedule to keep. We were expected at a bonfire at the Finland Community Center at 5:00. The plan was to meet Dave and Amy Freeman, on their dog team coming from Ely, just outside of Finland, and we would travel in together.

In spite of all our stopping on the trail, we arrived at the trail junction, just outside of Finland where we were going to meet Dave and Amy, at 4:30, a half hour early.

"Hey, ya seen a sled dog team?"

The snowmobiler was coming in on the trail from Ely and had slowed down as he passed my team tied off on the side.

"Yeah, but they're a ways back. Some guy's skiing with one of those big hairy dogs."

"Thanks."

It sounded like I had some time to wait, so I turned the leaders around the corner to the trail down to the Community Center and tied them off to a tree. Since we were going to be there a while I tied the wheel dogs, Ben and Jake, off to another tree, then dug in the sled for some dog snacks. I had some chicken chunks left. All their eyes were on me as I rummaged in the sled. Barks erupted when I pulled the bag out. Each dog caught the chicken chunk out of the air as I tossed it to them. There was no chewing either, just grabbing it out of the air, then barking for seconds.

"Sorry, guys. That's all I got for now. You'll eat a big dinner soon."

After stuffing the empty bag back in the sled, I gave a good neck-and-head scruff to them all, starting in the back with Ben and Jake, then Ajax, Moo, Esther, Rippie, Wolf, Nita, and the leaders Fly and Acorn.

"Remember the last time we were here, pups? We were a lot more tired then."

It had been over two years since we'd been at that very spot. For a moment I was back on that cold night of the Beargrease 2010. Ajax and Wolf were leading with Fly and Acorn right behind. An hour before our race had almost come to a cold dangerous end but Ajax had found a spark that got the rest of us going again.

"Ajax, you sweet prince, you saved us."

His whole body wagged with me saying his name.

"Nita and Esther, you were there and were only a year and a half old...how about that."

Sitting on my heels, the fatigue returned. I realized that I hadn't taken anything for my pneumonia since noon and would need to show my gratitude to our hosts and be social for a few more hours. Exhaling, I all of sudden didn't feel like I even had the energy to get up and look for some cold medicine in my bag.

"God, please give me the strength to get through this."

And I looked up at the sky. The boreal forest canopy rose high over our heads. At the crown was a long river of an opening that paralleled the trail below. In the fading late afternoon sunlight I saw shadows move over the opening in the trees. My eyes fixed on the gap and one shadow then another appeared again. It was two eagles circling overhead.

Minutes passed. Their circles got wider and higher. The dogs were quiet as I sat and watched the sky until the eagles vanished into the twilight.

Acorn began the howl, mouth up towards the sky. Once, twice, then on the third howl Ajax joined in. On the fourth all ten dogs howled in unison. Then twice more. The last one trailed off into silence.

In the distance I heard dogs barking. Immediately all my dogs' heads were turned back towards the trail. Nita barked a response. I looked at my watch. It was five o'clock exactly. I walked up to the trail and sure enough, some guy was skiing behind a big hairy dog. Following right behind was a team of six one-hundred-pound Canadian Inuits. On the sled adorned with large "Stop Sulfide Mining" banners stood Dave and Amy Freeman. They clearly had a different approach to spreading the message than I did and weren't sneaking up on anyone.

Smiling, we greeted each other by grabbing each other's arms and shoulders.

"It's so good to see you guys."

"Sorry it took us so long. It was pretty warm and these dogs can only go so fast."

I looked down at their dogs rolling in the snow. Each was twice the size of my smaller short-haired racing Alaskans but we were all there, at the agreed upon time.

They followed me down the trail and into the Finland Community Center parking lot where a bonfire was already going. About twenty-five people were gathered to greet us. My dogs ran right to the truck, knowing that's where their dinner was. Mark, Adam, Jerry, and Jill, Jerry's girlfriend and a close friend of ours too, all grabbed the gangline while I again embraced all the dogs thanking them for another day on the trail. I saw that Mark had already laid out the bowls and had the five-gallon bucket of the dogs' dinner mixed up.

"You guys want to hook the dogs up to the truck while I get their bowls ready?"

In a minute all the dogs were eating with Mark, Jerry, and Jill taking off their booties and harnesses. Adam stood next to me.

"How'd it go?"

"No problem really, but we've never been on the trail with so many snowmobiles."

"There'll be a lot more tomorrow. All we saw on Highway 61 was trucks with snowmobile trailers."

"Adam, I feel like hell. I'm going to go sit by that fire. Hey Mark, Jer, you guys got the dogs?"

They were both in the middle of a dog massage when they looked up. Mark just nodded.

Jerry said, "You go ahead. We've got them taken care of. After a quick massage I'll go through and check the musculoskeletal integrity of each dog, then..."

I couldn't hear the rest as I walked over towards the fire.

"Oh, I love you!"

Diadra Decker was squeezing me before I even noticed she was there. Diadra is a real gem, a wiry middle-aged hippie with a gleam in her eye and a heart of gold. She was the Board President for Water Legacy, the first group that was formed in Minnesota for the primary purpose of fighting against sulfide mining.

I forced a smile.

"Hi, Diadra. It's great to see you. I gotta sit down."

My attention was focused on a wood bench near the bonfire.

Soon I was on the bench, closer to the fire than anyone else in the circle, my parka visibly steaming.

"Hey, Frank. It's so cool you guys are doing this." It was Matt Tyler, another Water Legacy board member. "We've been trying to get people to listen to us for so long. This dog-sled trip might be the ticket. You want a hot dog? They're over on the picnic table. You can have my stick."

Matt was a large man in his thirties. He was a forester and—in his long, black beard, red-wool-flannel jacket and Carhartt pants— looked like the guy that would be cast in a movie to play the part. He and his wife Melinda lived near Finland. Melinda was smart and grounded. I felt comfortable around her from the second I met her. Melinda coordinated the event in Finland. She and Matt own their home and property but a year before realized that they didn't own the mineral rights under it, the State of Minnesota did. The State planned to lease those rights to the highest bidding mining company and there was nothing that Matt and Melinda could legally do about it. If a mining company leased the rights and decided to mine their property, they would have to sell their property to the company, for the price that the mining company said was fair. If Matt and Melinda refused, the state would foreclose. There was no bargaining power for the property owners at all. It was a sweetheart deal written into the law by the state politicians who represented the area. Matt, Melinda and many other local property owners wondered who the politicians really represented and where their campaign contributions came from. I already knew.

"Thanks Matt."

I struggled to my feet. On the table I found hot dogs, buns and a bottle of Coke. Without a thought I grabbed the Coke and half emptied it on the first drink. After the second it was almost empty. I stuck a couple of buns in my parka pocket, saw some cookies, put them in on top of the buns, and stuck a couple of hot dogs on the end of the stick. I sat back down next to Matt. He wasn't a big talker and that suited me fine. I ate the cookies, then the hot dogs that were scorched on the outside and still cold in the middle.

"Want some mustard?"

Matt was grinning at his own joke. I laughed as I put the last bite of the second hot dog in my mouth. He introduced me to some of the other locals who were sharing the fire with us. There was a little small talk before we all settled into watching the fire. Occasionally someone would get up to get a marshmallow to roast. The circle grew as the dogs were all cared for and few latecomers showed up. The group remained mostly quiet. I think we were all inwardly grateful for the chance to have a quiet communion. It was the first time I had sat in front of a campfire all winter. I was wondering when the last time was that I had sat in front of a campfire.

"We should get you inside."

I was shaken from my trance. Adam had been sitting next to me for how long I didn't know. "OK."

My whole body felt encased in concrete. I focused and forced myself to standing. The fire had a gravity but my mind slowly accepted that I needed to go inside the Community Center where wrestling mats were waiting for me and my sleeping bag.

My legs first guided me to the truck where Mark was taking the dogs out once more before we headed in for the night. I looked around.

"Where's Jerry and Jill?"

"They just left. He said they have friends near here with a couple of couches."

"I'll put the dogs back in their boxes. Thanks, Mark."

He gave Acorn one more good night scratch then went inside. We didn't have kids but putting our dogs to sleep at night must have been similar to how parents feel when they tuck their kids under the covers, shut out the light and close the door. I lifted each one up into its straw-lined dog box and closed the door, latching it tight. The dog curled up in the straw and after they stopped circling and lay down. Their eyes glowed in my headlamp through the grated openings in the doors. I walked around the truck once more, double-checking each door to be sure that the latch was fully locked. Knowing that the dogs were warm and secure, I grabbed my sleeping bag out of the truck and walked towards the community center.

Inside, sleeping bags were laid out all over the floor on top of a wrestling mat. Dave and Amy Freeman, some of their crew, and Mark and Adam were all in the process of taking off their wet clothes, and the place smelled like wet socks.

"Frank, we've got internet here. You wanna use my computer and send out an update?"

"Yeah. Thanks, Mark. Give me a minute. I got to get this wet stuff off."

Mark's eyes didn't leave his computer. He had agreed to upload pictures for Conservation Minnesota. Paul Austin, the Executive Director, was sending out daily blog posts about our trip and he was including the pictures that Mark was sending.

"OK, I'm done."

I sat down and logged onto my email. In my selfishness of focusing on our immediate team, me, Mark, Adam, Jerry and the dogs, I had forgotten about all who were at home cheering for us. The little note that I had sent that morning set off a flurry of responses:

Frank, Thank YOU for energizing us all. Good luck and safe travels!
Cathy

Sherry, the donut lady came up to Marco, Staci and I as things were closing down (see the photo sent)…and said that she and her friends felt that they were "watching history in process" - and Kathryn Nelson-Pedersen's students were right there, interviewing everybody for their "Social Studies" project! This was their Paul Wellstone moment, I think :) Jan

The Sierra Club just called my shop and got permission to use one of my photos from yesterday on their website …

THAT SO ROCKS!!!!! Congratulations Stephan.
Has anyone heard if Frank is in Finland?

Signed, the wife at home.

There were many more and my tears kept falling as I read through them all. I had sat down, totally spent, cold, tired, and homesick. But sitting there in Finland it started to sink in that I was just one part of something larger than I yet understood. I not only had to get those dogs and petitions to the Capitol in Saint Paul by Thursday, but I needed to be the one telling the story along the way. People wanted to hear it from the guy on the sled. I got up, found a cup of coffee and sat back down to begin the ritual that I would repeat every night for the rest of the trip. Paul Austin from Conservation Minnesota reposted my blog on their website and Facebook page. Thousands of people read and shared those posts.

Wolf (photo by Joi Electa)

Blog Posts

Friday, March 2

Hello from the Finland Community Center. We had a warm but easy trip in. We passed about 100 snowmobiles today on the trail and stopped to talk to many of them about sulfide mining. It was good to let the dogs cool off by rolling in the snow. With all the snow now on the trail, it's hard to believe that the Beargrease Sled Dog Marathon was cancelled this year. We got to run that same trail today and for a change weren't racing. The trail looks and feels different when you're just taking your time.

Today I had hours on my own with the dogs to think about all that brought us here to this moment. This trip to Saint Paul feels like a final adventure, the one that all the others have built up to. There's no way we could do it or even try, without all the trials and trails we'd been down before it.

Eagles showed up along the trail again today. They must be coming home for the spring in spite of all the new snow. Last week we were wondering how we were going to make it to Saint Paul with no snow on the trail. I was prepared to run on gravel the whole way. Now we've got plenty of snow and if it doesn't get too warm and melt all the snow we just might luck out and slide right up to the Capitol.

Our team waited outside of Finland for Dave and Amy's team to arrive and ran in ahead of them to the Community Center where we all shared a campfire, roasted hot dogs and marshmallows. Tomorrow morning we'll speak at the pancake breakfast with John Beargrease's Great Granddaughter, take the over 8,000 petition signatures we've collected so far and head to Two Harbors. Someone has offered us a yurt to sleep in there.

Good Night.

Acorn and Fly Leaving Finland (photo by Joi Electa)

Blog
Saturday, March 3

Hello from Two Harbors. All I've got to do before crawling into my sleeping bag is let the dogs out of their boxes one more time for the night. Our day started with the pancake breakfast, rally and sendoff from the Finland Community Center. There's only 160 people in Finland and 50 of them were there learning about sulfide mining pollution and eating pancakes. Jennifer, John Beargrease's great granddaughter, and I both addressed the group and then we loaded almost 8,000 signatures on petitions into the sled and hit the trail. Two eagles again sailed overhead as we pulled out of the parking lot.

The word is out we've got snow on the North Shore. Between Finland and Two Harbors we passed at least another 500 snowmobiles. The dogs, with Acorn and Fly in the lead, had no trouble. They Gee over, stay over to the far right side of the trail, so well. At first I was more nervous than they were. Soon we were waving to everyone and they were all respectful, glad to see a dog team out on the trail. I was happy to see so many people out enjoying the spectacular North Shore Trail. We stopped and talked to many of them and they even seemed interested. A few said they'd come see us arrive in Saint Paul. Good to see so many families out there on the trail together. The snow started falling again around noon, adding three inches to the foot we had a few days ago. It made for slow travel but since we weren't racing, it was OK to just take our time.

The team arrived in the Gravel Pit, another Beargrease checkpoint, outside of Two Harbors with heavy snow falling. Jerry found a deep cut on Esther's paw. It would heal but her trip is over. Sherri is coming to Duluth tomorrow, and hopefully I can get in touch with her tonight and ask her to bring another dog, maybe Tina.

Whoever said they had a yurt for us wasn't there, but Jerry's friends, Liz and Bill, lived nearby. They have plenty of floor space, warm cookies and promised us breakfast. So don't worry, Sherri, I'm not having to sleep out in the snow.

Tomorrow we'll leave here and head for Duluth for the rally at Lester Park. Time to go to sleep. The dogs need to eat in the morning at 6:00.

Good Night

Rippie and Esther (photo by Joi Electa)

Blog
Sunday, March 4

A light snow fell most of the day today and the trail was perfect. Again I spent the day seeing and talking to snowmobilers. I tried to count all the snowmobiles and gave up by lunch. I was already at 300. I invited them all to the Duluth event and a few actually showed up. We stopped at a snowmobile trail parking lot on the edge of Duluth. Sherri was going to meet us there with Tina and pick up Esther. Lisa came instead because Sherri is sick. She brought Tina and Winnie. Sherri said Winnie was depressed being left behind and wouldn't go in his house or eat. Ben had been getting a little surly with all the attention so we decided he needed a break. My friend Matt Weik showed up too. We needed the help. Winnie and Tina were nuts to go.

The Duluth event at Lester Park was bigger than I could have hoped. As we got close to the park I heard the Fond du Lac drum group, so I knew we were close. The dogs and I were fashionably late at 3:20, so I missed the other speeches. The dogs arriving in the park stole the show. I heard there were almost 300 people there and it seemed like they all descended on us. The dogs ate up all the attention. Both Duluth TV stations were there filming along with radio stations and the *Duluth News Tribune*. The TV stations said it was going to be their lead story.

The dogs were jumping and barking to go while we were waiting to leave from Lester Park, especially Winnie. It was hard to talk or hear over them at the rally. When we were about to leave I noticed that people were pointing up. I looked up and saw two eagles circling overhead, above the canopy of white pines. Staci (Drouillard) told me they are here because we are doing the right thing. They are taking our prayers up to the heavens. I pulled the hook and we headed back up the trail.

Leaving Lester Park I felt like we had already accomplished something. The Duluth-area media was all there and we had made it, without a major problem, yet. Standing on the sled, feeling pretty cocky, I didn't recognize the trail and soon we were dumped out onto the road to Hawk Ridge. As soon as I realized we were off the trail and after hooking a tree I turned the team around.

"Focus, Frank." Sure we made it to Duluth but the trail and traffic were going to get worse, probably much worse.

Mark remembered to pass around the buckets again at the rally and we collected over $200 for gas and food. We should be able to make it to Saint Paul on that. We left Grand Marais planning to camp the whole way and so far we've been offered a place to sleep and dinner every night. We must be doing something right. Tonight we even have hotel rooms at the Munger Inn!

Tomorrow morning we'll have an event there at 9:00 a.m. before we head down the trail to Hinckley, maybe camping at Banning State Park.

We're half way to Saint Paul.

Good Night.

Snow on the Trail (photo by Mark Luttinen)

Blog
Monday, March 5

This morning we had the pleasure of having breakfast at the Munger Inn with Will Munger Jr. whose father is one of Minnesota's conservation heroes. Will shared stories of environmental victories past while we waited for the children and families to show up for our morning program. It was an honor to be able to spend that time with Will and I hope to stay there again in the future, maybe at next year's Beargrease.

I had a couple of interviews today, including one with Cindy Brucato who now writes for *MinnPost*. A busload of kids showed up at 9:15 and we introduced them to all the dogs. After that they really weren't interested in anything else I had to say, so we pretty much just got ready for the trail while the students petted the dogs. I answered an occasional question while I did another interview with Duluth News Chanel 5. I pulled the hook and waved back at the kids in the parking lot. An eagle overhead caught my eye. I'm not superstitious, far from it, but seeing the eagles along the way has been comforting.

The Munger Trail begins in the boreal forest and climbs gradually out of the St Louis River Valley. I enjoyed watching the forest transition into a more mixed forest with the occasional farm sprinkled in. It reminded me of running the Soo Line Trail that we used to train on between Cass Lake and Remer, when we lived near Bemidji.

My friend Matt Wiek showed up again on the trail as it came into Carlton, and showed us a shortcut so we didn't have to run down Main Street. Matt rode on the sled with me until the edge of town. He got off and we shared a handshake and a knowing smile. At that moment Matt wanted to switch places with me and we both knew it.

The day was long but the dogs ran hard all day and by 5:00 p.m. we were in Sandstone, 67 miles from Duluth. And the dogs weren't tired. They were howling and lunging in their harnesses to continue. Today, more than ever, I felt so grateful to be able to have these beautiful, true animals in our lives, to have their trust and commitment. They are bringing the petitions to the Governor, not me.

We started the day with Wolf and Ajax in lead. After forty miles, Ajax decided he was more interested in Moo than leading, so I brought our super girl leader Nita up front. The team picked up its pace to match hers and we were going as fast at the end as when we started seven hours earlier.

Again, at the end of the day's trail my handling crew, Mark, Adam, and Jerry, were all waiting for us. They've been at every major road crossing to see that we get across safely; are staying up late and getting up early with me to take care of the dogs, and seem to be having fun doing it.

A retired couple, the Dybvigs, have been following our trip. They offered to put us up tonight. We walked into their house tonight to the smell of meatloaf and chocolate chip cookies. I get to sleep in a trundle bed. Staci's right. We must be doing something right.

We've already travelled 250 miles on the trail and have about 120 to go. I'm tired tonight but I know tomorrow, once I get out and see the dogs, they'll get me ready for another day. Tomorrow is supposed to be in the forties, so we're going to try and hit the trail before 8:00. That means a 5:00 a.m. wake-up call.

Good Night

Adam helping us cross 35W while being filmed by WCCO
(photo by Mark Luttinen)

On the Way to Pine City (photo by Mark Luttinen)

Blog
Tuesday, March 6

300 plus miles down and about 65 to go. It's still 40 degrees here and the snow that's on the ground is turning to mud but the dogs don't seem to mind. By the time we got to North Branch, the dogs, the sled, and I were all soaked. It seemed like a scene out of *Iron Will*. Somehow they knew we were coming and many locals lined the street and trail as we came into town. We got a similar reception in Harvey and Pine City. In Pine City the trail ended at a lake that was no longer frozen. Someone who showed up to greet us called the president of the local snowmobile club and he came down to give us directions out of town. That's really been the story of the trip. Whenever we needed help, it came.

The trail into Pine City was lined with large pines, some of the largest white pines I'd ever seen. In true Pine County fashion several had elaborate deer stands next to or in them. In the biggest white pine, above a deer stand, sat an eagle watching us as we passed under.

It's strange but the closer we get to the city, the quieter the trail is. I see people going about their lives as I pass by, but the team and I have the trail to ourselves.

As the day warmed the snow softened and turned to large puddles. The trail across farm fields exposed large areas of black soil. So much of the mud stuck to my boots, I thought I might bring it home and add to our garden. The temperature topped out at 50 degrees in the afternoon and we rested the dogs for a couple of hours and fed them some soup for hydration. The break did us all good and we finished the 60 plus miles by 5:00. We were wet, a little tired but will all be ready for the 45 miles that it looks like we have to make tomorrow. The snow will continue to melt through the night so we're prepared for a muddy, wet run tomorrow.

In the afternoon there were miles of trail that were along two-lane state highways, 23 and 11. Next to Hwy 11 we were on the left side of the road, sometimes only inches from oncoming 55-mile-an-hour traffic. Nita and Wolf kept their heads down, pulled with all they had and didn't seem to notice. I did notice and got pretty nervous. This was by far the most danger we had yet been in. Our small handling crew was maxed out trying to keep us safe when Jim and Cindy Hickey, from Pine City, showed up with two more cars to shadow the team for the rest of the day. I could relax a bit.

John Vitek showed up on the side of the trail in Harvey with a couple of bottles of Gatorade. He and his wife Judy have sled dogs and a farm outside of North Branch. They're letting us stay in their barn tonight. I guess the rooster will wake us up in the morning.

WCCO channel 4 was with us for a portion of the day. I'm not sure if I'll have internet tomorrow so this might be it until we arrive at the Capitol on Thursday at 11:00. Thank you all for the work you've put in to allow me to make this trip. Spending this time with the dogs, through new and difficult challenges, is a gift I'll treasure for the rest of my life.

Good Night.

Ice, mud, and wet pavement (photo by Mark Luttinen)

Blog
Wednesday, March 7

It's hard for me to believe that we'll arrive at the Capitol tomorrow. The dogs have pulled me and the petitions about 340 miles already, with just 19 to go tomorrow morning. Today was mostly on pavement, gravel, grass, with puddles often up to my knees and the dogs' shoulders. But they didn't stop. In fact the dogs were running as well today as they were a week ago when we left Grand Marais. It was slow going, though, and it's good we only needed to go 40 miles today. The sled doesn't move as well on pavement and gravel. Running through the standing water had us all soaked but again the dogs were unfazed. They seem to be on the mission to get the petitions to the Governor more than I am.

It is so humbling to be carried by them. They ask for nothing but good care, food, a dry place to sleep, and some love. In return they give their hearts and all they have. It's such a lesson for me and, nearing the end of this adventure, I know that we have succeeded just by making the journey. We have changed, and it seems like the debate about whether we should allow sulfide mining pollution in Minnesota or not is changing too.

John and Judy were along to help with some of the road crossings, which were the biggest yet. Going right through downtown Forest

Lake was crazy and we got some looks. Again we saw eagles. John said they're pretty common down here but I was still glad to see them.

Sherri and our friend and handler Steve arrived today to help bring us in. Coming up to a road crossing I saw Sherri and stopped the team. As the dogs barked and lunged I hugged her like it had been a lot longer than seven days since I'd last seen her. She handed me two cheeseburgers. Moo needed a break today so Sherri had brought Ben back down. It was good to see his big happy white face too.

The word was that the Governor was planning to meet with me and accept the petitions when we arrived. Now that's changed. He says he's too busy. I doubt that's what happened. I was pretty pissed off when I heard the news but then I got back on the sled and got to spend a few more hours with the dogs. They are amazing, so inspiring for me. They've given their all to get us here and the journey itself has great rewards. Meeting with the Gov or not is secondary. I'll put my best face on, walk up there and wait in his sitting area with the petitions. He'll eventually show up and I'm guessing the media will be with me. We've built great good will and it seems the press is on our side.

Again we had planned to camp tonight, but Mark's brother lives nearby in a big warm house. They think I'm crazy but I'm going to sleep outside. Sorry, Sherri. Thank you for all you've done to get us here. Time for me to climb into the truck and to sleep near the dogs. Now that our trek is almost over, I don't want it to end.

Good Night.

Jake (photo by Joi Electa)

To the Capitol (photo by Stephan Hoglund)

Blog
Thursday, March 8

At 7:00 a.m. this morning we stood at the beginning of the Gateway Trail in Pine Point County Park, twenty miles from Saint Paul. The trail was only covered with a little ice before turning to dry pavement that looked like it went all the way to Saint Paul. I guessed I'd have to run next to the sled most of the way to the Capitol. Walking up to the truck where the team was planning the last leg of our journey, I looked up to see two eagles flying overhead. It had clouded up and then begun to snow. The weather said it was supposed to be sunny this morning. As we bootied and harnessed the team the snow coated the trail, granting our entry to Saint Paul.

The next two hours were surreal. The dogs pulled me through neighborhoods, business parks and over interstate highway bridges. A quiet settled over us in the noise of the city. Most people didn't take their eyes from their lives to look, but some did, and the expressions were great. One poor guy was walking his Pomeranian that wanted to challenge the team. The look in his eyes said that he thought his pup was going to be breakfast. It almost was but the dogs quickly returned to business. They were on a mission.

Honestly I didn't know what to expect at the Capitol. I was just so focused on getting there. The dogs' determination the last few days and their ability to navigate the city streets in Saint Paul really blew me away. When we finished running up the walkway to the Capitol, watching the dogs, I couldn't contain my emotions anymore. They gave it everything they had. That moment at the Capitol steps was theirs and I wanted the world to stop, so I could spend hours of that moment with them. The crowd surrounded us, cameras and microphones. Starting in the rear, I hugged every dog, worked my way to the front where I kneeled in front of Wolf and Nita. I held them close and looked into their eyes. They knew they had done something great, led us through the streets of Saint Paul, city traffic and no snow, just pavement. Nita gave me a few quick licks and Wolf stood there looking up and smiling. In that instant, staring into each other's eyes, we were one. Standing up there was Sherri, tears also in her eyes. I held onto her and said, "We did it."

The drumming continued while I embraced Sherri. Through the drumming and cheers I heard Steve Morse, the Executive Director of the Minnesota Environmental Partnership, call me to the microphone. Sherri let me go and I climbed the stairs to the microphone. Just minutes ago we were solely focused on getting here, to the Capitol. Now I was standing in front of a crowd of hundreds, with no rehearsed speech. An eagle flew overhead. I whispered a "Hello" and "Thanks." Then I turned to the mic. The words came and I told the story of the trip down and what inspired it, but I kept looking down at the dogs that brought me there. Of course they were getting the best care from Sherri, Mark, and Adam, but my heart wanted to be down there sharing this time with them. I had a duty though, one that they'd given me the chance to fulfill, so I thanked everyone there, returned to the sled, pulled out the petitions and walked up the Capitol steps. I was going to wait in the Governor's office as long as it took for him to come out so I could hand the petitions to him, myself. I'd given my word.

As I walked up the Capitol steps I looked back at the truck, the dogs all tied up around it, waiting, sitting, looking around for what was next. How could I tell them what they'd done, accomplished what humans haven't yet been able to do by bringing attention to what sulfide mining would do to Minnesota? Those beautiful dogs delivered me and over 13,000 petition signatures, 362 miles to the Capitol in Saint Paul. They navigated a trail that for four days was dominated by snowmobiles; pulled through heavy snow, mud and deep water; then dragged a sled over a hundred miles of gravel and pavement; finishing by running right through the streets of downtown Saint Paul. They did this not because they were asked but because they had to, were born to. They didn't know anything else but to pull. Their drive and hearts had now given us a chance, the brief attention of Minnesotans, to remind them that our water was everything. Our jobs, our food, our lives depended on it.

The dogs didn't know the message. They just looked up at me as I walked up the steps, as if they were hoping I would come back and harness them up, for one more run.

I walked into the world I'd left four years ago as if I'd just been gone a day. The extreme pace and focus of the Capitol mostly ignored me in my musher's clothes, a foot high stack of petitions in my hands. Lobbyists and legislators rarely looked up from their iPods and Blackberrys as I went by. I walked into the Governor's front office and waited for the receptionist to get off the phone.

"Hi, my name's Frank Moe and I've driven my dog sled 362 miles from Grand Marais to bring these petitions to the Governor. Would you let him know that I'm here?"

She looked at me for a few seconds as she took in what stood in front of her. While I knew that members of the Governor's staff knew that I was coming, the receptionist clearly did not.

"Um…The Governor has a very busy schedule, but if you leave them here with me, I'll be sure that the appropriate person gets them."

"No, that's OK, I'll give them to the Governor myself. Would you just let him know that I'm here? I'll just sit over here and wait." I sat down on the couch across the office from her desk. She stared for a few seconds then picked up the phone and made a call.

There I was at the end of the most important adventure of my life. Sitting in the Governor's lobby, I was wearing the smell of eight days on the trail and hoping he'd decide to come out and accept this stack of muddy petition signatures. The mushing season was over. Eight days ago, we were hooking the team up in Harbor Park, downtown Grand Marais. Every cell in my body was screaming to get out of there, outside to the dogs and Sherri and head north.

"Just wait, Frank, a bit longer. Finish it like you said you would."

The Governor's Lobby (photo by Stephan Hoglund)

The media continued to come in, tweeting their messages that I was in there waiting for the Governor, and finally Dana Anderson, his Deputy Chief of Staff, came out.

"Frank, I'll hand them to him personally. He's very busy."

"Thanks, Dana, but I'll wait for the Governor. The dogs and I travelled 362 miles to get here and promised these 13,000 people that I'd hand them to the Governor myself. I can't just hand them to you after only waiting an hour. I gave my word. I'm sure you understand. "

Her look showed that she didn't.

For the next half hour I waited in the Governor's lobby. Several members of the media came and left. The Politics in Minnesota reporter blogged that I was sitting in the Governor's office and that he was refusing to meet with me. Behind the scenes my friend Molly Peterson, the Conservation Minnesota Governement Affairs Director, was working on the Governor's staff to let me in to see him. Then word came out that the Governor would meet with me but they didn't want any pictures taken. And then a minute later there he was. I thanked him for coming out and told him why I was there. He listened politely, nodded as I handed him the petitions and asked me about the trip. Before I could answer his question a few others came into the waiting room and began to confront him about potential sulfide mining and the current lack of enforcement by the Minnesota Pollution Control Agency. I was a little frustrated after having worked so hard to get this meeting and now didn't have a chance to say much but honestly wasn't too upset. Since I'd given him the petitions, as I said I would, I just wanted to get out of there.

The Governor soon retreated to the confines of his offices and I left the waiting room, breathing a sigh of relief. I'd done what I'd set out to do. A couple of reporters were waiting, including Dennis Anderson of the *Star Tribune*. Quickly realizing how important this was, I forced myself to sit down and gave him the story of the trip and why we did it. All this time my attention was more on the dogs. Sherri and Mark were out caring for them, I knew that, but they had been my sole focus for eight days. I tried to answer Dennis' questions, and when he said he'd like to have a picture, I jumped up and said, "Great, let's go outside. The dogs are in the truck right in front."

As we got up, a few men in suits, who had been following me since I walked up the steps to the Capitol, descended on Dennis to give him "their side of the story." The words of these mining executives and lobbyists found their way into every story done about our dog sled trip to the Capitol. As always, their endless money bought their views into the media.

After Dennis Anderson's picture of Ajax and me was taken, I finally got some time. The dogs were now in the truck and I opened every door, thanking them all. They all deserved the rest they were finally getting. Closing the last door I looked around the almost deserted Capitol grounds. It was now sunny and in the 40s. That sled dog truck couldn't have looked more unnatural. Sherri walked up to me with the smile that only she could give me. I put my arms around her, looked into her eyes and said, "Let's go home."

As I let Sherri go I really looked at her, her eyes, face, the way she was holding herself. I'd been so focused on getting to the Capitol, I hadn't had much time to think about my wife and now looking at her, I saw how tired she was. Here I was again, exhausting myself and getting all the attention for doing it, but there waiting for us at the finish to take care of us, pick up the pieces, was Sherri. And it was all she had. Sherri sighed, "I need to get my car."

I watched her walk off knowing that I now needed to take care of my wife, my selfless partner.

Sherri pulled around in front of the dog truck and rolled down the window, saying she'd follow me home.

"I don't know how far I can go, but let's get out of town. "

"Just let me know, Sherri. We can pull over whenever you need to."

Crazy as it sounds I also had in the back of my mind that I needed to get three teams ready for another short race in less than two days. My own energy clock was set to wind down on Saturday night after we got home from that race. Not racing for me because of fatigue or sickness had always seemed as crazy as a farmer leaving his crops in the field because he was too tired to harvest them. Our lives were designed to get these dogs to the races and safely home. But now the importance of getting to that next race faded. I was worried about Sherri. She had selflessly given her all, staying home working while suffering from a terrible cold. She had also been taking care of the rest of the dogs with Lisa and yet still made it down for our last leg into Saint Paul.

"There's no way I was going to miss it."

I needed to find her a bed, a meal and a long night's sleep. The snow started to fall again as our little caravan headed north, for home.

Driving out of Saint Paul on 35E, we crossed under the Gateway Trail bridge. Only a couple of hours earlier the dogs and I had crossed over the freeway right there. My exhaustion was still at bay. The buzz from having made the trip was being fueled by still more coffee and a Twin Cities rock and roll station. I wondered if the questions about the direction and worth of my life that normally dominated my mind at the end of the mushing season would return. Maybe this time they wouldn't now that I had something to work for beyond competing in sled dog races.

"What's next?" I wondered.

My adventures had mostly been about challenging myself, now it was time to bring others along with me, in a quest for something more.

The next chapter of Northern Minnesota's story is now being written. Maybe together, running as a team, we will write it. Clean water with fish, and rice we can eat, that our kids can eat, and eagles along on our journey. That's this story. We'll tell it to all who will listen and some day, maybe soon, Minnesotans and those who we elect to represent us, will hear it…and join us on the trail.

Ben at the Capitol (photo by Mark Luttinen)

Epilogue

"You takin' off, Frank?"

"Yeah, it's getting late. Thanks, Adam. This wouldn't have happened without you."

Standing outside of Stephan Hogland's shop on the Saturday night after our trip, Adam and I shared a knowing look. My words sounded trivial. Our adventure, that we had spent months planning and for eight days was our life, was over. With Mark, Jerry and the dogs, we had been a team with the sole focus of getting 13,000 petition signatures to the Governor in Saint Paul. Adam and I knew things about the trip, what it took, that no one else did.

For a moment I flashed back to the night before we arrived at the Capitol. Some of our friends and activists were outraged that the Governor had decided to not meet with us. They were threatening to storm the Governor's Office, stage a sit-in, get arrested, whatever it took. Adam and I knew what damage that would do to all the good press that we had worked so hard to earn. We'd abandoned our plans to camp out our last night on the trail because where we were planning to camp didn't have cell phone reception. Hours of phone calls were made that night from a pizza place in Stillwater, talking our friends off the cliff, convincing them that we needed the press at our rally on the Capitol steps.

"Please let the story be about the dogs arriving at the Capitol, not arrests being made in the Governor's Office."

Their intentions were noble and in the end they deferred and agreed to just come to the rally.

Looking at Adam, a week after it was all over, I shared a smile, remembering how close we were in the end, to failing.

"I think we should make a movie, about our trip."

He nodded his agreement.

"I'm in."

We shook hands and we both slowly turned and walked back to our lives. Adam rejoined the group around the fire at Stephan's patio. They had all helped plan the trip to Saint Paul and were celebrating our success.

I stood out on the sidewalk and looked across Wisconsin Street at Harbor Park. Closing my eyes I imagined the drumming, people smiling on that late winter day, the dogs barking, Sherri holding Cocoa, the Eagles flying overhead. It felt a lifetime ago…or it could have been just this morning.

A bark brought me back to the night, the quiet street. Harbor Park was empty. The lake was calm and dark. I turned and got into my truck then scratched my dog on his head.

"Let's go home, Gus."

Made in the USA
Middletown, DE
18 January 2016